The Educator's Guide to
Feeding Children with Disabilities

University of Colorado Health Sciences Center
JFK Partners
4200 E. 9th Ave. C221
Denver, CO 80262

The Educator's Guide to Feeding Children with Disabilities

by

Dianne Koontz Lowman, Ed.D.
Virginia Commonwealth University
Richmond

and

Suzanne McKeever Murphy, M.Ed., CCC-SLP
Private Practitioner
Richmond

with invited contributors

·P A U L·H·
BROOKES
PUBLISHING Co.

Baltimore • London • Toronto • Sydney

Paul H. Brookes Publishing Co.
Post Office Box 10624
Baltimore, Maryland 21285-0624

www.pbrookes.com

Typeset by PRO-Image Corporation, Techna-Type Division, York, Pennsylvania.
Manufactured in the United States of America by
Hamilton Printing Company, Rensselaer, New York.

The suggestions in this book are not intended as a substitute for professional medical consultation. The authors and publishers disclaim any liability arising directly or indirectly from the use of this book.

The vignette appearing on pages 21 and 22 represents an actual person and actual circumstances and is published with the individual's written permission. The other vignettes in this book are composites based on the authors' experiences; these vignettes do not represent the lives or experiences of specific individuals, and no implications should be inferred.

Readers are granted permission to photocopy the forms in the appendix of this volume for use in service provision to students with disabilities and their families.

Library of Congress Cataloging-in-Publication Data

Lowman, Dianne Koontz.
The educator's guide to feeding children with disabilities / by Dianne Koontz Lowman and Suzanne McKeever Murphy.
    p.   cm.
   Includes bibliographical references and index.
   ISBN 1-55766-375-0 (pbk.)
   1. Handicapped children—Nutrition.   2. School children—Food.   I. Murphy, Suzanne McKeever.   II. Title.
RJ233.L69   1999
371.91—DC21   98-17858
                                                             CIP

British Library Cataloguing in Publication data are available from the British Library.

Contents

About the Authors

Dianne Koontz Lowman, Ed.D., Assistant Professor, Department of Occupational Therapy, Virginia Commonwealth University, Post Office Box 980008, Richmond, Virginia 23298

Dr. Koontz Lowman teaches graduate and undergraduate occupational therapy students at Virginia Commonwealth University. She has 22 years of experience working with young children with disabilities, specializing in the inclusion of children with complex health care needs. Dr. Koontz Lowman conducts research, presents workshops, and has published numerous chapters and articles on topics related to feeding children with complex health care needs and with oral-motor problems. She is an active member of the Division of Early Childhood and the Division for Physical and Health Disabilities, subdivisions of the Council for Exceptional Children; American Occupational Therapy Association; and Virginia Occupational Therapy Association. These are professional organizations related to early childhood and children with physical and health-related disabilities.

Suzanne McKeever Murphy, M.Ed., CCC-SLP, Pediatric Speech-Language Pathologist, 1400 Cedar Crossing Trail, Midlothian, Virginia 23113

Ms. Murphy has a private practice as a pediatric speech-language pathologist in Midlothian, Virginia. She has worked with children from birth to 5 years of age with communication, oral-motor, and feeding problems for 17 years. Ms. Murphy received her Neurodevelopmental Treatment certificate in 1986. She was an adjunct professor in the Department of Early Childhood Special Education at Virginia Commonwealth University in Richmond for 7 years. Ms. Murphy works as a communication and feeding technical assistant consultant for the entire state of Virginia through the Virginia Department of Education. Each year, she conducts numerous workshops on the topics of communication and feeding disorders to professionals and parents. Ms. Murphy also has worked as a feeding research advisor for students receiving their master's degrees in occupational therapy at Virginia Commonwealth University.

Patricia M. Blasco, Ph.D., Associate Professor of Education, Department of Education, Bowie State University, 14000 Jericho Park Road, Bowie, Maryland 20715

Dr. Blasco teaches classes in early childhood and early childhood special education at Bowie State University. Dr. Blasco has extensive experience in the fields of early intervention and early education. She currently serves on the Board of Directors for the Division of Early Childhood (DEC) and is active on the local level as a member of the Baltimore County Interagency Coordinating Council and co-president of the Maryland DEC. She works on several projects addressing services for infants, toddlers, and their families.

Darbi Breath, LOTR, Pediatric Occupational Therapist, Clinical Instructor, Department of Interdisciplinary Human Studies, Human Development Center, Louisiana State University Medical Center, 1100 Florida Avenue, Building 124, New Orleans, Louisiana 70119

Ms. Breath, in addition to working as a pediatric occupational therapist and clinical instructor at the Louisiana State University Medical Center, writes and lectures on topics related to positioning and handling for young children with special needs. Ms. Breath is completing her master's of health sciences degree in occupational therapy at Louisiana State University Medical Center with an advanced clinical skills emphasis and is serving a second term as vice president of the Louisiana Occupational Therapy Association.

Vanessa Caretto, M.S., OTR/L, Occupational Therapist, Wake Forest University Baptist Medical Center, 1912-D Falcon Pointe Drive, Winston-Salem, North Carolina 27127

Ms. Caretto is a graduate of Virginia Commonwealth University, Department of Occupational Therapy. She has experience primarily with infants and preschool–age children, and she has completed specialized interdisciplinary training in the provision of early intervention services through the Virginia Institute for Developmental Disabilities. She has also conducted research and is a co-author of an article about parent education on infant care and feeding in the neonatal intensive care unit environment.

Gerard J. DeMauro, M.S., PT, Assistant Professor of Clinical Physical Therapy, Department of Physical Therapy, School of Allied Health Professions, Louisiana State University Medical Center, 1900 Gravier Street, New Orleans, Louisiana 70112

Mr. DeMauro is a physical therapist with more than 20 years of clinical and teaching experience in the area of pediatrics. At the time his chapter in this book was written, Mr. DeMauro held the position of Assistant Professor of Clinical Physical Therapy at the Louisiana State University Medical Center. He has extensive training in neurodevelopmental treatment, and he has served on the Board of Directors for the Neuro-Developmental Treatment Association. Mr. DeMauro has and continues to collaborate on interdisciplinary projects with Ms. Breath and Dr. Snyder.

Julie K. Jones, Ph.D., Director, Migrant Head Start Disabilities Services Quality Improvement Center, Academy for Educational Development, 1255 23rd Street NW, Washington, D.C. 20037

Dr. Jones has worked with children with sensory and multiple disabilities and deaf-blindness for more than 25 years. She has extensive experience with children who are learning to eat solid foods or to self-feed. She has written on a variety of topics related to young children with special needs, personnel preparation, professional development, and collaborative partnerships. Dr. Jones teaches graduate courses in special education and consults nationally and internationally on educating children with disabilities.

Mary Kientz, M.S., OTR, Occupational Therapist, 3890 Hancock Avenue, Williamstown, New Jersey 08094

Ms. Kientz is an occupational therapist who has worked extensively with children with autism and challenging behaviors. She emphasizes contextually relevant, family-centered, and positive approaches in her practice. She currently works part time for an early intervention program and lectures about using positive approaches with children with disabilities. Ms. Kientz has written about supporting individuals by using a sensory-based approach and has been an adjunct profesor in the Department of Occupational Therapy at Virginia Commonwealth University.

Patricia A. Snyder, Ph.D., Professor, Department of Occupational Therapy, School of Allied Health Professions, Louisiana State University Medical Center, 1900 Gravier Street, New Orleans, Louisiana 70112

Dr. Snyder teaches graduate and undergraduate students from a variety of allied health disciplines at Louisiana State University Medical Center. Dr. Snyder has more than 22 years of experience in early intervention, specializing in topics related to infants and toddlers who have significant motor and communication challenges. She is an associate editor for the *Journal of Early Intervention,* serves as the personnel preparation representative on the State Interagency Coordinating Council for Part C in Louisiana, and is an active member of several professional organizations related to early childhood.

Rebecca Anderson Weissman, M.S., Private Consultant, 507 Jackson Street, Falls Church, Virginia 22046

Ms. Weissman has worked in the field of special education for 15 years. She has taught young children with severe disabilities, supervised special education programs serving children with severe disabilities, coordinated a home-based early intervention program serving infants and their families, and served as consultant and trainer on numerous topics that have included assessment of the extensive scope of feeding needs of children with disabilities as well as other topics that emphasize family-centered practices and the prevention of secondary disabilities. As an adjunct professor in the field of special education, she has taught graduate courses on the topics of severe disabilities, neuromotor development, and behavioral strategies. At the time of her contribution to this book, she is enjoying her newest role, that of mother to Joseph Charles and newborn Lowell Meyer.

Foreword

Shauna is home from school! Shauna's mom, Chris, having just returned from a busy 3-day stint for her airlines job, walks out the back door of the house to greet Shauna. Chris can tell it has been a good day because Shauna is smiling, vocalizing, and gesturing about the news from school. Shauna, who just turned 20 years old, has been attending school longer than most people; her education started shortly after she was born, and she is still 2 years shy of graduation. Shauna has cerebral palsy and significant visual impairments. She uses a wheelchair for much of the day and communicates in many ways—sounds, facial expressions, gestures, words, yes/no responses, and a communication device called the Dynovox with auditory scanning and a hand switch—whatever works to get the message across to her partner. At 20 years of age, Shauna is tall and lean; likes to tease and joke; and has clear preferences about her daily and weekly activities, her friends, and her life. But right now, the message is "I'm hungry!"

Chris asks Shauna, "So, do you want some cheese?"

Shauna says, "Yeah."

"What about some Pepsi?" Chris asks.

"Yeah," Shauna replies.

"And some turkey?" Chris asks as she takes some lunchmeat and cheese from the refrigerator.

"Yeah."

"Gee, you're hungry!"

Shauna laughs.

Chris folds a slice of cheddar cheese and holds it out to Shauna while touching her hand. "Here's the cheese."

Shauna extends her hand and opens it slightly; Chris opens Shauna's hand wider and places the slice of cheese in her grip. Shauna takes the cheese immediately to her mouth, and it is gone almost instantly.

"Want more?" Chris asks.

"Yeah," Shauna answers.

Chris gives Shauna a cheese "refill," then pours some Pepsi into Shauna's sports cup, replaces the lid and straw, and puts the cup into its holder on the right side of Shauna's tray. "Pepsi's served!"

Shauna smiles, eats another bite of food, and leans forward for a sip of Pepsi, but she is interrupted by several coughs. She sits up straight, clears her airway, and then takes a drink.

"Not so fast, girl!"

Shauna giggles and then consumes two pieces of turkey.

"So what happened for the past 3 days?" Chris asks. "I've missed you! Dad says you went back to the job at the day care center, and you lead games with the kids. Do you like working there?"

"Yeah," Shauna says loudly, but then she frowns.

"Oh-oh, we need your voice," Chris says as she notices Shauna's frown.

In order to really talk, Shauna needs more than a "yes" or "no" response. Chris wipes off Shauna's tray and hands Shauna the wet cloth to clean her hands. Next, Chris takes the Dynovox out of Shauna's backpack, places it on the tray, turns it on, and sets up the switch.

"OK, now tell me what happened at work!" Chris says.

If one were to analyze this after-school snack scene from a feeding standpoint, many things are happening and working well:

- *Positioning*—Shauna sits in an upright 90°–90°–90° position in her adapted chair. She moves with the most control in this position.

- *Adaptive equipment*—In addition to her wheelchair and tray, Shauna uses a simple sports cup with a straw and a lid; the cup is positioned in a holder within reach. Shauna uses an electric self-feeder for meals at home and for some meals at school, where she works on increasing her ability to eat with little assistance from others.

- *Communication*—Shauna uses gestures, words, and facial expressions during her rapid exchanges with her mom about what to eat and the day's events. Whenever Shauna self-feeds, the hand switch and Dynovox cannot be used, so Chris phrases her questions to Shauna so they can be answered by a simple "yes" or "no." Once Shauna is finished eating and her hands are clean and free, the Dynovox and a hand switch are put in place for Shauna to use. Chris wonders about revisiting the knee switch Shauna used years ago so she can be more precise in communicating during meals when she self-feeds. No one should have to choose between eating and communicating.

- *Respiration*—Shauna breathes easily in the 90°–90°–90° position; clearing her airway, as she did today, is not always easily accomplished, but Shauna has learned to gauge the amount and rate of eating and drinking so there is less choking.

- *Vision*—Shauna follows verbal and tactual cues easily, which Chris uses liberally.

- *Diet, food preferences, and approach*—Shauna's tastes and appetite are similar to many others her age; regular table food is cut into bite-size pieces and either fed to Shauna or placed on her electric self-feeder. At other times, finger foods are placed in Shauna's right hand or on a plate within her reach.

- *Drinking*—Shauna drinks independently through a straw from a secured cup placed within her reach.

- *Social interaction*—Snacktime works very well. Eating does not get in the way of interacting and catching up on one another's day, and Shauna still can satisfy her basic hunger.

Has eating and talking with Shauna always been so easy? "No way," says Chris. Shauna and her dad, Bob, agree. Along with Shauna's changing medical and educational team over the past 20 years, Shauna's parents have learned the answers to many questions about drinking and feeding, diet, positioning, communication, and health:

- How should we hold or position her?

- How do we feed her, and when do we feed her?

- What spoon, cup, plate, or electric self-feeder should we use?

- Can she learn to feed herself?

- How much do we grind or cut her food? What foods can she eat?

- Is she getting enough to eat? Is she getting enough to drink?

- What do we do when she gags, coughs, chokes, refuses food, cries, or when we don't know what she wants?

As Shauna got older, she changed—and so did some of her parents' questions and concerns. Moving from grade to grade and from one school to the next meant that team members came and went. With these changes, professionals' priorities changed, progress on some issues stopped, and new issues were raised. Shauna's parents can tell stories about having to defend their priorities or recreate old solutions whenever anyone new joined the team. Unfortunately, this "changing of the guard" on educational teams is typical; but when schools have a coordinated system for moving students from school to school and from year to year, the negative impact of team member changes is minimized.

The collaborative process is a complex one: The team of parents and professionals must identify concerns and questions, pool information, discuss possibilities, try out options, and create solutions. This process is usually highly successful when team members work toward common goals, respect one another's talents, take turns listening and speaking, are responsible in their roles, are both trustworthy and trusting of one another, cooperate without competition, and share celebrations and humor. Throughout her 20 years, Shauna's successes have depended a lot on her team's successes with collaboration.

The readers of this book vary extensively in their experiences with individuals whose daily eating routines are dependent on others or are complicated by medical, muscular, or behavior difficulties. Many of you are at the beginning of your careers as teachers or therapists. Some of you already work with students who present unusual needs in eating, moving, and interacting with others. As you read the 12 chapters of this book, 10 different authors with an extensive array of knowledge will guide your understanding of the challenges Shauna and her parents, teachers, therapists, and friends have faced and resolved during the past 20 years and the challenges they have yet to face. The answers to many of the questions about Shauna's positioning, eating routines, and communication were woven together from several sources:

- Medical/physical/physiological (e.g., her health, breathing, and swallowing patterns; seizure control; extension of functional vision; muscle tone; drooling; allergies)

- Communication/psychological (e.g., her understanding and expression of language, her knowledge of things around her)

- Social/psychological (her likes, dislikes, choices, fears, expectations)

- Assistive equipment and technology (e.g., adaptive seating, feeding equipment, communication devices and switch access)

With each new week, more knowledge is added to each source of information—discoveries and clues that may hold promise for answering the questions that Shauna's team raises. Weaving together these pieces of information, however, is often more cumbersome for team members than finding the information itself. Weaving is accomplished by several pairs of hands working at the loom, and each pair of hands may be operated by someone with a personal design in mind. Only when the creative process involves harmonious exchange and coordinated actions among team members can the outcomes be useful and satisfactory. First, team members reach consensus on the concerns. Next, they work together to create potential solutions. Finally, their group decisions are acted on, the outcomes are evaluated, and some reweaving occurs as team members rework the design until it suits the situation.

You might think that it would be much easier just to master all of these sources of information and take total control. Why depend on multimember teams and the fragile nature of human dynamics? Unfortunately, there is too much information to know in order to attain such independence. Also, many people have discovered that solutions resulting from collaborative teaming are often better than those devised by individuals. Understanding how the information in this book about feeding applies to a variety of children and young adults with disabilities will be part of your responsibility; however, the more complex part of this task involves the collaborative teaming process by which most decisions about feeding, positioning, and communication are made, implemented, and evaluated.

Martha E. Snell, Ph.D.
Department of Curriculum, Instruction, and Special Education
Curry School of Education
University of Virginia
Charlottesville

Acknowledgments

This book would not have been possible without the support of many people who are acknowledged here. We would like to take this opportunity to thank them. First and foremost, we wish to thank Suzanne Evans Morris and Rona Alexander for sharing their wisdom and compassion with so many of us in the field of feeding that, in turn, has allowed us the opportunity to carry on their pioneering efforts.

There are numerous teachers, therapists, and classroom assistants who helped us realize that we can make a difference in a child's life. Thank you to Suzanne's fellow therapists, Lourdes Sanabria, OT; Mary Lundy, PT; and Ann Losak, PT. We would also like to thank the parents of children we have worked with over the years. Thank you for inviting us into your lives and for teaching us all we needed to know about feeding.

Thanks go to Shelly Lane, Chair of the Department of Occupational Therapy, Virginia Commonwealth University (VCU), for her support, understanding, and calm words during the development of this book. Special thanks go to the VCU occupational therapy graduate students who spent hours compiling information in the library and conducting research: Krista Francois, Catherine McKinney, Jennifer White, Margaret Smith, Tara Reidy, Jeanne Dougherty, Holly Ernouf, Becky Hundley, Rob Gerkin, Marc Samuels, and Steve Wasilewski.

We would like to thank the following people for their help in proofreading and editing this material: our husbands, George Lowman and John Flynn Murphy; Suzanne's mother, Barbara McKeever; and "best friends" Maureen Seifert and Kim Wesdock, PT. We are grateful to Marti Snell for reviewing the manuscript and for providing the foreword. Special thanks go to Rebecca Anderson Weissman, who assisted in the development of the original proposal.

The staff of Paul H. Brookes Publishing Co. provided many hours and words of support throughout this process. We are especially grateful to Lisa Benson and Scott Beeler, who encouraged us when we were most tired. In addition, we would like to thank Cassidy and Connor Valenti, ages 5 and 7 respectively, who created the artwork for the cover.

Finally, we would like to acknowledge the contributing authors for the significant role each played in the creation of this book. Thank yous go to Patti Blasco, Darbi Breath, Vanessa Caretto, Gerard DeMauro, Julie Jones, Mary Kientz, Pat Snyder, and Rebecca Anderson Weissman for all of the time and effort spent to meet tight deadlines. Thank you for sharing your expertise with us.

To my husband, George,
who is the wind beneath my wings
DKL

and

To my wonderful parents, Joseph and Barbara McKeever,
who have always encouraged me to reach for the stars,
follow my dreams, and make a difference in the world.
I love you more than you will ever know!
SMM

The Educator's Guide to
Feeding Children with Disabilities

chapter one

Introduction
The Reasons Why
Educators Should Learn Feeding Skills

Dianne Koontz Lowman

No single activity is as critical to the health, education, and happiness of children with disabilities as feeding. In the best instances, meals combine nutrition needed for survival and growth, opportunities for experiencing social interactions, and a chance for children with disabilities to become independent. For those children with disabilities who also have difficulties with feeding, however, attempting to complete a meal without choking or gagging can be very stressful for both the child and the feeder (Orelove & Sobsey, 1996). This book is written for educators who feed children with disabilities who also have feeding problems and for educators who want the mealtime experience to be as pleasant as possible for the children and themselves.

WHY DO EDUCATORS NEED TO KNOW
HOW TO DEVELOP FEEDING PROGRAMS?

In the general school environment, classroom teachers and assistants are responsible for feeding a growing number of children with disabilities who also have feeding problems. Educators also serve as critical members of the planning team for feeding children with disabilities. Many teachers and assistants report, however, that they feel unprepared to deal with oral-motor feeding problems in the general classroom.

Prevalence of Children with Feeding Difficulties in the Classroom

In 1990, Blackman estimated that 25% of children with disabilities consumed an inadequate diet, 90% had some type of nutritional problem, and 15%–25% had a weight-for-length ratio below the 5th percentile. Blackman further estimated that 70% of children with developmental delays also had some form of feeding problem. In a study of children with cerebral palsy between the ages of 12 and 72 months, Reilley, Skuse, and Poblete (1996) found that 36% of the children had severe oral-motor dysfunction, 21% had

1

moderate dysfunction, and 34% had mild impairments (9% did not have feeding difficulties). Feeding problems may be caused by a variety of conditions or factors, including neurological problems (e.g., cerebral palsy), congenital anomaly syndromes (e.g., Down syndrome), gastrointestinal disorders (e.g., gastroesophageal reflux), metabolic disorders (e.g., phenylketonuria), intrauterine growth retardation (e.g., fetal alcohol syndrome), chronic illness (e.g., cystic fibrosis), environmental influences (e.g., prenatal exposure to substances), and psychosocial factors (e.g., failure to thrive) (Batshaw, 1997; Berkow & Fletcher, 1992; Klein & Delaney, 1994; Singer, 1990; Starrett, 1991; Walter, 1994). In fact, many childhood diseases and disabilities have the potential to negatively affect feeding (Bazyk, 1990). Clearly, there is a significant number of children attending school who require some form of assistance with feeding difficulties.

Because of the growing number of children with feeding difficulties in the classroom, preservice teacher training programs in disability areas (e.g., early childhood special education [ECSE] and Severe Disabilities programs) have begun to address feeding difficulties. Anecdotal data from educators, however, indicate that most knowledge on feeding skills is still gained "on the job." In a study of 234 ECSE teachers, Lowman (1993) found that 78% of the teachers conducting gastrostomy feedings in the classroom environment indicated that their training was received through in-service or demonstration.

The Educational Team

In addition to the direct responsibility for feeding children in the classroom, educators are important members of the planning team. Difficulties in the feeding process may be complex and may require planning by a team of individuals from various disciplines (Hall, Yohn, & Reed, 1992). Educational team members come from a variety of disciplines, including but not limited to occupational therapists (OTs), physical therapists (PTs), speech-language pathologists (SLPs), nurses, special educators, and family members. Ultimately, the individuals who have the primary responsibility for feeding the child with a feeding difficulty on a daily basis will be the child's family members, the teacher, and the classroom assistant. For this reason, the educator assumes the role of team leader within the educational environment. Within this capacity, educators need good observational and problem-solving skills to aid in the development of feeding plans. This book is written for the classroom staff and is designed to be a tool to assist in the development of observational skills and problem-solving skills related to feeding problems.

DEFINITIONS

The purpose of this book is to provide specific information to educators who will be feeding children with disabilities. All aspects of feeding are discussed throughout this book, including feeding children with oral-motor problems, children with behavioral issues related to feeding, and children who are receiving supplemental tube feedings. Because there are considerable differences in terminology, the following definitions are used:

- *Eating* refers to the child's being able to actively bring food to his or her mouth independently (Avery-Smith, 1996).

- *Feeding* refers to the child's being assisted in the activity of eating (Avery-Smith, 1996).

- *Oral-motor control* relates to the child's ability to use his or her lips, cheeks, jaw, tongue, and palate (Wolf & Glass, 1992). *Oral-motor development* refers to feeding, sound play, and oral exploration (Morris & Klein, 1987). Feeding is a part of oral-motor skills, but there are oral-motor skills that may not involve food at all, such as oral-motor awareness and exploration (Clark, 1993). This book focuses on oral-motor skills as related to feeding.

UNDERSTANDING FEEDING SKILLS FROM DIFFERENT PERSPECTIVES

Feeding and eating skills are essential to survival; all people must eat to stay alive and healthy. Difficulties in feeding skills may affect all aspects of a child's life, including growth, learning, and communication and interactions with others within the environment (Case-Smith & Humphry, 1996). Oral-motor movements used during feeding are the same movements used in smooth, coordinated speech. Feeding skills have a long-term effect on the quality of life and on the degree of independence a child is able to achieve (Caretto, Francois, & McKinney, 1996). In addition to these general statements about the importance of feeding and eating skills, each member of the planning team approaches feeding issues from a slightly different perspective.

Child's and Family's Perspective

The feeding process is critical for family members. All species feed their offspring; all good caregivers feed their children. Imagine how devastating it is for caregivers when they cannot feed their own child. Feeding and eating difficulties that affect the child's health and growth can be extremely upsetting for caregivers. In addition to the nutritional aspects, the feeding process is a social process that helps caregivers and family members form relationships and impart culture, traditions, and values (Case-Smith & Humphry, 1996). Disruptions in the feeding process can upset parent–child, family, and mealtime interactions.

Educator's Perspective

Sometimes educators do not realize the emotional impact that feeding problems have on the family. Take a moment to read the vignette at the end of this chapter (see page 7). As can be seen from Jan's situation, it is critical for educators working with families to first recognize and acknowledge the emotional impact of feeding problems. Educators must also respect different methods that individual families have for coping with stressful situations. In the vignette, Jan came to realize that Brittany's parents were coping with Brittany's multiple problems by holding on to oral feedings as a symbol of something their daughter could do that was "normal."

In addition, educators must remember that while teachers, therapists, and services will change and vary over the child's life span, family members will remain the only constant in a child's life (Shelton & Stepanek, 1994). These and the other elements of family-centered care, which are presented in Table 1, are critical for educators working with children with feeding problems.

Because cultural implications affect all interactions with children and families, the cultural umbrella should always cover all aspects of working

Table 1.   Elements of family-centered care

- Recognizing that the family is the constant in the child's life while the service systems and personnel within those systems fluctuate
- Facilitating parent–professional collaboration at all levels of care:
    Care of an individual child
    Program development, implementation, and evaluation
    Policy formation
- Honoring the racial, ethnic, cultural, and socioeconomic diversity of families
- Recognizing family strengths and individuality as well as respecting different methods of coping
- Sharing with parents, on a continuing basis and in a supportive manner, complete and unbiased information
- Encouraging and facilitating family-to-family support and networking
- Understanding and incorporating into service delivery systems the developmental needs of infants, children, adolescents, and their families
- Implementing comprehensive policies and programs that provide emotional support that responds to the needs of families
- Designing accessible service delivery systems that are flexible, culturally competent, and responsive to family-identified needs

---

Adapted with permission of the Association for the Care of Children's Health, 7910 Woodmont Avenue, Suite 300, Bethesda, Maryland 20814, from Shelton, T.L., & Stepanek, J.S. (1994). *Family-centered care for children needing specialized health and developmental services.* Bethesda, MD: Association for the Care of Children's Health.

with children (Lowman & Lane, 1998). Before making any recommendations or developing the feeding plan, educators should determine whether their recommendations respect the family's beliefs and values.

Therapists' Perspective

Two therapists who usually are responsible for the development of oral-motor feeding programs are OTs and SLPs. The American Occupational Therapy Association (AOTA) has issued a position paper on eating dysfunction that states "because eating is an important daily living skill, essential to health and well-being, and critical throughout a person's life span, it falls within the occupational therapy domain of concern" (Avery-Smith, 1996, p. 846). AOTA summarized that OTs may be involved in the planning and development of a feeding plan as well as in direct evaluation and intervention of feeding difficulties. Oral-motor feeding, however, is viewed as a specialty and not as an entry-level skill. Many OTs who have just graduated from school do not have extensive training in oral-motor feeding difficulties.

In a document defining the scope of practice of speech-language pathology and audiology, the American Speech-Language-Hearing Association (ASHA) stated that the practice of speech-language pathology includes "screening, identifying, assessing and interpreting, diagnosing, and rehabilitating disorders of oral-pharyngeal function (e.g., dysphagia) and related disorders" (1990, p. 7).

Medical Practitioner's Perspective

Members of the educational team who are medically trained include the nurse, the OT, the PT, and the SLP (Hall et al., 1992). If these individuals are not comfortable with the information available in the school's medical records or if they suspect specific medical concerns (e.g., malnutrition or aspiration due to swallowing difficulties), a comprehensive medical evaluation may be recommended. Members of a medical pediatric feeding and swallowing disorders team may include a pediatric gastroenterologist, a developmental pediatrician, a diagnostic radiologist, a dietician, and a nutritionist (Hall et al., 1992; Walter, 1994). The primary role of this medical team is to determine what is "safe" for each child, provide that information, and educate those providing direct care for children with feeding problems (Walter, 1994).

CONTENT AND ORGANIZATION OF THIS BOOK

Because feeding and eating are dynamic skills, this book emphasizes the use of an observational/interview process to gather as much information as possible about all aspects of the feeding, eating, and mealtime process. The Process for Developing a Holistic Feeding Plan in the appendix to this chapter is provided in a problem-solving format that helps team members consider all components that might interfere with feeding, eating, and mealtime (Lowman & Lane, 1998). By using the questions on the Process for Developing a Holistic Feeding Plan as a guide, team members can gather information from a variety of sources about

- The family's feeding routine, issues, and cultural implications

- The presence of any respiratory issues

- Physical development and positioning during feeding and eating

- The child's oral-motor and sensory development

- Communication, behavioral, and socialization skills during the feeding process

There are numerous assessment scales available. At present, there are no universally accepted single-assessment exits for feeding evaluations (Arvedson, 1993). For this reason, the ongoing problem-solving process highlighted in the Process for Developing a Holistic Feeding Plan is recommended.

Chapter Content

The goal of this book is to provide educators with the necessary information to design and implement comprehensive feeding plans for children with disabilities. The goal of each chapter is to identify and explore a separate component of feeding, especially any problematic ones, frequently encountered in a school-based situation. Each chapter discusses one component of the Process for Developing a Holistic Feeding Plan in detail. All components are incorporated in Chapter 12, which provides a completed example of a Holistic Feeding Observation Form.

Chapter 2 emphasizes the important role of collaboration among educators, caregivers, and medical professionals when designing a feeding plan. The transdisciplinary model, in which active teaching across disciplines takes place, is described throughout the sequence of a child's daily activities and environments.

In Chapter 3, anatomy of the mouth and throat is translated into lay terminology and descriptions. Here, the focus is on how the anatomy and physiology of the mouth, throat, and respiratory system interrelate to all aspects of feeding. A developmental perspective is described that presents typical as well as atypical progression. In Chapter 4, the anatomy and physiology presented in Chapter 3 are interwoven with oral-motor considerations. Typical and atypical development as well as common feeding concerns are described for the jaw, lips, tongue, cheeks, and palate. The motor abilities necessary for adequate feeding skills also are highlighted. Chapter 5 describes the key components for high-quality positioning and subsequent facilitation of better eating skills. A description of various feeding positions and their benefits also are provided.

Chapter 6 examines the sensory issues related to feeding. The roles of taste, texture, temperature, and touch are explored, including how to incorporate each of these "4 T's" into a comprehensive feeding plan. The importance of communication and communication control on the part of the child throughout the feeding process is emphasized in Chapter 7. An overview of communication strategies and the social aspects of feeding also is provided. The use of adaptive equipment specific to feeding and the importance of working with therapists comprises the context of Chapter 8.

Chapter 9 emphasizes the positive behavioral strategies needed to address common as well as rare, yet serious, feeding problems. Behavioral issues include picky eating, refusing to eat, rumination, and pica. Literature related to the communicative intent of challenging behaviors also is highlighted. In Chapter 10, the topic is on feeding children with complex health care needs and how health-related needs affect feeding. This chapter also describes what teachers need to know with respect to feeding children with a feeding tube, ventilator, or tracheostomy. The development of a Health Services Plan also is emphasized.

Chapter 11 focuses on feeding issues common to children with sensory disabilities, such as children with vision impairments and children requiring hearing accommodations. The chapter also focuses on the rare, yet challenging, population of children with dual sensory impairment and the accommodations children with deafblindness need.

The final chapter, Chapter 12, culminates the book by showing how to incorporate each of these necessary components into a comprehensive feeding plan. This feeding plan utilizes significant family input as well as a team approach. Such a comprehensive feeding plan results in successfully addressing each child's individual communication, sensory, and motor needs specific to feeding. Practical forms for educators and their colleagues are provided to facilitate the development of a holistic feeding plan for children in their care.

Vignettes and Practice Exercises

At the end of each chapter in this book, vignettes are presented to illustrate creative problem solving for the needs of children of different ages and different types of disabilities. Each vignette is supplemented by a Practice Exercise to assist educators in the development of the skills needed to function as a team leader in the feeding plan developed for each child. The practice exercise at the end of the chapter includes questions specific to the children with problems highlighted in that chapter. These exercises will give the reader an opportunity to use new information, in practice, before putting all of the components together to design an entire feeding plan in Chapter 12.

SUMMARY

Educators are being asked to feed increasing numbers of students with feeding problems in the school environment. Although preservice training in this area has increased, most of the training educators receive is "on the job." All personnel involved in planning for children with feeding problems want the feeding process to be as safe and pleasant as possible for both the feeder and the child. Although the educator is typically the primary person responsible for daily feeding in school, planning must be conducted by a team of professionals that takes into consideration all aspects of the feeding process. The overall importance of holistic team planning is emphasized throughout this book.

Jan

Jan was an ECSE teacher in an integrated child care center located in an urban area. The school system rented classroom space in the child care center for the ECSE program; the child care center also housed a Head Start program. Jan had taught for 6 years before Brittany was placed in her class. Brittany was a preschooler with multiple disabilities who aspirated food when she was fed orally. Brittany's parents refused the doctor's recommendation to place (insert) a feeding tube and instead asked the school staff to feed Brittany orally. After the first 3 months of school, Jan asked the principal if she could stop feeding Brittany orally at school:

> I had to cease feeding her because I couldn't [continue] to feed her, knowing she was choking every time. . . . After the [fourth] time she had pneumonia. I just asked [the parents] to please feed her at home. Or come in. . . . This could be a child that dies in my arms. And I don't want to be responsible for that. (Lowman, 1994, p. 106)[1]

The concerns voiced by Jan are echoed by many educators who daily feed children with oral-motor difficulties. Jan was prepared to feed children with disabilities and wanted to have Brittany and other children with complex health care needs in her class:

> They are children first. And if you look at the child and think this child really needs me to do this . . . if you could look at the kid, I think you can overlook the fear. . . . Just do it. (Lowman, 1994, pp. 110–111)

Jan wanted to feed Brittany, but she was not prepared for how scary Brittany's frequent choking episodes would be. Brittany's frequent hospitalizations for pneumonia (caused by aspiration) were also very disturbing. Jan questioned the parents' motives for insisting on oral feedings; in fact, she believed that Brittany's parents' refusal to use a feeding tube was an attempt to starve Brittany. After Jan worked with the family, she realized that the family didn't want to starve their daughter; they only wanted Brittany to eat "normally" like other children:

> It's the only normal thing that this low-functioning child did was feed. . . . and to put [in] a feeding tube was the end of my normal children. (Lowman, 1994, p. 106)

Fortunately, Jan and Brittany's story has a happy ending. After much discussion with the doctors, Brittany's family did agree to use a feeding tube. Brittany began to grow and thrive in school. Jan and the therapists worked closely together to develop a plan to continue oral feedings with Brittany.

---

[1]The quotations used in this vignette were gathered during a qualitative study of teachers of students with complex health care needs. The experiences of one teacher, Jan, are used to illustrate many of the points discussed in this chapter. The authors would like to thank Jan for allowing us to learn from her story.

PRACTICE EXERCISE

- It is important to acknowledge your own beliefs, emotional reactions, and biases regarding the feeding process before working with families of children with feeding problems.

  What are your personal beliefs about the feeding process?

  Do you believe that a child must eat everything on his or her plate?

  Do you believe that a child's picky eating reflects on the parenting?

- Jan's emotional reaction to the feeding situation with Brittany was fear. Jan was afraid that Brittany would die while she was feeding her.

  If you were in Jan's place, what would you have done when asked to orally feed Brittany in school?

- Sometimes educators do not realize the emotional impact that feeding problems have on the family.

  What steps could Jan have taken to learn and attempt to understand the family's feelings?

- Jan believed that her past experiences and training helped prepare her to work with children with complex feeding problems. She also realized that most of her knowledge was gained "on the job."

  What resources might be available to help Jan deal with this initially difficult situation?

REFERENCES

American Speech-Language-Hearing Association. (1990). Scope of practice, speech-language pathology and audiology. *Asha, 32*(Suppl. 2), 1–22.

Arvedson, J. (1993). Oral-motor and feeding assessment. In J.C. Arvedson & L. Brodsky (Eds.), *Pediatric swallowing and feeding: Assessment and management* (pp. 249–291). San Diego, CA: Singular Publishing Group.

Avery-Smith, W. (1996). Eating dysfunction positions paper. *American Journal of Occupational Therapy, 50*(10), 846–847.

Batshaw, M.L. (Ed.). (1997). *Children with disabilities* (4th ed.). Baltimore: Paul H. Brookes Publishing Co.

Batshaw, M.L., & Perrett, Y.M. (1992). *Children with disabilities: A medical primer* (3rd ed.). Baltimore: Paul H. Brookes Publishing Co.

Bazyk, B. (1990). Factors associated with the transition to oral feeding in infants fed by nasogastric tubes. *American Journal of Occupational Therapy, 44*(12), 1070–1078.

Berkow, R., & Fletcher, A.J. (Eds.). (1992). *The Merck manual of diagnosis and therapy* (16th ed.). Rahway, NJ: Merck Research Laboratories.

Blackman, J.A. (1990). *Medical aspects of developmental disabilities in children birth to three*. Gaithersburg, MD: Aspen Publishers.

Caretto, V., Francois, K., & McKinney, C. (1996). *Facilitating oral motor feeding.* Unpublished master's thesis, Virginia Commonwealth University, Richmond.

Case-Smith, J., & Humphry, R. (1996). Feeding and oral motor skills. In J. Case-Smith, A.S. Allen, & P.N. Pratt (Eds.), *Occupational therapy for children* (2nd ed., pp. 430–460). St. Louis: Mosby.

Clark, G.F. (1993). Oral-motor and feeding issues. In C.B. Royeen (Ed.), *AOTA self-study series: Classroom applications for school-based practice* (Vol. 9). Rockville, MD: American Occupational Therapy Association, Inc.

Hall, S., Yohn, K., & Reed, P.R. (1992). *Feeding students in school: Providing guidelines and information on safe feeding practices for special students.* Salem: Oregon Department of Education.

Klein, M.D., & Delaney, T.A. (1994). *Feeding and nutrition for the child with special needs: Handouts for parents.* San Antonio, TX: Therapy Skill Builders.

Lowman, D.K. (1993). Preschoolers with complex health care needs: A survey of early childhood special education teachers in Virginia. *Topics in Early Childhood Special Education, 13*(4), 445–460.

Lowman, D.K. (1994). *Integrating preschoolers with complex health care needs into early childhood special education programs: The teacher's perspective.* Unpublished doctoral dissertation, University of Virginia, Charlottesville.

Lowman, D.K., & Lane, S.J. (1998). Children with feeding and nutritional problems. In S. Porr & E.B. Rainville (Eds.), *Pediatric therapy: A systems approach.* Philadelphia: F.A. Davis Company.

Morris, S.E., & Klein, M.D. (1987). *Pre-feeding skills: A comprehensive resource for feeding development.* San Antonio, TX: Therapy Skill Builders.

Orelove, F.P., & Sobsey, D. (1996). *Educating children with multiple disabilities: A transdisciplinary approach* (3rd ed.). Baltimore: Paul H. Brookes Publishing Co.

Reilley, S., Skuse, D., & Poblete, X. (1996). Prevalence of feeding problems and oral motor dysfunction in children with cerebral palsy: A community survey. *Journal of Pediatrics, 129*, 877–882.

Shelton, T.L., & Stepanek, J. (1994). *Family-centered care for children needing specialized health and developmental services.* Bethesda, MD: Association for the Care of Children's Health.

Singer, L. (1990). When a sick child won't—or can't—eat. *Contemporary Pediatrics, 12*, 67.

Starrett, A.L. (1991). Growth in developmental disabilities. In A.J. Capute & P.J. Accardo (Eds.), *Developmental disabilities in infancy and childhood* (pp. 181–187). Baltimore: Paul H. Brookes Publishing Co.

Walter, R.S. (1994). The multidisciplinary approach to management of swallowing disorders in the pediatric patient. In D.N. Tuchman & R.S. Walter (Eds.), *Disorders of feeding and swallowing in infants and children: Pathophysiology, diagnosis, and treatment* (pp. 251–257). San Diego, CA: Singular Publishing Group.

Wolf, L.S., & Glass, R.P. (1992). *Feeding and swallowing disorders in infancy: Assessment and management.* San Antonio, TX: Therapy Skill Builders.

Appendix
Process for Developing a Holistic Feeding Plan

The questions provided under each heading are suggestions to help guide your observations.

I. Collaboration with the Family

- Has a positive family dialogue been established?
- What is the feeding routine at home? What is the feeding routine in the school or child care center?
- Issues identified by the caregiver
- What is pleasurable specific to the feeding interaction?
- What is difficult specific to the feeding interaction?
- What cultural implications are important to consider?

II. Respiratory Issues

- Is the gag reflex present and effective (i.e., not over or under responsive)?
- Is the swallow reflex present and effective (i.e., not inhibited or delayed; no paralysis)?
- Is the feeding pace determined by the child (not the feeder)?
- Is swallowing relaxed and without gagging, coughing, or aspiration?
- If a respiratory infection is present, is enough extra time allowed for coordination of breathing and swallowing?
- Is the coordination of breathing, swallowing, and talking difficult?

III. Oral-Motor Development

- Has overall muscle tone been determined (e.g., low, normal, high)?
- Have muscle tone issues specific to the face and mouth been determined?
- Have needs for oral-motor treatment been identified? Some common examples include

    Jaw—thrust, clenching, retraction, instability

This plan was adapted with permission of Rebecca Anderson Weissman, 507 Jackson Street, Falls Church, VA 22046.

Tongue—retraction, thrust, limited movement

Lip and Cheek—low tone, lip retraction

Palate—nasal reflux, cleft

Other

IV. Physical Development/Positioning

- Is 90°–90°–90° position achievable?
- Are feet and arms supported by a flat surface (i.e., not dangling)?
- Are knees at a comfortable 90° angle?
- Are hips resting symmetrically against a supportive surface?
- Is trunk upright and symmetrical?
- Is a neutral head position ensured for most effective swallow and eye contact?

V. Sensory Development

- Are any limitations of the sensory modalities present (e.g., visual, auditory, tactile, gustatory, olfactory, proprioceptive)?
- Which **textures** are most easily tolerated (e.g., thick liquids, thin liquids, smooth solids, lumpy solids, chewy solids, crunchy textures, mixed textures)?
- Which **tastes** are most easily tolerated (likes versus dislikes)?
- What **temperatures** are most easily tolerated? (Note preferences.)
- What type(s) of **touch** is (are) most easily tolerated (arousing versus calming)?

VI. Communication, Behavioral, and Socialization Skills

- Does the child have the maximum control possible?
- How does the child indicate hunger? Does food need to be present?
- How does the child indicate his or her need for a change of pace/pause in feeding?
- How does the child indicate a choice of food or liquid?
- How does the child indicate readiness for more food?
- How does the child indicate that he or she is finished eating?
- How does the child indicate a desire for social closeness/distance?

VII. Feeding Process and Implementation Plan

- Have the family, all feeders, and needed specialists participated in the development of this plan?
- Has needed medical information (including physician orders and nutrition requirements) been received and factored into this feeding plan?
- Has needed feeding equipment been identified and obtained?
- Has the most effective sequence (i.e., the best order to present food to the child) been determined?

chapter two

Collaboration and Teams

Patricia M. Blasco

This chapter addresses the importance of collaboration and team effort in effectively meeting the needs of children and young adults, ages birth–21 years, who are diagnosed with feeding difficulties. Families of children and young adults with feeding difficulties are often barraged by an onslaught of services. Federal legislation under the Individuals with Disabilities Education Act (IDEA) of 1990 (PL 101-476) and its 1997 amendments (PL 105-17) have reinforced the need for comprehensive, coordinated efforts on the part of the service delivery teams and state agencies in delivering services to children and young adults and their families.

Recommended practices within the field of special education have long advocated for collaboration among families, service providers, and agencies (Buysse & Wesley, in press; Odom & McLean, 1993; Rainforth & York-Barr, 1997; Rowan, McCollum, & Thorp, 1993). Collaboration is a process through which multiple stakeholders can constructively explore their differences and search for solutions beyond their own limited vision (Friend & Cook, 1996; Gray, 1989). Collaboration involves shared visions intended to advance the collective good of all stakeholders, interdependence among stakeholders that allows a give-and-take to produce solutions, joint ownership in the decision-making process, and the ability to engage in constructive conflict resolution (Gray, 1989).

In order to achieve collaboration, many agencies have adopted a team approach to services. *Collaborative teamwork* is defined as a process of problem solving by team members who share their knowledge and skills to work toward a solution (Rainforth et al., 1992). According to Rainforth et al., "Collaborative teamwork is work accomplished jointly by a group of people in a spirit of willingness and mutual reward" (1992, p. 11). Collaborative team models have been adopted as effective practices by professional groups working with children who have disabilities (American Occupational Therapy Association, 1989; American Physical Therapy Association, 1990; American Speech-Language-Hearing Association, 1990; Division for Early Childhood, 1993). The collaborative team model works best when team members share equal status within the group. The approach to teaming and how status is determined may, however, vary across educational, medical, and community environments.

TEAM PROCESS

Models of team organization from medical, educational, and business sectors were developed and refined in the 1980s and early 1990s as many agencies reorganized to incorporate a team approach. Important aspects of teams include how they are structured (i.e., membership), how they function as a unit, and how they interact as individuals and team members.

Based on seminal work by Tuckman (1965), Briggs (1991) provided a model for understanding the growth and development stages of teams:

1. Stage One is the *forming* stage, when the members determine the rules, expectations, and methods of functioning as a team. At this time, individuals decide their level of commitment to the team.

2. Stage Two is the *storming* stage, when team members express resistance to other members' ideas or tasks that are mentioned. An identity for the team emerges during this time.

3. Stage Three is the *norming* stage, when a sense of cohesion develops; the cultural norms of the group are set. There is a sense of team spirit and pride. Trust and open communication continue to develop.

4. Stage Four is the *performing* stage, when the team's mission and internal relationships are established. The work of the group is now accomplished, using positive problem solving and decision making.

Another aspect of team function is related to team identity. How teams conduct their interactions can be influenced by the philosophical approach to teaming. Three models provide distinct approaches to teaming and are discussed in the literature:

- The *multidisciplinary team* represents a group of professionals who work independently of each other and share information to present the goals and plans of each discipline (McGonigel, Woodruff, & Roszmann-Millican, 1994). A disadvantage of this approach is that services may not be coordinated, and families may undergo the same evaluation and assessment procedures by different team members.

- The *interdisciplinary team* represents a group of professionals and family members who work together or as a group to evaluate a child. They share information to reach consensus on a plan for the child and family. They also support each other in efforts to coordinate services to the family. Family members may be invited to participate as members of the team.

- The *transdisciplinary team* is a group of professionals and family members who not only share information and coordinate services but also share roles through role release. *Role release* involves the transfer of information and skills traditionally associated with a specific discipline to other team members (McGonigel et al., 1994; Rainforth et al., 1992). For example, an occupational therapist (OT) teaches an early intervention teacher the necessary skills to implement a feeding program for an 18-month-old child in a center-based program. Parents are members of the team and, if desired, play an active role in the assessment, implementation, and evaluation of services (Antoniadis & Videlock, 1991; Bailey, McWilliam, & Winton, 1992; Salisbury, 1992; McGonigel et al., 1994). It is important to realize that families are both participants and recipients of services and should have the opportunity to choose their level of involvement on any team.

All teams go through a process of team stabilization that requires time and commitment from team members. As new team members are added or team members leave, the team may go through a period of adjustment before it restablizes as a cohesive unit. Service providers who work on teams often refer to "strong" teams and "weak" teams. Typically, they are referring to how well the team operates as a unit to provide the most efficient and effective intervention for the child and his or her family. When teams have not gone through the process of "forming, storming, norming, and performing" (previously described in the Briggs [1991] model for understanding the growth and development stages of teams), they may have difficulty operating as an efficient unit. When this happens, problems develop that make teaming difficult or even impossible. Some teams may never move beyond the storming stage, and difficulties continue to disrupt their work.

CHALLENGES AND OPPORTUNITIES OF THE TEAM-BASED APPROACH

Since the late 1980s, training efforts have been utilized to help teams evolve toward a transdisciplinary approach to services. Despite enormous training efforts, service providers often need to be flexible in their approach to teaming. Here is one service provider's assessment:

> As a physical therapist, I've had training in the multidisciplinary approach. When I began working in early intervention, the program was using an interdisciplinary approach. Then we were trained in the transdisciplinary approach. If you asked me today which approach we use, I'd say it depends on the child, the program, and the other agencies we are dealing with. You have to be flexible and change your approach to meet the needs of the child and family. (L. Eliason, personal communication, February 21, 1995)

In the previous statement, the physical therapist was expressing her need to engage in flexible behavior when interacting with different teams. Families of children with feeding concerns also find themselves dealing with several teams that offer services. For example, a feeding team may be associated with a health care facility and function in a multidisciplinary fashion. The early intervention or special education team may be associated with a school system or community organization and function as an interdisciplinary or transdisciplinary group. It is important that teams recognize the role they play in the families' lives and that coordinated services ensure children and families optimal benefits from all agencies. In Figure 1, a feeding team model is shown that is associated with a health care facility. In Figure 2, a feeding team model is shown that is inclusive of service providers working with the family at home or in the community.

Young children with feeding difficulties may need the concerted efforts of highly skilled specialists in the health care field. Often these specialists are

The Medical Feeding Team Model

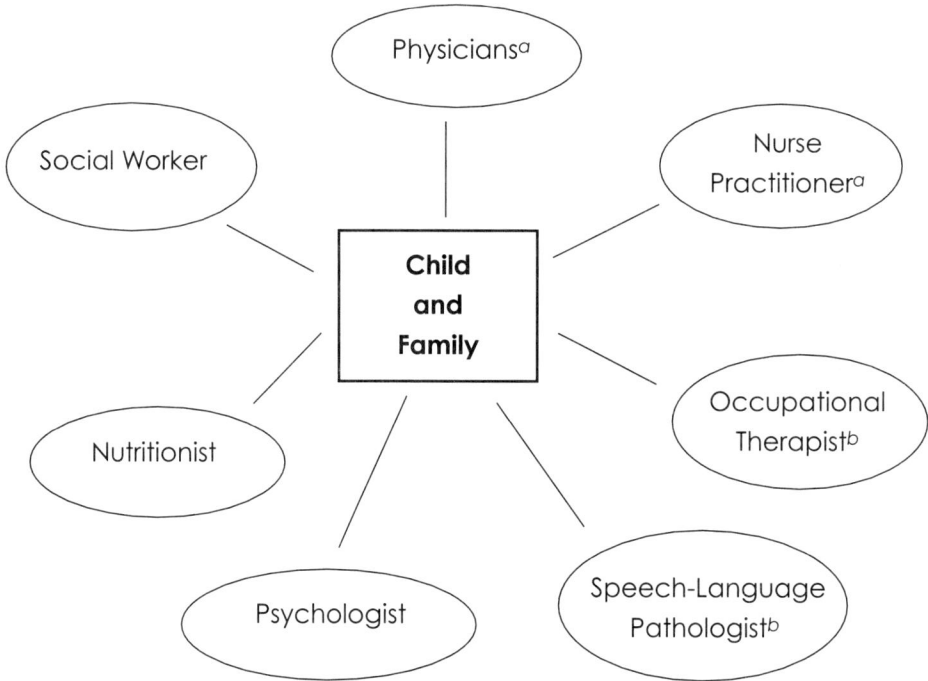

Figure 1.   The medical feeding team model, which varies in size depending on resources, the child's and family's needs, and the philosophical orientation of the program. ([a]Most teams in health care centers include a number of physicians, including pediatricians and/or pediatric gastroenterologists and/or developmental pediatricians. Nurses include the nurse practitioner as well as the local community health nurse. [b]Most teams in health care centers have either a speech-language pathologist or an occupational therapist, and some teams include a behavioral psychologist as well.)

linked to health care facilities and rehabilitation centers and may function as separate units from the "community-based" (i.e., early intervention or school-based) team. The feeding specialist collaborates with local service providers to ensure that recommendations are carried out in the home and community. Sometimes, this type of approach leaves parents negotiating with different teams who may or may not agree on a final plan. In the following vignette, an OT from a nationally recognized rehabilitation center describes her role as a member of the feeding team.

Sarah

Sarah is an OT working with a feeding team at a major rehabilitation center. An important part of her role is to interpret videofluoroscopic swallowing evaluations with a team of highly specialized health care personnel. Sarah contacts team members in each child's community to follow up on the implementation of a feeding plan. Typically, the recommendations are welcomed by the home team. Recently, however, Sarah saw Matthew, a 3-year-old boy who was born prematurely and has a significant feeding disorder. Matthew

The Inclusive Feeding Team Model

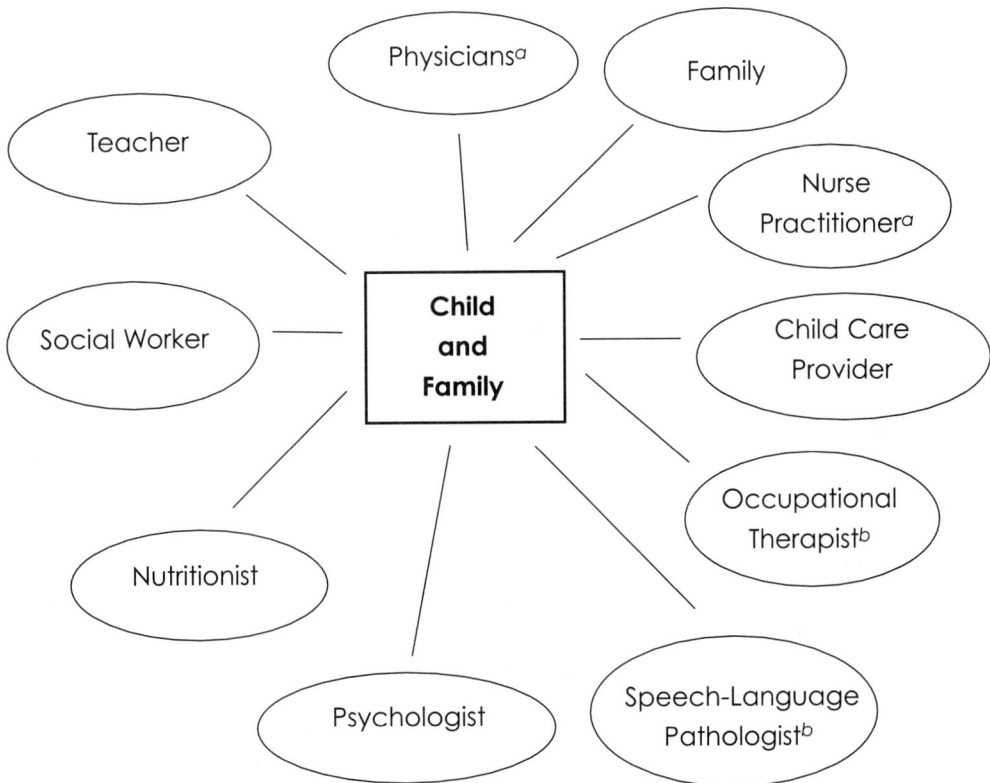

Figure 2.   The inclusive feeding team model includes the teacher and child care provider in addition to the other team members. Family members are equal team players in this model. ([a]Most teams in communities include a number of physicians, including pediatricians and/or pediatric gastroenterologists and/or developmental pediatricians. Nurses include the nurse practitioner as well as the local community health nurse. [b]Most teams in communities have either a speech-language pathologist or an occupational therapist, and some teams include a behavioral psychologist as well.)

was seen by the feeding team, who came up with a plan that Sarah shared with the home therapist. Despite several telephone conversations and faxing of medical reports, Sarah and the therapist could not agree on Matthew's treatment. Ultimately, Matthew's mother and the local primary care physician made the decision on which treatment plan to follow. Sarah expressed her frustration with the increasing difficulty within the present managed health care system in providing consultation and collaboration with local intervention teams. She said, "I used to spend time with these other team members or talk with them on the telephone. Now much of my time is spent getting preauthorization by both the primary care physician and the insurance company. In addition, the reimbursement does not cover indirect costs, such as team collaboration and telephone time required to implement a complex plan."

In the previous vignette, the parent had to step in and, with the help of one service provider, make the final decision in regard to treatment. The efforts of the OT to resolve differences with the community therapist were hampered by the lack of consultation time and loss of direct contact. Health maintenance organizations (HMOs) may discourage referrals for specialized treatment.

In an ideal scenario, the local team members, including the parents, could attend the medical team meeting, offer input to the discussion, and jointly decide on a plan. Gray (1989) noted, however, that institutional disincentives often work against a collaborative approach. With the advent of managed health care, indirect costs are not reimbursed, which limits the time for collaboration within teams and for collaboration between teams. In addition, because some facilities are no longer listed under certain HMOs, professionals find themselves competing for dollars. Thus, "turf issues" and ideological differences may surface when financial resources become scarce, and professionals are increasingly held accountable for their services.

One strategy to help improve communication under the present system is to utilize the service coordinator as a liaison between different teams. The service coordinator acts as a link between the family and service delivery professionals (Bennett, Nelson, Lingerfelt, & Davenport-Ersoff, 1992). Teams need to find consensus despite different philosophical approaches to teaming. An important goal is to ensure that communication is facilitated in an efficient and productive manner.

Building Collaborative Relationships

"Real change will occur only when a comprehensive, long-term systematic approach is taken and when those who will be affected by change participate in the decisions about its implementation" (Bailey et al., 1992, p. 74). In order to develop more inclusive teams, a team-based model for change was developed and tested by Bailey and his colleagues (Bailey et al., 1992; Winton, McWilliam, Harrison, Owens, & Bailey, 1992). This approach was designed to promote family-centered practices among members of teams. The model is based on the following assumptions about how change among team members occurs:

- Change is a difficult process.

- Change is a gradual, long-term process.

- Change is more likely to occur in small steps that blend existing ideas with new ones.

- Training to promote change should focus on the entire team, rather than on the individual.

- Training to promote change should empower team members to identify their own change strategies and solutions.

- Parents and other consumers should have input about changes that will affect them (Buysse & Wesley, in press).

When the feeding team applies this model, it is easier to accept that things may move at a slow pace. Team members are more likely to work on problem solving as a cohesive unit rather than as a group of individuals. Parents are more likely to carry out the plan at home, and child care workers are more likely to carry out the plan in a center- or home-based program. Obstacles include the lack of total participation by all team players and possible negative effects because of repeated absenteeism by some members (Winton et al., 1992). As we enter the 21st century, options such as teleconferencing need to be explored as a means of bringing teams together without the expensive and extensive time commitment required for face-to-face meetings. By including options for conference calls and/or video conferencing, information can be shared efficiently and quickly with team members.

Another significant challenge to effective teaming occurs when there is dissatisfaction among a few team members, but not the entire team, regarding team goals, roles, or process (Buysse & Wesley, in press). When an individual is not satisfied, he or she may behave in ways that can be counterproductive to teaming. Each individual brings his or her own interpersonal skills to the team. A team member who feels ownership as the "feeding expert" may want to dominate decisions regarding the feeding plan. In a worst-case scenario, team members may attempt to "win" the family over to their side of a disagreement and inadvertently promote unnecessary problems and confrontations for the family.

It is important for teams to realize that conflict is a part of collaboration (Gray, 1989). Johnson and Johnson (1997) pointed out that people who avoid conflicts may do so because they do not trust the other team members. People who are afraid of conflict may be fearful of being rejected. Johnson and Johnson identified several outcomes of constructive conflict. These outcomes include the following:

- Relationships among participants are strengthened so they are able to work collaboratively.

- Participants increase respect and trust for each other.

- Participants are satisfied with the results of the conflict (i.e., goals and needs are met).

- Participants have increased their ability to resolve future conflicts.

Developing Communication Skills for Team Members

Many of the problems in teaming can be averted if team members take the time to reflect on their own values and skills in negotiating with others. Good communication skills are essential for all team members. Communication includes listening skills that are related to effective interactions with other team members, including the family (Friend & Cook, 1996; Winton, 1988). Some communication strategies are

- *Minimal encouraging*—Ability to use words, phrases, silence, and so forth that show the team member is listening, interested, and nonjudgmental (Winton referred to these skills as *reflective listening.*)

- *Paraphrasing*—Ability to give feedback to the speaker, essentially repeating everything the speaker just said (e.g., "You're not sure if he did a thorough examination")

- *Reflecting*—Ability to acknowledge the speaker's feelings (e.g., "You sound angry about this, but I think we can find a solution we can all live with")

- *Clarifying*—Ability to confirm the speaker's comments (e.g., "So you definitely feel unsure about the results of the test")

- *Elaborating*—Ability to enhance what the speaker says by adding more details

- *Summarizing*—Ability to integrate and synthesize all of the relevant information that was shared (Friend & Cook, 1996; Winton, 1988)

Team members, knowingly or not, also communicate nonverbally through body movements, facial expressions, eye contact, posture, and gestures (Friend & Cook, 1996). Team members should consider the impact of their body language through role play with another team member or by videotaping themselves during a conference and completing a self-evaluation. For example, a team member who is shuffling through papers while another team member or parent is speaking is not showing respect for the speaker.

Many team members will admit discomfort with silence. As a result, they may interrupt a speaker or immediately introduce another topic to keep the team moving. It is important for team members to allow some time for silence in order to synthesize what has been shared in the meeting and to let the speaker know that the team members are interested in his or her comments (Friend & Cook, 1996).

Evaluating the Team Process

In order to reflect on one's own contribution to the team and evaluate the roles of individuals on the team, one should understand the different types of roles team members may play. The following descriptions of team members' styles of interaction indicate some of the many roles that are played during teaming:

- The *contributor* is task-oriented. This individual may be a mentor to other team members and a disseminator of technical knowledge.

- The *collaborator* is goal-oriented. This individual may be a supporter and synthesizer of information.

- The *communicator* is process-oriented. This individual may be a monitor, consensus builder, and active listener.

- The *challenger* is values-oriented. This individual will question team process, take risks, and seek creative solutions (Buysse & Wesley, in press; Parker, 1990).

An understanding of the roles members play may help the team to assess and evaluate the team's behavior. For example, too many people of any one type of personality may lead to increased conflict within the team. When problems are complex, as feeding problems often are, conflicts within the team are inevitable (Gray, 1989). Teams need to acknowledge the potential for conflict and act accordingly to resolve situations that could result in escalating and deeply polarizing problems.

In describing effective teams, several researchers have found that certain characteristics are essential for success (Briggs, 1993; Buysse & Wesley, in press). Similarly, many of these capabilities are validated in the literature on establishing collaborative relationships. Table 1 describes the functions of effective teams.

Effective teams enjoy and celebrate collaborative relationships. They set ground rules; when bickering occurs, they reexamine their mission. Effective

Table 1.   Functions of effective teams

- Establish a clear mission, purpose, and goals
- Involve all key stakeholders in the development of a plan
- Provide sufficient resources to engage in teaming
- Recruit qualified team players
- Promote open communication and a climate of trust
- Evaluate both individual and team performance
- Engage in constructive conflict resolution and problem-solving strategies (Briggs, 1993; Gray, 1989)

teams engage in ongoing evaluation through self- and group-reflection exercises. They may ask themselves, "How are we doing?" and "What has been accomplished today?" The approach to formative evaluation procedures varies widely from informal meetings held over lunch to structured activities, surveys, or focus groups. In the appendix at the end of this chapter, resources for team reflection and team-building activities are listed.

FAMILIES AS PARTNERS IN COLLABORATION

The use of positive communication strategies is particularly important in working with families. Following a family empowerment model, Dunst, Trivette, and Deal (1988) suggested that parents and professionals work together to secure and maximize services. As team members, families may or may not feel equal in the partnership, depending on the approach used by the team. Families often state that they are not considered equals. For example, parents of children with failure to thrive (both organic and nonorganic) may believe that they have done something wrong to their children (Family Network on Disabilities of Florida, 1995). In order to avoid negative connotations for families, professionals should show sensitivity to family members. For example, professionals should avoid terms such as "inadequate weight gain" when discussing a child with failure to thrive with the child's family (Dawson, 1992). The professional should make a special point of acknowledging positive features about the child as well as the child's strengths. In the following vignette, one parent describes her experience with her infant daughter, who is now a young adult.

Kimberly

Imagine for a few minutes that you are a new mother. Since coming home from the hospital, your baby has experienced most of the following symptoms:

- Takes one or more hours to finish a bottle
- Frequently vomits everything he or she just painstakingly drank
- Often refuses to eat
- Has frequent episodes of diarrhea
- Does not sleep much
- Cries often and is hard to settle down
- Is exhibiting very slow weight gain

What would you do?

Let me tell you about my daughter, Kimberly, an infant who was unable to eat. By the time Kim was 17 months old, she had been hospitalized 12 times. The first hospitalization was when she was 2 weeks old. During each hospitalization, Kim was put through a lot of tests—stomach, neurological, blood, and so forth. She was often hooked up to an IV (intravenous catheter). She would refuse to eat and vomited in the hospital just as she did at home. Kim's team included pediatricians, surgeons, a gastroenterologist, nurses, social workers, and clergy. They would have weekly meetings with us. It was very frightening and frustrating for us because no one could come up with a solution. Some of the doctors fought with each other as to the best treatment for Kim. One surgeon proposed flying her to Boston to have a specialist stitch her abdomen to her esophagus to stop her from vomiting, but the pediatricians argued she would die on the operating table due to her low weight.

By this time, my husband and I had both dropped out of college, and I had to quit my part-time job. I stayed at the hospital around the clock to be with Kim. I became so exhausted that I had to be hospitalized myself for 4 days. My husband and I argued about which treatment plan Kim should follow. He thought we should take her out of the hospital and seek new doctors. I wanted to keep Kim's doctors and follow their treatment plan. Eventually the strain was just too hard on our marriage, and we separated and divorced.

Kim typically took 1½ hours to complete a feeding. At 17 months old, she weighed 19 pounds (see Figure 3). It often took two people to feed Kim; one person played games with her while the other person would sneak her the food. This had to be done because Kim began to associate eating with vomiting. This scenario went on for 6 months until an astute radiologist noticed on an X ray that Kim had esophageal reflux—stomach contents flowed upward in her esophagus. Kim was finally diagnosed with organic failure to thrive at 2 years of age. Due to her late diagnosis, she was delayed in her development. For example, Kim did not walk until she was 20 months old. She continued to receive special education services throughout her elementary school years.

Kim is now 19½ years old. She is in her first year of college and has many friends. She works part time, and she would like to be a news reporter. She recently landed a job at a local newspaper. It has been a long, hard road for Kim, myself, and our family, but we made it! Hopefully, future children and their families will not have to go through the difficulties we encountered, given current research and medical advancements.

Collaboration with Families from a Family Systems Approach

Relationships within a family are driven by interacting subsystems (Minuchin, 1988; Turnbull & Turnbull, 1990). Different members of the family make up several subsystems that are mutually influential. For example, the marital subsystem is composed of the interaction of two primary caregivers (traditionally the parents of the children within the marriage). Other subsystems include the parent–child, sibling, and extended family interactions.

Understanding the influence of these interacting subsystems helps service providers work with families in a more effective way. All families follow rules of interaction that are embedded in the individual cultural and ideological beliefs of the family (Blasco & Pearson, 1995; Salisbury, 1992). It is important to acknowledge family rules and boundaries established to delineate membership within a subsystem. Boundaries may keep service providers outside family interactions or allow them into the inner core of the family. Families may respond differently to service providers at different times in

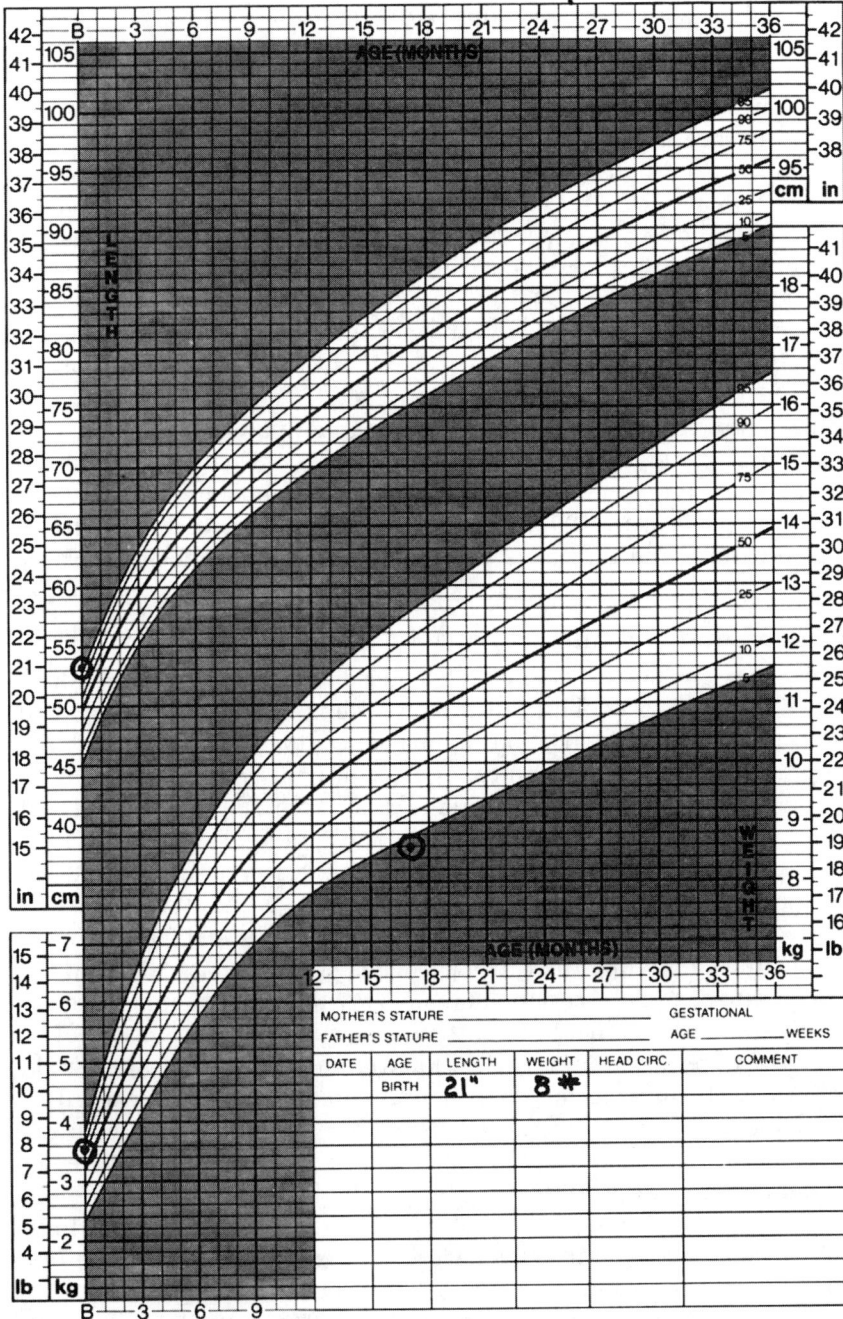

Figure 3. Kimberly's growth chart (Adapted from Hamill, P.V.V., Drizd, T.A., Johnson, C.L., Reed, R.B., Roche, A.F., & Moore, W.M. [1979]. Physical growth: National Center for Health Statistics percentiles. *American Journal of Clinical Nutrition, 32,* 607–629; used with permission of Ross Products Division, Abbott Laboratories, Columbus, OH 43216; from NCHS Growth Chart Girls Birth To 36 Months, © 1982 Ross Products Division, Abbott Laboratories.)

their child's development. For example, when a family is in crisis, boundaries may be confused, inconsistent, or nonexistent (Minuchin, 1988). Thus, a service provider may be closed out of the family at a time when services could be most helpful. Acknowledgment of the family's wishes and desires and a willingness to follow the family's lead help establish the trust necessary for a continued working relationship between the service provider and the family.

Parents under a great deal of stress may not have the emotional availability to engage in positive feeding interactions. At an early age, these reciprocal interactions are often precursors to active engagement for the child with others (Satter, 1992). As stated in Chapter 1, feeding is a social endeavor that can promote or discourage positive relationships between the child and caregiver. It is also a time when cultural traditions and values are shared (Case-Smith & Humphry, 1996).

When a parent or caregiver cannot feed his or her child for a variety of reasons, problems may develop across many aspects of the relationship. This may be further compounded in families experiencing poverty and lack of informal resources (e.g., friends, relatives) and formal resources (e.g., agencies, religious groups). In some situations, parents may need help with basic information on proper nutrition and resources for obtaining nutritious food for their child (Dawson, 1992). Service providers can advocate for resources and help parents and caregivers to help themselves in achieving a plan for their child.

Understanding Parent–Child Interaction

Children and families experiencing feeding difficulties are often evaluated together in order to establish an understanding of the complexity of the relationship and how the relationship may affect the child's feeding abilities. Aspects such as pacing, preference, or capability in terms of food readiness are examined for both the parent and the child. According to Barnard (1997), each partner's responses are contingent on one another. This interactive partnership should be rich in affection and mutual pleasure. The Nursing Child Assessment Satellite Training Feeding and Teaching (NCAST) scales (Barnard, 1979) were developed around six constructs of parent–child interaction. The four constructs reflecting the caregiver's behavior are 1) sensitivity to cues, 2) response to distress, 3) social-emotional growth fostering, and 4) cognitive growth fostering. The other two constructs examine the child's clarity of cues and the child's responsiveness to the caregiver. In numerous research studies, the NCAST scales have been used to identify three risk factors associated with problematic parent–child interaction. These are 1) low maternal education, 2) adolescent motherhood, and 3) preterm birth or infants with severe medical conditions (Barnard, 1997).

One criticism of quantitative scales to assess feeding is that these instruments quantify the amount of behaviors on a binary scale. This type of assessment may not take into account the quality and appropriateness of the interaction or other extenuating circumstances. For example, if a parent is asked to feed his or her child in a clinical environment, the parent may not exhibit the types of interactions that are natural in the home environment. In addition, the scale is based on the scoring by the professional, who may or may not be attuned to the influence of cultural differences.

Researchers have attempted to apply a partnership approach to examining parent–child interaction. Lawhon (cited in Barnard, 1997) designed an intervention study in which the parents decided the amount and timing of intervention. The researcher provided guidance of the parents' impression of their infant's behavior. Similarly, Haas, Baird, McCormick, and Reilly (1994) used videotapes of parent–child interaction to help parents identify their own interactive style.

In reality, teams will differ in their approach to family involvement. In addition, families will differ in their interest in involvement. As stated in Wolf and Glass, "The chronicity of the feeding problem combined with the stress of dealing with it many times per day can erode the spirit of even the most invested parent" (1992, p. 287). Using active listening techniques and avoiding professional jargon help the service provider and the family find common ground. Another consideration is the complexity of the feeding difficulty. If the infant develops bradycardia (i.e., slower heart beat) or experiences apnea (i.e., passing episodes of stopped breathing) during feeding, then the number of individuals responsible for feeding may need to be limited. The team, including the family, must feel comfortable with individuals entrusted with feeding a child who has complex health care needs.

THE FEEDING PLAN

Once all team members have participated in a full evaluation of the child with a feeding disorder, the team can move forward with a feeding plan. This plan can be incorporated into the child's individualized family service plan (IFSP) or individualized education program (IEP). It is important to approach the identification of strategies as an ongoing process that changes with the child's needs (Wolf & Glass, 1992). It is equally important to consider the parents' preferences and to include those preferences in the plan. For example, one mother expressed the desire to breast-feed her child who was experiencing difficulty with feeding. The team developed strategies to address the child's needs while adopting a plan so that the mother's strong desire to breast-feed her infant could be accommodated as well.

Straka and Bricker (1996) advocated five team competencies that will result in an effective program for all children. The first competency, communication, has already been discussed in this chapter. Communication skills, however, are important in facilitating a smooth IFSP or IEP process. The second competency is related to the need to streamline assessment procedures. Collaborative teamwork during the assessment process should reduce redundant testing and provide more functional outcomes. The third competency is related to the development of the IFSP or IEP. According to the authors, collaborative discussion and joint decision making in the development of outcomes and objectives will result in more cohesive and functional goals. The fourth competency is related to a coordinated intervention plan that utilizes the IFSP and IEP in activities that are most meaningful for the family and can be generalized across multiple environments. The fifth competency is related to the evaluation process. The team should jointly conduct an evaluation to determine whether both child and family goals have been met. The evaluation process should include both formative (i.e., ongoing) evaluation of the child's and family's progress as well as overall evaluation of team function and family satisfaction. Families should have the opportunity to participate in all competency areas. Professional team members should identify supports for families so they can participate in team activities to the extent that they want to be involved.

ECOLOGICAL INVENTORY

An ecological inventory is one strategy for developing a comprehensive feeding plan (Noonan & McCormick, 1993; Snell, 1987). This method focuses on the natural environment both as a source for developing an effective plan and as a source for implementing the plan. The ecological inventory includes five phases:

1. Identify feeding issues.

2. Identify current and future natural environments.

3. Divide the relevant environments into subenvironments.

4. Inventory those subenvironments for relevant activities performed there.

5. Examine the activities to identify the skills needed to perform the task.

In Figure 4, an ecological worksheet is used to demonstrate a plan that includes the natural environment and activities that are likely to be carried out by the caregiver and family members. This plan can be developed by the team, including the parents or caregivers. The inventory can be a formal or informal set of questions to assess both current and future environments. For

---

Steps
1. Identify current environments.
2. Identify subenvironments.
3. List activities that occur in subenvironments.
4. Identify the skills necessary to participate in the activity.
5. Assess the abilities of the child to perform those skills.

Environment: Home

Subenvironment #1	Subenvironment #2	Subenvironment #3
Kitchen	Family room	Patio

Activities

Breakfast	Television or movie snack	Lunch
Lunch		Dinner
Dinner		

Skills
Participate in family meals.
Participate in family recreation time, including snacks.
Engage in social conversation and interaction during meals.

Specific
Eat food with partial participation by a family member.
Eat food, using adaptive utensils.
Stay seated during meals.
Pass food to other family members.
Wipe face and hands after eating.
Carry plate and utensils to the sink.

Figure 4.   An ecological worksheet.

example, if the family is concerned that the child be capable of sharing a family meal, then part of the plan could address strategies and materials to enable the child to sit upright at a table and eat with appropriate assistance from family members.

Incorporating Feeding Goals into the IFSP or IEP

One goal of collaborative teamwork is to develop the IFSP or the IEP (Straka & Bricker, 1996). The ecological inventory and the feeding plan can be used as part of the IFSP and IEP process. Families can help team members specify the outcomes in relation to feeding activities and set the time lines to address these activities. For older children, feeding goals may not be listed on an IEP; however, these are functional goals that will affect all other educational domains for the child experiencing difficulty.

SUMMARY

This chapter addresses collaboration among team members working with children experiencing feeding difficulties and their families. Collaborative teamwork has long been advocated in educational as well as health care environments. In order to engage in successful teaming, an understanding of team dynamics and team styles are important. Teams should engage in periodic individual and group reflection as a part of ongoing evaluation of services.

The role of the family as a member of the team is presented in this chapter. Family members play an important role in carrying out the feeding plan and should be involved in the design, implementation, and evaluation of the plan. At the same time, family members vary in the amount of time they can contribute to the team; therefore, schedules should be flexible to include family input.

Teams can incorporate an ecological framework for developing a feeding plan that includes natural environments for the child and family. In many situations, feeding goals are incorporated into the IFSP or IEP by team members. This practice may facilitate implementation of goals across environments.

Amber

Karen sat in the conference room shuffling papers as she tried to compose herself. There was a team meeting in 15 minutes, and she knew that she would have to confront one of her teammates. Karen, an OT with an early intervention team, has been working with one family for over 14 months. The family was referred to early intervention after Amber, 2½ years old, was admitted to the hospital with gastroesophageal reflux. In addition to her feeding problem, Amber had been removed from a child care center the previous spring. The family often falls behind on child care payments, and Amber's behavioral concerns are challenging to the staff. Amber lives with her father, grandmother, two aunts, and one uncle. Amber's father and grandmother both work, so Amber is often cared for by her aunts. At the last team meeting, Karen had requested a behavioral observation in Amber's home by Cathy, the special education teacher. The team agreed that this would be an important step prior to the next IFSP meeting. Karen noticed that Cathy appeared unhappy.

Cathy said her workload was already reaching her limits, and she didn't know where she would find the time to visit Amber's home. Karen and Cathy agreed that Cathy would visit on a Tuesday morning. Because Karen was interested in behavioral observation procedures, she thought she would meet Cathy at the family's home. Karen thought about stopping by the office to let Cathy know she would be there, but she was running late from her previous visit, so she just drove over to Amber's neighborhood. Karen arrived 10 minutes early and chatted with Amber's dad, Nigel, who had gotten time off from work to participate in the observation/interview. Cathy failed to arrive at the appointed time, and Karen became annoyed because she had heard complaints from other families that Cathy was often late. After 20 minutes, Karen decided to call the office. She got Cathy's voice mail and left a message reminding Cathy of the appointment. Karen apologized to Amber's family and suggested that perhaps there was a mix-up.

The next day at the office, Karen approached Cathy to inquire about her absence. Cathy informed Karen that she had heard that Amber lived in a bad neighborhood and chose not to go there. Cathy said that she called the police precinct, and they told her it was not a safe place to go alone. Cathy also thought that Amber's feeding needs should be the main concern right now and that Amber's behavior would improve once she was eating well. Cathy reminded Karen of Maslow's theory of need hierarchy and how basic needs, such as nutrition, had to be met before other needs were met. Karen was furious with Cathy. She couldn't believe that Cathy could be so irresponsible. Karen was too upset to confront Cathy at the time, and now they would have to deal with the problem during the team meeting. Maybe it was just as well; Cathy's behavior in the past several months had been an issue for all of the team members. Karen just didn't know how to get started.

PRACTICE EXERCISE

. . . .

1. What should Karen say or do during the team meeting?

2. Was there anything Karen could have done prior to the meeting?

3. How could this situation be resolved so that Amber's family does not need to be caught in the middle?

4. What communication skills could Karen use to engage in this conflict in a constructive manner?

5. What communication skills could Cathy have used to avoid the incident altogether?

6. Do you agree that the team meeting is a good place to resolve this conflict?

7. Do you think that the team can adequately address the issues? Think of some strategies to solve the problems of 1) Cathy's missing an appointment without calling the family and 2) Cathy's belief that Amber doesn't really need a behavior program until her feeding issues are resolved.

REFERENCES

American Occupational Therapy Association. (1989). *Guidelines for occupational therapy services in the public schools* (2nd ed.). Rockville, MD: Author.

American Physical Therapy Association. (1990). *Physical therapy practice in educational environments.* Alexandria, VA: Author.

American Speech-Language-Hearing Association. (1990). The roles of speech-language pathologists in service delivery to infants, toddlers, and their families. *Asha, 32*(Suppl. 2), 4.

Antoniadis, A., & Videlock, J.L. (1991). In search of teamwork: A transactional approach to team functioning. *Infant-Toddler Intervention: The Transdisciplinary Journal, 1*(2),157–167.

Bailey, D.B., McWilliam, P.J., & Winton, P.J. (1992). Building family-centered practices in early intervention: A team-based model for change. *Infants and Young Children, 5*(1), 73–82.

Barnard, K.E. (1979). *Instructor's learning resource manual.* Seattle: University of Washington, NCAST (Nursing Child Assessment Satellite Training Feeding and Teaching) Publications.

Barnard, K.E. (1997). Influencing parent–child interactions for children at risk. In M.J. Guralnick (Ed.), *The effectiveness of early intervention* (pp. 249–268). Baltimore: Paul H. Brookes Publishing Co.

Bennett, T., Nelson, D.E., Lingerfelt, B.V., & Davenport-Ersoff, C. (1992). Family-centered service coordination. In T. Bennett, D.E. Nelson, & B.V. Lingerfelt (Eds.), *Facilitating family-centered training in early intervention* (pp. 145–177). San Antonio, TX: Therapy Skill Builders.

Blasco, P.M., & Pearson, J.A. (1995). Working with families. In T.J. Zirpoli (Ed.), *Understanding and affecting the behavior of young children* (pp. 219–241). Upper Saddle River, NJ: Prentice-Hall.

Briggs, M.H. (1991). Team development: Decision-making for early intervention. *Infant-Toddler Intervention: The Transdisciplinary Journal, 1*(1), 1–9.

Briggs, M.H. (1993). Team talk: Communication skills for early intervention teams. *Journal of Childhood Communication Disorders, 15*(1), 33–40.

Buysse, V., & Wesley, P.W. (in press). Models of collaboration for early intervention: Laying the groundwork. In P.M. Blasco (Ed.), *Early services for infants and toddlers with disabilities.* Needham Heights, MA: Allyn & Bacon.

Case-Smith, J., & Humphry, R. (1996). Feeding and oral motor skills. In J. Case-Smith, A.S. Allen, & P.N. Pratt (Eds.), *Occupational therapy for children* (pp. 430–460). St. Louis, MO: Mosby.

Dawson, P. (1992). A feeding problem. *Zero to Three, 12*(5), 21–23.

Division for Early Childhood Task Force on Recommended Practices. (1993). *DEC recommended practices: Indications of quality in programs for infants and young children with special needs and their families.* Reston, VA: Council for Exceptional Children.

Dunst, C., Trivette, C., & Deal, A. (1988). *Enabling and empowering families: Principles and guidelines for practice.* Cambridge, MA: Brookline Books.

Family Network on Disabilities of Florida. (1995). *Building family strengths: An educational and skill building workshop for families of children with or at risk for developmental delays* [Brochure]. Clearwater, Florida: Author.

Friend, M., & Cook, L. (1996). *Interactions: Collaboration skills for school professionals.* White Plains, NY: Longman.

Gray, B. (1989). *Collaboration: Finding common ground for multiparty problems.* San Francisco: Jossey-Bass.

Haas, L., Baird, S.M., McCormick, K., & Reilly, A. (1994). Infant behaviors interpreted by their mothers. *Infant-Toddler Intervention: The Transdisciplinary Journal,* 203–220.

Hamill, P.V.V., Drizd, T.A., Johnson, C.L., Reed, R.B., Roche, A.F., & Moore, W.M. (1979). Physical growth: National Center for Health Statistics percentiles. *American Journal of Clinical Nutrition, 32,* 607–629.

Individuals with Disabilities Education Act (IDEA) of 1990, PL 101-476, 20 U.S.C. §§ 1400 *et seq.*

Individuals with Disabilities Education Act Amendments of 1997, PL 105-17, 20 U.S.C. §§ 1400 *et seq.*

Johnson, D.W., & Johnson, F.P. (1997). *Joining together: Group theory and group skills* (6th ed.). Needham Heights, MA: Allyn & Bacon.

McGonigel, M.J., Woodruff, G., & Roszmann-Millican, M. (1994). The transdisciplinary team: A model for family-centered early intervention. In L.J. Johnson, R.J. Gallagher, & M.J. LaMontagne (Eds.), *Meeting early intervention challenges: Issues from birth to three* (2nd ed., pp. 95–131). Baltimore: Paul H. Brookes Publishing Co.

Minuchin, P. (1988). Relationships within the system: A systems perspective on development. In R.A. Hinde & J. Stevenson-Hinde (Eds.), *Relationships within families.* New York: Oxford University Press.

Noonan, M.J., & McCormick, L. (1993). *Early intervention in natural environments: Methods and procedures.* Pacific Grove, CA: Brooks/Cole.

Parker, G.M. (1990). *Team players and teamwork.* San Francisco: Jossey-Bass.

Rainforth, B., & York-Barr, J. (1997). *Collaborative teams for students with severe disabilities: Integrating therapy and educational services* (2nd ed.). Baltimore: Paul H. Brookes Publishing Co.

Rowan, L.E., McCollum, J.A., & Thorp, E.K. (1993). Collaborative graduate education of future early interventionists. *Topics in Language Disorders, 14,* 72–80.

Salisbury, C. (1992). Parents as team members: Inclusive teams, collaborative outcomes. In B. Rainforth, J. York, & C. Macdonald *Collaborative teams for students with severe disabilities: Integrating therapy and educational services* (pp. 43–66). Baltimore: Paul H. Brookes Publishing Co.

Satter, E. (1992). A feeding problem. *Zero to Three, 12*(5),18–19.

Snell, M. (1987). *Systematic instruction of persons with severe handicaps.* Upper Saddle River, NJ: Prentice-Hall.

Straka, E., & Bricker, D. (1996). Building a collaborative team. In D. Bricker & A. Widerstrom (Eds.), *Preparing personnel to work with infants and young children and their families* (pp. 321–345). Baltimore: Paul H. Brookes Publishing Co.

Tuckman, B.W. (1965). Developmental sequence in small groups. *Psychological Bulletin, 63,* 384–399.

Turnbull, A.P., & Turnbull, H.R. (1990). *Families, professionals, and exceptionality: A special partnership* (2nd ed.). New York: Merrill/Macmillan.

Winton, P.J. (1988). Effective communication between parents and professions. In D.B. Bailey & R.J. Simeonsson (Eds.), *Family assessment in early intervention* (pp. 207–228). Columbus, OH: Charles E. Merrill.

Winton, P.J., McWilliam, P.J., Harrison, T., Owens, A.M., & Bailey, D.B. (1992). Lessons learned from implementing a team-based model for change. *Infants and Young Children, 5*(1), 49–57.

Wolf, L.S., & Glass, R.P. (1992). *Feeding and swallowing disorders in infancy: Assessment and management.* San Antonio, TX: Therapy Skill Builders.

Appendix
Teams: An Annotated Resource List

Administrative (Team) Challenges in Early Intervention
Garland, C.W., & Linder, T.W. (1990). Administrative (team) challenges in early intervention. *Early childhood special education: Birth to three.* Washington, DC: ERIC Clearinghouse on Handicapped and Gifted Children. This is a chapter in a three-chapter monograph. It addresses administrative aspects of teaming, including interviewing potential team members and assessing team effectiveness.

Collaborative Team Planning in Early Intervention
Kjerkland, L., & Trimbach, K. (1989). *Collaborative team planning in early intervention.* Eagan, MN: Project Dakota Outreach. Describes a method of collaboratively building a holistic description of a child in functional language and a method of generating clear, practical goals/outcomes and strategies. Available through Project Dakota, Training and Consultation Services (612/455-2335; FAX 612/455-8972).

Collaborative Teams for Students
with Severe Disabilities: Integrating Therapy and Educational Services
Rainforth, B., & York-Barr, J. (1997). *Collaborative teams for students with severe disabilities: Integrating therapy and educational services* (2nd ed.). Baltimore: Paul H. Brookes Publishing Co. This guidebook discusses how to choose team members, define responsibilities, and implement team strategies. Issues discussed include developing an ecological curriculum, conducting collaborative assessment, designing a collaborative IEP, scheduling the logistics of integrated therapy and education, and developing action plans for change.

Consultation-Based Programming:
Instituting the Collaborative Ethic in Schools
Phillips, V., & McCullough, L. (1990). Consultation-based programming: Instituting the collaborative ethic in schools. *Exceptional Children, 56*(4), 291–304. This article discusses program development, proposes "informal standards for ecological evaluation of specific formats" of collaborative service provision, and identifies factors that contribute to the success of such programs.

Drexler/Sibbet Team Performance Model
Drexler, A., & Sibbet, D. (1994). *Drexler/Sibbet team performance model.* San Fransisco, CA: Graphic Guides Inc. This four-page, two-color folder includes an overview of the seven stages of the team process, as described by this model. Each stage includes behavior indicators for determining resolved and unresolved issues.

Getting Started Together: Developing an Interdisciplinary Team
Bataillon, K. (1990). *Getting started together: Developing an interdisciplinary team.* [videotape]. Omaha, NE: Meyer Rehabilitation Institute. This videotape addresses the development of an interdisciplinary team, the elements of effective team meetings, managing conflicts, and in-

Compiled by Karen Lewis and Patricia Mulhearn Blasco, University of St. Thomas, St. Paul, Minnesota.

volving parents. It provides examples of team meetings. The video can be used for self- or group-instruction. A manual is included that contains study guides, worksheets, additional readings, and evaluation forms. The first section is dry with a single presenter; the later section, with examples of team meetings, is very effective in illustrating important aspects of team meetings.

Getting to Yes
Fisher, R., Ury, W., & Patton, B. (1991). *Getting to yes.* New York: Penguin Books. Offers methods for negotiating personal and professional conflicts with objectivity and fairness.

Getting Together
Fisher, R., & Brown, S. (1989). *Getting together.* New York: Penguin Books. Gives guidelines for initiating and sustaining effective relationships in work and personal situations.

Graphic Guide to Team Performance Principles and Practices
Sibbet, D., & Drexler, A. (1994). *Graphic guide to team performance principles and practices.* San Francisco: Graphic Guide, Inc. This introductory guide includes discussion about outlining strategies for defining teams, determining interdependence, selecting leaders, and initiating performance improvement. A catalog section describes stages of the model in detail and reviews recommended practices in paragraph form. It can be used to give teams ideas for managing the team process.

'I Beg to Differ': Conflict in the Interdisciplinary Team
Sands, R.G., Stafford, J., & McClelland, M. (1990). 'I beg to differ': Conflict in the interdisciplinary team. *Social Work in Health Care, 14*(3), 55–72. This article demonstrates conflict and conflict resolution, using three examples as illustrations. The article discusses covert and overt expressions of disagreement and the different ways individuals address these situations. It is also suggested that one difficulty encountered by interdisciplinary teams is that members often see themselves as representatives of their discipline, rather than as members of the team.

Implementing Family-Centered Services: A Team-Based Model for Change
Bailey, D.B., McWilliam, P.J., Winton, P.J., & Simeonsson, R.J. (1992). *Implementing family-centered services: A team-based model for change.* Boston: Brookline Books. This resource provides a team-based decision-making workshop for implementing family-centered services.

Indirect Service Delivery Through Consultation:
Review and Implications for Early Intervention
File, N., & Kontos, S. (1992). Indirect service delivery through consultation: Review and implications for early intervention. *Journal of Early Intervention, 16*(3), 221–233. This article draws information from the fields of school psychology, counseling psychology, organizational theory, and special education and looks at three aspects of consultation models: input, process, and outcome.

Instructional Solutions: A Computerized Tool that Supports Collaboration
Warger, C.L., Aldinger, L.E., & Eavy, P.W. (1993). *Instructional solutions: A computerized tool that supports collaboration.* Reston, VA: Council for Exceptional Children. Contains both DOS and Macintosh formatted software and a user's guide. This package includes information that can be used to generate discussions and reflections by teams of service providers in the areas of early childhood instruction, general classroom instruction, classroom management, and cooperative learning.

Interactions: Collaboration Skills for School Professionals
Friend, M., & Cook, L. (1996). *Interactions: Collaboration skills for school professionals.* White Plains, NY: Longman. Useful for a variety of environments, roles, and service models to address skills for collaboration. Contains case studies and samples of interactions as well as other practice and application exercises.

Introduction to Type
Myers, I.B. (1987). *Introduction to type.* Palo Alto, CA: Consulting Psychologists Press, Inc. Related to the Myers-Briggs Type Indicator tool, an instrument for determining team strengths and tendencies.

Managing Quality Through Teams: A Workbook
Miller, L., & Howard, J. (1991). *Managing quality through teams: A workbook.* Methuen, MA: GOAL/QPC. This workbook can assist teams in working toward ongoing improvement. Topics covered include process management, decision making, action planning, managing team meetings, facilitating participation, and problem solving.

Parker Team Player Survey
Parker, G.M. (1991). *Parker team player survey.* Tuxedo, NY: XICOM. This is a tool for helping individuals determine their primary style and strengths as team members.

Reaching Out: Interpersonal Effectiveness and Self-Actualization
Johnson, D.W. (1990). *Reaching out: Interpersonal effectiveness and self-actualization.* Upper Saddle River, NJ: Prentice-Hall. This book introduces the reader to theoretical and experiential elements of effective interpersonal relationships.

Skills Inventory for Teams (SIFT)
Garland, C., Frank, A., Buck, D., & Seklemian, P. (1992). *Skills inventory for teams (SIFT).* Lightfoot, VA: Child Development Resources Training Center. The SIFT is an inventory of skills that enhance the effectiveness of early intervention teams. It is divided into Team and Team Member sections. The Team section looks at team functioning, as a whole; the Team Member section examines skills necessary for an individual's effectiveness on teams. Each section contains a screening scale, which helps the team and team members to identify areas of need and strength, and an assessment checklist, which helps to clarify and prioritize for improvement in the identified areas. Forms for creating development plans are included.

Strategies for Teacher Collaboration
Adlinger, L.E., Warger, C.L., & Eavy, P.W. (1991). *Strategies for teacher collaboration.* Reston, VA: Council for Exceptional Children. This resource provides 18 in-service activities to help demonstrate the dynamics of collaboration. These activities apply the problem-solving model to teacher consultation and provide opportunities for participants to learn how to work through conflict and resistance toward effective teamwork.

Teams and Teamwork: Academic Settings
McFarlane, L., & Hagler, P. (1993, June–July). Teams and teamwork: Academic settings. *Asha, 35,* 37–38. The emphasis of this article is on interdisciplinary teamwork, based on a clinical training program out of the University of Alberta, Edmonton.

Thomas-Kilmann Conflict Mode Instrument
Thomas, K.W., & Kilmann, R.H. (1991). *Thomas-Kilmann conflict mode instrument.* Tuxedo, NY: XICOM. This tool assists individuals in identifying their own responses to conflict and for planning conflict resolution strategies.

Transdisciplinary Arena Assessment
Process Viewing Guide: A Resource for Teams
Frank, A., & McCollum, J. (1992). *Transdisciplinary arena assessment process viewing guide: A resource for teams.* (ERIC Document Reproduction Service No. ED 361 959). [Videotape EC 302 430]. Lightfoot, VA: Williamsburg Area Child Development Resources. This guide accompanies a 43-minute video that introduces early intervention teams to the transdiciplinary (TD) assessment process.

Transdisciplinary Teamwork
and Integrated Therapy: Clarifying the Misconceptions
York, J., Rainforth, B., & Giangreco, M.F. (1990). Transdisciplinary teamwork and integrated therapy: Clarifying the misconceptions. *Pediatric Physical Therapy, 2*(2), 73–79. This is a good brainstorming tool for groups to look at common misconceptions of teamwork. This tool also provides clarification.

chapter three

Anatomy of the Oral and Respiratory Structures Made Easy

Suzanne McKeever Murphy and Vanessa Caretto

Before an educator can understand the skill of eating, he or she must understand the anatomical structures and functions for both eating and respiration. The information available on this subject is vast and complex; however, this chapter presents anatomical information in a simple, meaningful way. Anatomical definitions associated with eating and respiration are provided as is a brief overview of the typical anatomical progression of eating and respiration. A discussion of the more common compensatory patterns resulting from anatomical abnormalities concludes the chapter.

EATING

The skill of eating is often taken for granted because it is accomplished with very little conscious thought. In fact, it is a very complex process that combines adequate oral control with precise timing and coordination of breathing. There are numerous oral and respiratory structures, each having specific functions that help make eating both carefree and enjoyable.

Structures and Functions for Eating

The mouth functions as the receptor of food and liquid and prepares food and liquid for swallowing and digestion. The muscles and structures of the mouth that are most often attributed to eating are the lips, cheeks, teeth, tongue, jaws, and palate. Normal development of these structures is necessary for both eating and speech (Blackman, 1990). In addition to the mouth, other digestive system muscles and structures help make swallowing possible, including the pharynx, larynx, epiglottis, and esophagus. (See Figure 1 for a diagram of the four phases of swallowing.) The following list is a brief, simplified look at these main anatomical muscles and structures involved in the eating process:

- The *lips* consist of muscles and sensory receptors that judge the temperature and texture of food and liquid (Hole, 1993). They are the entryway

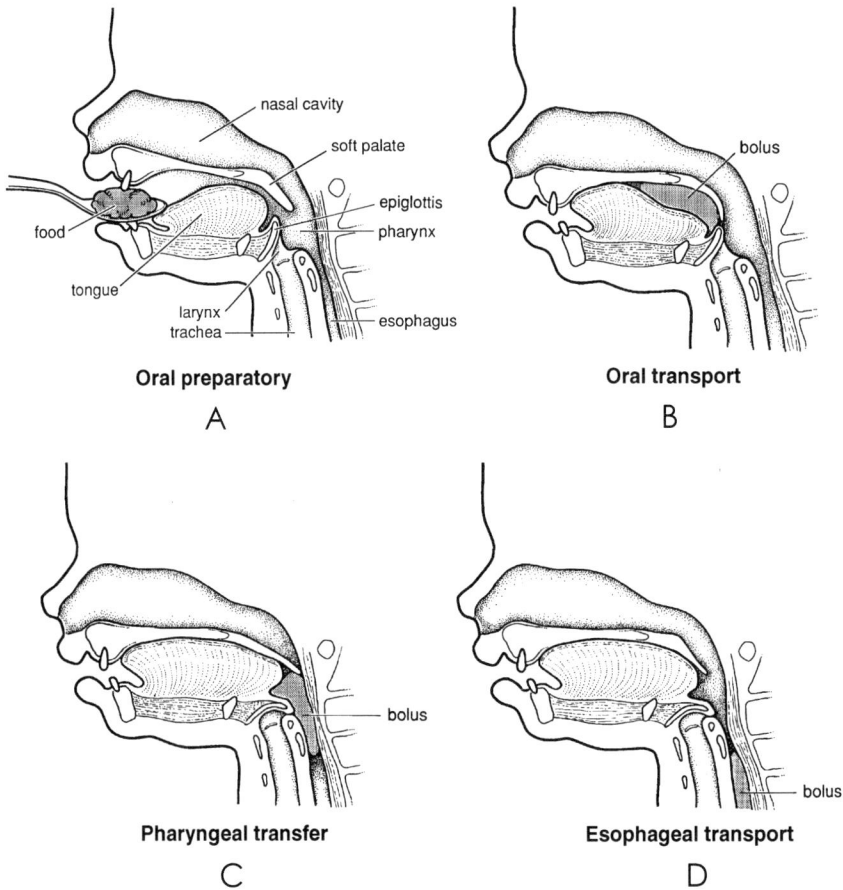

Figure 1.   The four phases of swallowing. A) Oral preparatory: Food is taken into the mouth, processed to a manageable consistency, and then collected into a small parcel, or bolus. B) Oral transport: The bolus is then pushed backward by the tongue toward the pharynx. C) Pharyngeal transfer: As swallowing begins, the epiglottis normally folds over the opening of the trachea to direct food down the esophagus and not into the lungs. D) Esophageal transport: The peristaltic wave moves the bolus down the esophagus toward the stomach. (From Eicher, P.S. [1997]. Feeding. In M.L. Batshaw [Ed.], *Children with disabilities* [4th ed., p. 622]. Baltimore: Paul H. Brookes Publishing Co.; reprinted by permission.)

for food and liquid, help control food and liquid in the mouth, and help create suction to assist in the movement of food and liquid to the back of the mouth in preparation for swallowing (Blackman, 1990; Hunter, 1990).

- The *cheeks* are the walls of the mouth and contain muscles that aid with chewing, creating negative pressure in the mouth, and controlling the movement of food and liquid (Hunter, 1990).

- The *teeth* are necessary in order for food to be broken down in preparation for swallowing and digestion. Teeth also assist in production of sound during speech. During fetal development, the growth of teeth stimulates growth of the jaw. Typically, a child grows his or her first primary tooth by 6 months of age and has 20 teeth by 2–4 years of age. Permanent teeth begin to emerge by the age of 6, and the adult mouth holds 32 permanent teeth (Batshaw, 1997; Hole, 1993).

- The *tongue* is a large muscle attached to the floor of the mouth, which almost totally fills the mouth when it is closed. The tongue assists in the control of sucking, the mixing of food with saliva during chewing, and the movement of food and liquid during swallowing (Hole, 1993; Hunter, 1990).

- The *palate* is the roof of the mouth and has hard and soft portions. The *hard palate* lies between the mouth and nasal passage as a divider. The *soft palate* is a soft continuation of the hard palate that acts with the walls of the pharynx to close off the mouth and nasal cavity during eating, drinking, and speaking (Blackman, 1990). The soft palate elevates during swallowing to keep liquid from entering the nasal cavity.

- The *pharynx* is a partially muscular and partially membranous tube that connects the mouth, nose, and esophagus. In the infant, the pharynx follows a curve from the top (nasopharynx) to the bottom (laryngopharynx), and the pharynx changes to a 90° angle by adulthood (Arvedson & Brodsky, 1993). The muscular walls of the pharynx are known as the *pharyngeal constrictors* because they constrict during swallowing.

  The pharynx has three parts that are known as the nasopharynx, oropharynx, and laryngopharynx. The *nasopharynx* is above the soft palate. The Eustachian tubes run from the ears and connect to the nasopharynx (Hole, 1993; Hunter, 1990). The nasopharynx opens into the nasal cavity and provides a route for air to travel during respiration (Hole, 1993). The nasopharynx is typically closed off during swallowing to keep liquid from entering the nose. The adenoids are in the top of the nasopharynx, and if their size increases significantly, they can partially or fully close off the airflow to and from the nose. This is very dangerous in the infant and can interfere with feeding. The *oropharynx* is a continuation of the mouth that runs between the soft palate and the base of the tongue near the epiglottis and connects to the nasopharynx. The oropharynx is a passage for food, liquid, and air. Between the base of the tongue and the epiglottis lie two small spaces that are known as the *vallecula*. These spaces are areas where food or liquid can get trapped before or after swallowing. If a swallow is adequate, the food and/or liquid are washed away. If a swallow is delayed, uncoordinated, or absent, however, the food or liquid can stay until the space fills up and then may spill over into the airway, leading to a potentially dangerous situation. The *laryngopharynx* (or *hypopharynx*) connects to the oropharynx and runs from the top of the epiglottis to the top of the esophagus. There is a sphincter here that is closed during talking, breathing, and at rest; and it opens when the swallowing reflex is triggered to allow food to enter the esophagus. Above this sphincter are the *pyriform sinuses*, which are also small spaces where food and liquid can collect and spill over into the trachea if the swallow is incomplete. Coughing, choking, and aspiration can occur when this happens.

- The *Eustachian tubes* are the canals that run from the middle ear to the pharynx and help adjust the air pressure within the middle ear to match the pressure outside the eardrum. In the infant, the Eustachian tubes are horizontal, and feeding the infant in a supine position or a failure of the nasal cavity to be closed off by the soft palate during swallowing can cause an increased incidence of middle-ear infections in the young child (Hunter, 1990). Liquid from the mouth often leaks into the nasal cavity and on to the Eustachian tubes. As the child's head and neck grow and the child becomes more upright against gravity, the angle of the Eustachian tubes becomes more vertical, and middle-ear infections typically decrease in frequency.

• The *larynx* is located at the base of the tongue and connects the laryngopharynx and the trachea. The larynx, a valve to help keep food or liquid from entering the trachea, is made up of muscle, cartilage, and ligaments. The larynx is responsible for voice production and plays a part in respiration. The larynx consists of many sets of small muscles that are known as the *true vocal cords,* the *false vocal cords,* and the *aryepiglottic folds.* These are three levels of valves at the top of the larynx that close off the airway and keep food and liquid from entering the larynx during swallowing.

• The *epiglottis,* a piece of cartilage at the top of the larynx that hangs over the opening to the trachea (i.e., airway), helps keep food and liquid from entering the trachea during swallowing. In the infant, the epiglottis and soft palate touch, which allows liquid to pass around the outer edges of the epiglottis and then continue down the pharynx and esophagus (Morris & Klein, 1987). The epiglottis protects the airway, allowing the infant to swallow and breathe simultaneously. The infant's survival depends on the placement of these anatomical structures until the neurological coordination and timing are mature (Morris & Klein, 1987).

• The *esophagus* is a muscular tube, which is approximately 23–25 centimeters in length, that connects the pharynx and the stomach. It is closed off at each end by a sphincter, and its peristaltic (i.e., wave-like) movements help move food from the oral area to the stomach. The esophagus remains empty between swallows. The *lower sphincter* keeps food and liquid from reentering the esophagus from the stomach, preventing gastroesophageal reflux.

Phases of Eating

There are four phases of eating and swallowing food and liquid: 1) the oral preparatory phase, 2) the oral phase, 3) the pharyngeal phase, and 4) the esophageal phase. The first two phases rely on voluntary control and involve skills in which intervention can help to decrease or alleviate dysfunction in the eating process. The pharyngeal phase has both a voluntary and an involuntary component, and the esophageal phase is totally involuntary. During the last two phases, which occur after food and liquid have passed beyond the mouth, interventions are ineffective in treating dysfunction because of the reflexive nature of these phases. Positioning, however, can be effectively used to help decrease the effects of dysfunction in these final two phases.

1. The *oral preparatory phase* involves the collection and control of food in the mouth in order to form a *bolus* (i.e., a rounded mass of food). The length of time it takes to complete this phase depends on the type of food being eaten. Sucking and swallowing of liquid in the young child happens very quickly. As the child begins to accept more textured foods, the length of time it takes to break down the food and then gather it back into a bolus can last up to several seconds. The bolus is formed in the front of the mouth and held between the tongue and hard palate while the swallow is initiated. The soft palate lowers in order to help prevent liquid from entering the pharynx before the swallow has taken place (Arvedson & Brodsky, 1993). The airway remains open, and the child can breathe through his or her nose until the swallow occurs.

2. The *oral phase* begins as the food is moved backward by the tongue, and the phase is complete when the swallow is occurring. This phase begins voluntarily, yet it ends as the swallow becomes involuntary. The presence of food or liquid causes a voluntary initiation of a swallow; however, the swallowing of saliva has a more automatic component (Arvedson & Brodsky, 1993). This is evidenced by the continued ability to swallow saliva while sleeping (Arvedson & Brodsky, 1993). The backward movement of the tongue helps propel the bolus toward the pharynx for swallowing. The tactile stimulation from the bolus as it moves inside the mouth triggers the swallow reflex, allowing the pharynx to open for the swallow to occur (Vergara, 1993). As the bolus moves toward the pharynx, the soft palate elevates to close off the nasal cavity, thus keeping food and liquid from entering the nose. The timing of the oral phase does not vary with the type of food, and the phase lasts less than 1 second when occurring normally (Arvedson & Brodsky, 1993).

3. The *pharyngeal phase* begins as the swallow is initiated and as the soft palate closes off the nasal cavity. The bolus enters the esophagus and is moved through the esophagus by contraction of the pharyngeal constrictors. The sphincter at the top of the esophagus closes to prevent food or liquid from reentering the pharynx. At the same time, the epiglottis moves back to cover the opening of the larynx to protect the airway from aspiration.

4. The *esophageal phase* involves the movement of the bolus to the stomach by peristaltic movement within the esophagus. The gastroesophageal sphincter (at the bottom of the esophagus) closes in order to prevent the reflux of the stomach contents back into the esophagus. The process is repeated with specific delays between swallows to allow the system to remain well-coordinated.

RESPIRATION

The primary function of the respiratory system is to ventilate the lungs for oxygen–carbon dioxide exchange (Langley & Lombardino, 1991). Although respiration is performed automatically, the timing and control must be precisely coordinated with oral-motor skills during eating. There are many structures involved in the respiratory process that allow for successful eating.

Structures and Functions for Respiration

The structures and muscles that compose the respiratory system are a series of passages for air and gases in the body. These include the nose, nasal cavity, pharynx, larynx, trachea, bronchial trees, and the lungs (Hole, 1993). (See Figure 2 for a diagram of the airways and lungs.) The following is a simple explanation of these anatomical muscles and structures involved in the respiration process.

- The *nose* has two openings (i.e., *nostrils*) for the passage of air into and out of the body. The nostrils have numerous tiny hairs that function to filter out large particles in the incoming air (Hole, 1993).

- The *nasal cavity* is a space behind the nose, located above the mouth and separated from the mouth by the palate but open to the pharynx at the posterior of the cavity during respiration. The nasal cavity is divided into

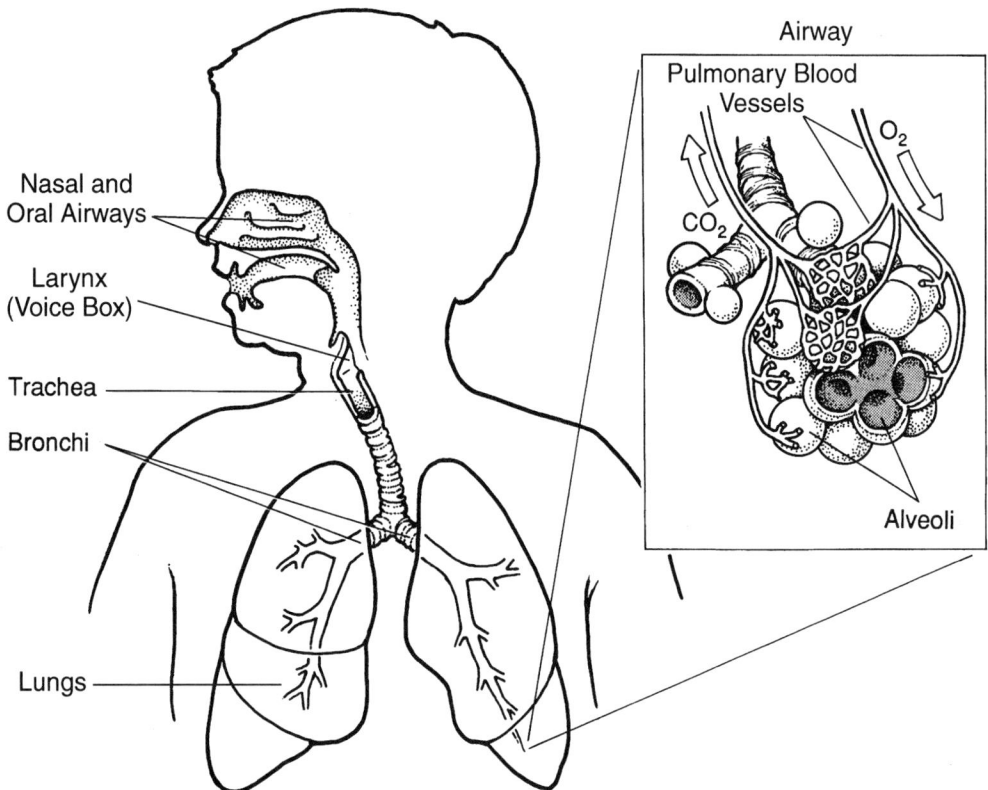

Figure 2.   The airways and lungs. The airways conduct inhaled gas from the atmosphere to the alveoli. Beginning at the mouth and nose, air enters the nose (and/or mouth), and then the voice box. It then descends into the chest via the windpipe or trachea. The trachea divides into two bronchi, one serving each lung. The main bronchus to each lung divides repeatedly into a series of progressively smaller tubes that ultimately deliver gas to the alveoli, where gas exchange occurs. (From Batshaw, M.L., & Perret, Y.M. [1992]. *Children with disabilities: A medical primer* [3rd ed., p. 143]. Baltimore: Paul H. Brookes Publishing Co.; reprinted by permission.)

upper, middle, and lower passages. The upper portion has smell receptors, whereas the lower portions conduct air to and from the nasopharynx. *Sinuses* (or openings) in the cranial bones open into the nasal cavity and drain secretions through the pharynx, often affecting feeding (Hunter, 1990). The nasal cavity also warms and filters incoming air.

- The *trachea* (i.e., windpipe, airway) is a tube that connects the larynx and the bronchial trees. It also functions to filter and conduct air in the respiratory system.

- The *bronchial trees* are continuations of air passages within a series of branches leading to the lungs. The branches terminate in *bronchioles* that enter the lungs and have microscopic, thin *alveoli* (i.e., tiny air sacs) that are surrounded by *capillaries* (i.e., tiny blood vessels) in the lungs. The alveoli operate in the gas exchange process between the incoming air and the blood in the capillaries.

- There are two *lungs* (left and right) that are separated by the heart. The right lung has three lobes, and the left lung has two lobes, with each *lobe* being attached to a bronchial tree and to blood vessels. Each lobe is divided into *lobules* that contain the bronchioles, alveoli, and capillaries.

The Respiratory Process

Respiration is the process that living organisms use to take in oxygen and expel carbon dioxide. The function of respiration is to provide adequate energy to the cells within the body. Respiration begins when air is breathed into the lungs via the nose and/or the mouth through the expansion of the chest muscles and ribs. Oxygen-depleted, waste-product–rich blood is carried to the lungs from the right side of the heart through the *pulmonary artery,* and oxygen in the air is then transferred to the blood by gas exchange between the alveoli and the capillaries in the lungs. The oxygen-rich blood is then carried from the lungs through the pulmonary veins to the left side of the heart and is then pumped out of the heart by the *aorta* (i.e., a large blood vessel) to the tissues and organs of the body. During *circulation,* blood passes through tiny capillaries within the body's tissues, where it releases the oxygen and gathers waste products (i.e., carbon dioxide and water) from the body's cells. Within the cells, glucose and oxygen interact to provide energy to power the cells, and glucose is transformed into the waste products (Clayman, 1989). The carbon dioxide waste travels in the blood to the right side of the heart and is then pumped out to the lungs. In the lungs, the gas exchange occurs, and carbon dioxide waste is transferred to the air in the lungs, which is then expelled from the body on expiration. When there is a buildup of carbon dioxide, the respiratory rate increases, but when the carbon dioxide level is low, the respiratory rate decreases.

DEVELOPMENT OF EATING AND RESPIRATORY COORDINATION/CONTROL

The full-term infant is structurally prepared to obtain adequate nutrition for growth and development. The infant's jaw is small and retracted with restricted movement, which is due to its position on the upper chest. The oral area is small, which makes the tongue appear to be large. The infant's tongue fills 80% of the oral area and touches the floor and roof of the mouth as well as the lateral gums and inside of the cheeks (Morris & Klein, 1987). Therefore, the movement of the tongue is limited, resulting in an anterior/posterior movement known as "suckling." With the mouth filled by the tongue, the infant must use his or her nose for breathing; therefore, the infant is referred to as an *obligate nose breather*. This airflow restriction helps protect the infant from choking and aspirating while allowing the child to suck, swallow, and breathe simultaneously. The infant's cheeks are a source of stability from which the remaining oral muscles can work. At birth, the full-term infant has a bulk of fatty tissue in each cheek muscle known as "sucking pads" that create a firm, stable base from which the entire oral system can work. Cheek activation helps increase intraoral pressure for compression and suction during sucking.

Typically, changes in the oral and facial structures are visible in the 4- to 6-month-old infant. The area inside the infant's mouth increases as the jaw grows down and forward. The sucking pads decrease because they are no longer needed due to more active stability of the muscles themselves and at the temporomandibular joint. This allows the cheeks and lips to have increased movements. The mouth elongates as the infant's head increases in size. The sucking reflexes decrease as cortical development improves, and more active control of the muscles begins to develop. The larger oral area makes more room for the tongue to move at the same time it is gaining more active control. This allows the "true suck" to develop because the tongue can then move up and down as well as forward and backward. Lip control also increases at this point in the infant's development. Because there is more oral space and increased mobility of the tongue, sensory exploration of the oral area is more active. With greater control of the jaw, lips, cheeks, and tongue comes a decreased need for deep grooving of the tongue (seen in early suckling and sucking) to move food and liquid toward the back of the mouth for a swallow (Morris & Klein, 1987). The increased muscle control helps move food and liquid back, which prepares the mouth to accept and control strained baby food (Morris & Klein, 1987).

Next, the infant's larynx begins to move downward, which increases the space between the epiglottis and the larynx. Food is directed over the epiglottis, rather than around it (Morris & Klein, 1987). With anatomical changes occurring in the oral/pharyngeal mechanism, the infant's coordination of breathing and swallowing is more difficult. Choking and coughing are often observed as the infant adjusts to these anatomical changes. From this age on, each of the oral muscles takes on more isolated functions, and they can modify their movements more independently of each other. (See Chapter 4 for more detailed information on oral-motor development.)

In utero, the first lung buds begin to appear at approximately 3 weeks' gestational age. Lung division is typically seen within 28–30 days. Airways and capillaries form within 17–24 weeks' gestation, and alveoli appear after 24 weeks' gestation. Lung growth appears to be influenced by liquid filling the lungs (amniotic fluid from the fetus) and by the fetal movements of the diaphragm (Vergara, 1993). Surface tension within the lungs is important for adequate breathing and is maintained by a protein known as *pulmonary sur-*

factant. This protein helps prevent the collapse of the lungs after birth and is present in full-term neonates. All of these developmental occurrences help prepare the lungs for functioning immediately after birth and increase the likelihood that the infant will be successful at coordinating breathing, sucking, and swallowing. Respiratory coordination that ensures adequate oxygen and carbon dioxide exchange will provide the foundation for successful feeding at birth.

PROBLEMS AFFECTING EATING

Children with neurological impairments, cardiovascular disorders, and congenital abnormalities often have complications with eating. Feeding difficulties can occur with all phases of eating. Difficulties in the oral preparatory stage and in the oral stage of eating involve a weak sucking pattern, loss of food, decreased movement of food within the mouth, pocketing food in the cheek area, and getting food stuck on the palate. Difficulties in the pharyngeal stage of eating include gagging, choking, coughing, and respiratory distress during meals (Arvedson & Brodsky, 1993). Problems often associated with the gastroesophageal phase of eating include spitting up, vomiting, esophagitis (i.e., inflammation of the esophagus), and irritability. Difficulties in the first two stages can be identified through observation of eating, whereas difficulties in the last two stages should be ruled out through the use of a modified barium swallow study. This test involves the child's eating or drinking food that has been laced with radioactive barium so that it shows up on X ray. The test is used for proper diagnosis of swallowing disorders and can aid in implementing appropriate treatment and feeding processes.

Anatomical Abnormalities

There are numerous anatomical abnormalities and anomalies that can cause feeding difficulties. These are typically identified at birth or shortly thereafter and often affect the ability of the infant to suck, swallow, and breathe effectively. Therefore, these abnormalities make breast and bottle feeding more difficult, if not impossible, and greatly affect the future eating abilities of the child. Several of the more common anatomical abnormalities and anomalies identified at birth are discussed briefly in the following list. Some of these problems may only require modifications in positioning, feeding techniques, or equipment, whereas others may require surgical correction so that the child can live and thrive. Many of these abnormalities will improve as the infant grows and matures; however, some will last longer and may affect all aspects of feeding skill development.

- The presence of a cleft lip and/or cleft palate is apparent at birth. These are typically caused by a disturbance during formation of soft tissues and bones in the upper lip and roof of the mouth from the 6th week through the 13th week of fetal development (Blackman, 1990), where the lip and/or palates fail to fuse normally (Batshaw, 1997). A *cleft lip* is a vertical split in the upper lip that can occur as a small notch in the lip or can extend all the way to the nose (Clayman, 1989). A *cleft palate* is an opening in the roof of the mouth that runs along the mid-line. There are different classifications of clefts. A child can have a *unilateral cleft* of the lip/palate, which involves only one side of the lip/palate, or a *bilateral cleft*, which involves both sides of the lip/palate. In some children, the cleft is beneath the palatal tissue and is not visible, which is known as a *submucous cleft*. Children with clefts often have difficulty coordinating the suck, swallow, and breathe pattern. They often gulp air, snort, or choke while eating, resulting in an ineffective swallowing pattern. Some children actually have nasopharyngeal regurgitation, which involves loss of liquid and/or food up through the nose. A child with a cleft lip/palate can have numerous related problems including dental malalignment or malocclusion, a susceptibility to upper respiratory infections, middle-ear dysfunction and hearing impairment from effects to the Eustachian tubes, eating and nutritional problems, delayed speech development, psychosocial problems, and decreased self-esteem (Blackman, 1990). Improved positioning and use of specific feeding materials can help the child with a cleft lip/palate eat more effectively. Repair of the lip is usually done by the time the infant has reached a weight of 10–12 pounds (Morris & Klein, 1987). Repair of the palate is more controversial and can occur anytime from 6 to 30 months of age. The later the palatal correction occurs, the more impact the cleft will have on feeding.

- *Micrognathia* refers to a small jaw structure. It is often seen in children with Pierre-Robin sequence and in children with Down syndrome. When the child's jaw is small, the tongue often appears large. The normal resting place for the tongue is on the floor of the mouth; therefore, when the mouth structure is reduced in size, the tongue often either protrudes or retracts while at rest. The retracted pattern of the tongue can obstruct the airway, which is especially risky during feeding. The jaw will typically grow as the child increases in age, and the impact on eating textured foods should diminish with time.

- *Tongue asymmetry* is often seen in children who have neurological dysfunction. The tongue is pulled toward its stronger side, which affects control of liquid and food within the mouth. Stimulation to the weaker side of the tongue as well as food positioning helps improve the symmetry and activity of the tongue during feeding.

- *Malocclusion,* or *malalignment,* is a condition in which the teeth do not sit in the mouth properly due to malformation. The condition can be caused from teeth growing in through the gums at odd angles or erupting outside of their usual place. Another cause of this condition is a poor swallow pattern, resulting in the tongue forcefully pushing on the teeth at rest or during a swallow. Malocclusion, or malalignment, can cause difficulty with spoon feeding, cup drinking, and biting and/or chewing skills.

- The *tonsils* and *adenoids* are composed of lymph tissue. This tissue helps to filter out bacteria that are obtained through the mouth and nose, blocking the bacteria from invading further into the body until the body has built its fighting abilities. Typically, the tissue should atrophy over time and all but disappear. In some children, however, numerous childhood infections actually cause the tissues to *hypertrophy* (i.e., enlarge), and they may actually become the source of infection or occlude the airway and interfere with breathing and eating. This condition may become so severe that the child does not gain weight (e.g., failure to thrive), or the child may develop *sleep apnea* and have interrupted breathing.

• Cardiopulmonary disorders can severely affect feeding in the infant and child because they often compromise respiration during the feeding process. Chronic lung disease (e.g., respiratory distress syndrome, bronchopulmonary dysplasia) and congestive heart failure can result from an increase in respiratory rate or fatigue during feeding. The child can often be observed eating well during the first part of a meal and then become irritable or fall asleep during the latter part of a meal. This is also seen in the child who has cardiac problems. Some of these abnormalities correct themselves over time, but others require surgery once the child is stable or reaches a specific age and weight.

• One of the greatest concerns when dealing with anatomical abnormalities is the fear of *aspiration,* or the intake of food or liquid into the lungs. Aspiration occurs from poor coordination or weak muscle contractions during swallowing, when the epiglottis fails to cover the opening of the trachea and food or liquid is inhaled into the lungs (Batshaw, 1997). Aspiration can cause recurrent pneumonia, which can further compromise the respiratory process and, in rare cases, can even cause death. At birth, many infants with anatomical abnormalities are at risk for aspiration until the abnormality is identified. Many abnormalities are first discovered when there is an interruption in the feeding process and further exploration is performed. Abnormalities that interfere with the suck, swallow, and breathe coordination are often found first, whereas other abnormalities are discovered when the baby has difficulty breathing or becomes cyanotic (i.e., turns blue). If the child has or is at risk for aspiration, alternative feeding measures for the child must be explored.

Other Anatomical Abnormalities

There are many other abnormalities that the educator does not typically see because they are usually so severe that they require surgery at birth to repair. Some of these abnormalities include *laryngeal stenosis* (narrowing of the larynx), *tracheoesophageal fistula* (an opening between the trachea and esophagus allowing food to enter the trachea), and *laryngomalacia* (softening of the larynx that may lead to a collapsing larynx). The symptoms of these abnormalities, which all indicate a problem with the airway, include *stridor* (upper airway noise indicating that air is moving through a narrowed space), snorting, grunting, frequent need to pause while eating, increased respiratory rate, and coughing while eating. The diagnosis is typically given following a procedure called *flexible endoscopy,* in which a lighted tube is used to help view the airway and any existing abnormalities.

SUMMARY

This chapter provides the educator with simple anatomical definitions of the body's oral and respiratory structures. The four phases of eating and swallowing, along with the respiratory process, are discussed. The educator is provided an opportunity to examine the development of eating and respiratory coordination and control. The chapter concludes with some of the more common problems associated with eating. (See Chapter 4 for specific techniques to improve eating skills.)

Jody

Jody is a 3-year-old girl with a diagnosis of failure to thrive. Although Jody typically eats a good variety of foods, she consumes only small amounts of food during each meal and becomes fatigued very quickly. Within an hour, she requests more food. Jody's oral-motor skills are good with the exception of her tendency to munch with her mouth open. She often loses food from her mouth and typically makes grunting noises while chewing and swallowing. Her swallow is generally followed by a large intake of air as if she is out of breath.

Before a feeding program can be implemented with Jody, the following questions should be addressed.

Collaboration

- Has the feeding team sat down with Jody's parents / caregivers to discuss their concerns as well as to obtain any previous medical information?

Anatomy

- Are there any structural anomalies that would interfere with eating?
- Are there any visible structural causes for Jody's open-mouth posture during eating?

Positioning

- How is Jody positioned while eating?
- Do changes in Jody's positioning improve her ability to keep food in her mouth?
- Do changes in Jody's positioning result in respiratory changes?

Sensitivity

- Does Jody's open-mouth posture appear to be the result of increased oral sensitivity?

Oral-Motor Skills

- Does the loss of food appear to be the result of Jody's poor oral coordination?
- Does the loss of food appear to be the result of Jody's poor muscle tone?
- What changes does the feeder see when the quantity of each bite is decreased?

Communication

- Is the feeder able to read Jody's cues of fatigue and fullness?
- Is the feeder adjusting the rate and volume of feeding to Jody's individual needs?

Behavior

- What reactions does Jody get when she becomes full too quickly?
- What behavior changes does the feeder notice when Jody is showing fatigue?

Medical Issues

- Has Jody received a thorough medical examination to rule out a medical cause of fatigue and satiation?
- Have enlarged tonsils and adenoids been ruled out?

Jody was referred to an otolaryngologist (i.e., ear, nose, and throat doctor) and was found to have abnormally large adenoids that were interfering with her breathing, especially while eating. This was causing Jody's fatigue as well as Jody's inability to close her mouth when it was full of food. Her respiration was constantly being compromised. Because this feeding problem was related to a medical/anatomical cause, intervention techniques would not apply. It is important, however, to note that the educator is very often the first person to notice the changes in a child's eating and overall behavior; therefore, close contact with the family is essential.

REFERENCES

Arvedson, J.C., & Brodsky, L. (Eds.). (1993). *Pediatric swallowing and feeding: Assessment and management.* San Diego, CA: Singular Publishing Group.

Batshaw, M.L. (Ed.). (1997). *Children with disabilities* (4th ed.). Baltimore: Paul H. Brookes Publishing Co.

Batshaw, M.L., & Perret, Y.M. (1992). *Children with disabilities: A medical primer* (3rd ed.). Baltimore: Paul H. Brookes Publishing Co.

Blackman, J.A. (1990). *Medical aspects of developmental disabilities in children birth to three* (2nd ed.). Gaithersburg, MD: Aspen Publishers.

Clayman, C.B. (1989). *The American Medical Association encyclopedia of medicine.* New York: Random House.

Eicher, P.S. (1997). Feeding. In M.L. Batshaw (Ed.), *Children with disabilities* (4th ed., pp. 621–641). Baltimore: Paul H. Brookes Publishing Co.

Hole, J.W., Jr. (1993). *Human anatomy & physiology* (6th ed.). Dubuque, IA: William C. Brown Publishers.

Hunter, J.G. (1990). Pediatric feeding dysfunction. In C.J. Semmler & J.G. Hunter *Early occupational therapy intervention: Neonates to three years* (pp. 124–141). Gaithersburg, MD: Aspen Publishers.

Langley, M.B., & Lombardino, L.J. (1991). *Neurodevelopmental strategies for managing communication disorders in children with severe motor dysfunction.* Austin, TX: PRO-ED.

Morris, S.E., & Klein, M.D. (1987). *Pre-feeding skills: A comprehensive resource for feeding development.* San Antonio, TX: Therapy Skill Builders.

Vergara, E.R. (Ed.). (1993). *Foundations for practice in the neonatal intensive care unit and early intervention: A self-guided practice manual.* Rockville, MD: American Occupational Therapy Association.

chapter four

Oral-Motor Considerations for Feeding

Suzanne McKeever Murphy and Vanessa Caretto

The development of mature oral-motor skills is crucial in gaining the ability to be an independent oral eater as well as an independent verbal communicator. The oral and pharyngeal structures and mechanisms allow an individual to breathe, eat, and produce speech in a highly orchestrated manner. These structures and the musculature must be intact and well-coordinated for the development of these sophisticated skills to occur. This chapter looks briefly at the normal development of oral-motor patterns as they relate to feeding skills. Muscular and structural influences of oral-motor skill development are discussed. Atypical patterns that result from various muscular and structural deficits are discussed as well as common feeding concerns associated with these atypical patterns. Issues that affect oral-motor skill development in the education environment are presented. Also included is a chart of specific feeding techniques that explores possible causes of feeding problems commonly found within the school-age population and suggested interventions to help the educator improve feeding skills.

EARLY DEVELOPMENT OF ORAL-MOTOR PATTERNS

A child's ability to develop adequate oral-motor skills for eating and speaking begins before the child is born. The oral and pharyngeal mechanisms of the newborn are prepared for the feeding process during fetal development (Alexander, Boehme, & Cupps, 1993). The lungs begin developing at about 24 days postconception and begin preparation for postnatal functioning (Vergara, 1993). The lungs are filled with amniotic fluid and are developed through fetal breathing movements of the diaphragm. Sucking the thumb and swallowing amniotic fluid are experienced by the fetus in utero to help prepare the child for the skill of feeding at birth.

Reflexes

The full-term infant is typically prepared to initiate feeding immediately following birth. The ability to do so is determined by many factors. Sucking activity depends on reflex development, muscle strength, and coordination of the oral-motor mechanism (Vergara, 1993). Reflexes are present for survival and are coordinated to allow the infant to locate the source of food, suck, and then swallow the nourishment. The infant's reflexes that have an effect on oral-motor development are discussed next.

- *Rooting reflex*—This reflex allows the infant to search for the food source. When the infant's cheek or lips are stroked, the infant will turn toward the stimulus. This response initiates the infant's preparation for feeding. The reflex is maintained for a longer period in breast-fed babies because they actually utilize it during feeding.

- *Suck–swallow reflex*—This response is seen when an infant's lips are given a light touch. The newborn's mouth opens, and sucking movements begin. A newborn's sucking pattern is referred to as a "total sucking pattern" because the cheeks, jaw, lips, and tongue work together as a whole unit for several weeks.

- *Gag reflex*—This reflex is present and highly sensitive at birth and can be elicited on the back three fourths of the tongue. It involves a forceful movement of the tongue and reversed peristaltic movement of the pharynx to bring up anything that may be dangerous to swallow or that may threaten the airway (Morris & Klein, 1987). The gag reflex gradually moves back to the posterior one fourth of the tongue through oral stimulation from fingers, toys, and food. On this section of the tongue, the gag reflex is retained through adulthood.

- *Transverse tongue reflex*—This reflex is observed when the lateral borders of the infant's tongue are stimulated. The result is a movement of the tongue toward the stimulus. This is the foundation for tongue lateralization, which is seen later in an infant's development.

- *Phasic bite–release reflex*—This reflex is seen when the infant's gums are stimulated; the reflex consists of a rhythmic up-and-down movement of the jaw. This response is the basis of chewing, which is seen later in the infant's development.

There are several other reflexes that are not as well-known in the infant; however, these reflexes build the foundation for the child to become a self-feeder as he or she learns to bring food or utensils toward his or her mouth.

- *Palmomental reflex*—This reflex is elicited by touching the infant's palm. The result is a wrinkle in the chin (the mentalis muscle). This response represents the early relationship between the hand and the mouth.

- *Babkin reflex*—This response is seen when the baby's palm is pressed. The infant's response is an opening of the mouth, closing of the eyes, and flexion of the head. Again, this demonstrates the early relationship between the hand and the mouth.

- *Grasp reflex*—This reflex is more functional and is often used by lactation consultants (professionals trained to work with mothers and their breast-fed babies) to enhance breast feeding because of its close relationship to the sucking reflex. When a finger is pressed into the infant's palm, he or she will grasp the finger and hold it tightly. As the baby sucks, the grasp tightens naturally, showing the connection between sucking and the grasp reflex. These automatic responses are the foundation from which active, voluntary movements will emerge to help in the infant's development of smooth, coordinated, connected oral-motor skills. Most of the early reflex patterns begin to modify (change or disappear) between 4 and 6 months, when cortical development occurs (Morris & Klein, 1987).

Muscular and Structural Influences

Muscle tone is basically the underlying tension of the muscles that allows the child to have smooth, controlled movements and is also important in the development of oral-motor skills for feeding. A child with typical muscle tone automatically changes muscle tension to adapt the amount of work needed from one activity to the next (Arvedson & Brodsky, 1993). For example, he or she is able to adjust the amount of muscle tension in the mouth needed to chew a potato chip versus the tension needed to chew a piece of steak. Abnormal muscle tone, however, results in either increased tension or decreased tension. This imbalance of muscle tension results in uncoordinated oral patterns while eating. It is extremely important to determine the overall muscle tone in infants because abnormal muscle tone has been linked with neurological abnormality in infants at high risk (Vergara, 1993). Furthermore, a weak, uncoordinated sucking action at birth has been found to be the primary indicator of a damaged central nervous system. The cause of a poor suck is typically abnormal muscle tone.

When examining the development of a newborn's oral-motor skills, it is important to look at the newborn's body as a whole. The position of the full-term newborn is known as *physiological flexion,* which is the term describing the flexion of the newborn's body, head, neck, and limbs. This position allows the newborn to eat and breathe simultaneously and provides maximum stability for the head, neck, and extremities by keeping the newborn in a compact position. Deep, firm pressure and natural stimulation to the newborn's face and oral areas is easily achieved as the weight of the body is displaced forward and the flexed hand is close to the mouth.

A newborn's oral and pharyngeal structures and musculature are uniquely suited for breathing and eating. The oral cavity is small; the tongue fills up to 80% of the oral cavity space. A newborn's tongue touches the floor and top of the mouth, the gum ridges, and the cheeks. Because the newborn's mouth is filled with the tongue, there is a need to breathe through the nose; therefore, the newborn is referred to as an "obligate nose breather." The airflow is directed through the nose, which allows the newborn to coordinate breathing with the suck–swallow pattern. The full-term newborn has fatty tissue deposits in the cheeks, known as "sucking pads," that provide stability for the entire oral system. The newborn's jaw is small, slightly retracted, and rests on the chest for further stability, which minimizes movement. Tongue movement is restricted to moving forward and backward because of the small oral cavity. All of these anatomical traits combine to allow the newborn to be an effective feeder.

Once the infant loses the stability and passive control of physiological flexion, there is an increase in achieving more active stability, organization, and control of the body. This is achieved by stability that develops proximally. Proximal stability allows the child to have improved mobility and distal control. Oral mobility is dependent on the development of neck and shoulder girdle stability, which are, in turn, dependent on trunk and pelvic stability (Morris & Klein, 1987).

The movement pattern progresses from a total unit, in which the oral mechanism moves as a whole, to a pattern of separate, refined movements of the articulators (i.e., jaw, cheeks, lips, and tongue). In other words, there is a movement from gross to fine control. This progression allows for the development of eating skills. Although the oral structures and muscles develop the ability to move independently of each other, the act of eating involves precise coordination of these structures in relationship to each other.

TYPICAL ORAL-MOTOR SKILL DEVELOPMENT

The child typically progresses through the following skills as he or she moves out of physiological flexion and begins to gain proximal stability and distal mobility.

- *Total sucking pattern*—As discussed previously, the advantage the newborn gains from the physiological flexion at birth allows the newborn to breathe and eat simultaneously. The jaw, cheeks, lips, and tongue move together as a whole unit. Highly sensitive lips allow the newborn to search out the source of nutrition, thus beginning the preparation for sucking. The newborn's lips help to form a strong seal around the nipple without allowing liquid loss. The jaw gains stability from the proximity of the chest, and the cheeks gain stability from the sucking pads. The newborn's small mouth allows only minimal movement of the tongue.

- *Suckling*—Once the physiological flexion decreases, a suckling pattern emerges. This is a backward and forward "licking" movement of the infant's tongue in conjunction with exaggerated opening and closing of the jaw. The infant's tongue does not extend beyond the lips during the forward movement. Retraction of the tongue is the stronger phase, while protraction moves the tongue back to the starting position. The sucking pads contract to increase the pressure inside the mouth (i.e., intraoral pressure), while the infant's jaw opens and closes, which aids in stripping the milk from the breast or nipple. The retraction pulls the liquid back toward the infant's throat (i.e., pharynx) for swallowing, and the tactile input from the liquid triggers a swallow reflex.

- *Sucking*—By 6 months of age, "true" sucking begins to emerge. It consists of a raising and lowering of the tongue body and smaller up and down movements of the jaw. Improved lip and jaw strength allows increased negative pressure in the mouth to build. Improved lip control and tongue movement independent of the jaw allows the infant's tongue to change from suckling to sucking.

- *Spoon feeding*—As a child begins to gain more head and neck control and trunk stability, there is also an increase in mobility in the facial and oral muscles. This allows for the introduction of spoon feeding. Foods that are puréed are not typically given to young children younger than 4 months of age because of the immaturity of the child's digestive system. Saliva-producing glands located between the cheek muscles and mucous membrane help aid in the breakdown of food within the infant's mouth. Initially, the food is placed into the infant's mouth by the feeder. Food is scraped off onto the infant's upper lip or gums until his or her lips become active. Because the infant is still using the suckling movement, the food usually comes right back out of the mouth. The feeder and infant continue this dance of the feeder putting food in and the infant pushing food out until enough food has been received. By 6 months of age, the infant opens his or her mouth in anticipation of the spoon, and if spoon feeding has been used for a while, a nice rhythm between the feeder and the infant is apparent. This is also the time when the infant's upper lip becomes active in removing the food from the spoon. By 12–15 months of age, the child is successfully removing food from the spoon with the upper lip, cleaning the food from the teeth with the lower lip, and sucking the food back. From 15 months to 2 years of age, the child becomes skillful at spoon feeding and often plays with the spoon. Food that is eaten from a spoon is primarily suckled or sucked before swallowing; therefore, more mature textures are typically fed to the child by hand.

- *Munching*—When infants first begin to "chew," around the age of 5 months, they use a phasic bite–release reflex pattern. With chewing experience, the up-and-down movement of the jaw, combined with the up-and-down movement of the tongue, changes the phasic bite into a more active skill known as munching. The acquisition of this skill is the beginning of learning to chew food. The lips are typically open during munching, and food within the mouth can be seen. Observing the lip activity is a great way to visually compare munching versus chewing.

- *Chewing*—This skill is typically seen at about 9 months of age. It involves more separate, refined movements of the lips, cheeks, jaw, and tongue. The sides, center, and tip of the infant's tongue begin to differentiate in the process of collecting and swallowing a bolus of lumpy food (Morris & Klein, 1987). The tongue has the ability to move from the center of the mouth to either side in order to place the food. The tongue then maintains pressure against the pressure of the cheeks, and the lips actively close to help keep the food on the surface of the gums for munching. By 15 months of age, the coordination of food within the mouth improves, allowing some diagonal, rotary movements of the tongue and jaw in order to help break down the food. This is typically seen when food is transferred to the infant's gums or placed there manually. Circular, rotary chewing develops between the second and third year of life and allows the child to eat almost all adult foods.

- *Cup drinking*—This skill can begin around the age of 4–6 months, when the infant begins removing food from the spoon during feedings. Most infants, however, are not given a cup until after 6 months of age. The interest in cup drinking typically begins when the infant reaches for the cup from which a parent is drinking. Spilling is to be expected because of the rapid flow of liquid from a cup. The child is often caught off guard and typically coughs and chokes when drinking from a cup. Experience, along with better tongue, jaw, lip, and cheek control, allows more proficiency to be achieved in cup drinking. By the age of 9 months, lip closure has improved, allowing the child to take up to three simultaneous sucks, although he or she may bite down on the cup rim for improved external stability. At the age of 12 months, a child is typically holding the cup independently, with spillage typically happening when the cup is removed from the child's mouth. The 2-year-old child generally drinks without difficulty, allowing for longer sequences of drinking and mature swallowing with tongue tip elevation.

ATYPICAL ORAL-MOTOR SKILL DEVELOPMENT

The typical development of oral-motor skills is carried out in a smooth, well-coordinated manner. When obstacles on the normal path of oral-motor skill development are encountered, progression is awkward and may be limited to the earliest patterns of coordination (Morris & Klein, 1987). Although no two children take food in and manipulate food in the same way, there are variations that may limit the further development of mature oral-motor skills. In turn, this may limit the quantity and variety of food consumed by the child. It is important to look at the possible causes of limited oral-motor control.

Most pediatric feeding disorders are caused by prematurity, whereas the second most common cause is neurological impairment (Vergara, 1993); both causes typically lead to muscle tone and muscle strength disorders. Other common causes of pediatric feeding disorders are structural deformities (e.g., cleft lip and palate) and syndromes that have associated oral, facial, and pharyngeal deformities; failure to thrive (FTT); acquired brain injury; and dysphagia. Although these causes are varied, the resulting problems have similar effects on eating. Discussed next are the typical disorders affecting the feeding process.

Muscle Tone Disorders

Muscle tone disorders include hypertonicity (increased muscle tone), hypotonicity (decreased muscle tone), and fluctuating muscle tone (alternating increased and decreased muscle tone). These problems affect the ability to achieve the appropriate balance of mobility and stability. The most typical muscle tone disorder is *hypotonia.* Children with hypotonia typically lack proximal stability and will often use compensatory positions and patterns of movement in order to gain some stability. The positions these children use are often ones that increase the tone and stability in more distal muscles. For example, a typical movement pattern is with the head and neck hyperextended, shoulders elevated, hands clenched in fists, upper extremities pulled back, and pelvis tilted forward. (See Chapter 5 for more information on positioning.) As a result of compensatory positioning, the muscles of the face and oral areas increase in muscle tone for stability, but these muscles lose the mobility needed for well-coordinated feeding.

Muscle Strength Disorders

Muscle strength is important for achieving and maintaining lip closure, jaw control, cheek control, and tongue control. Without strength in these muscles, the child will most likely have difficulty achieving and maintaining intraoral pressure for sucking and swallowing; lip closure for sucking and swallowing; jaw and cheek control for sucking, munching, and chewing; and tongue control for manipulating food within his or her mouth. Muscle strength disorders and endurance are often seen in the infant who is born prematurely or the infant who is born with central nervous system damage. The weak, uncoordinated suck will typically result in the infant's need for tube feeding. (Various types of feeding tubes are presented in Chapter 10.) Fatigue expressed by a child during eating can result in decreased nutritional intake and should be carefully monitored.

COMMON FEEDING CONCERNS
ASSOCIATED WITH ATYPICAL DEVELOPMENT

Atypical oral-motor development is often seen in patterns of oral movements. Some patterns interfere minimally with oral-motor development, but other patterns prevent the child from developing along the typical progression in feeding. The most common feeding patterns observed as a result of atypical oral-motor skill development are discussed next.

Jaw/Cheek/Lip/Tongue Retraction

Jaw/cheek/lip/tongue retraction is a common compensatory pattern that is most often observed in the child with hypotonicity proximally. The child attempts to compensate for poor trunk stability by increasing the tone in the facial and oral musculature. The result is a whole pattern of retraction of the jaw, cheeks, lips, and/or tongue, resulting in too much stability. The consequence is reduced oral mobility for eating. The child who uses this pattern typically prefers puréed foods that require only minimal oral mobility to manipulate and swallow. Jaw retraction can make it difficult to fully open and close the mouth. Cheek and lip retraction make it difficult to suck from a bottle or breast, remove food from a spoon, drink from a cup, keep food in the mouth, chew, or transfer food within the mouth. Tongue retraction can interfere with breathing, sucking, food manipulation, chewing, and drinking.

Inadequate Lip Closure

The inability to keep the lips closed makes it difficult to use a suck, swallow, and breathe pattern adequately. It is also difficult to keep food inside the mouth, and children with this problem tend to drool.

Tongue Protrusion

Tongue protrusion is when the tongue moves or rests beyond the gum or tooth line. It is typically seen in a child who has hypotonicity. The child's tongue often appears larger than normal because of the low muscle tone. Some children using this pattern will elect to protrude their tongue in an effort to keep their airway in a more open position. Children with Down syndrome, respiratory difficulties, enlarged adenoids or tonsils, or a large tongue may be observed to protrude their tongue in an exaggerated fashion.

Tongue Thrusting

Tongue thrusting is different from tongue protrusion, although many people incorrectly use these terms to mean the same thing. In tongue thrusting, the child's tongue is bunched and forced out of the mouth, which makes feeding difficult because it is hard for the feeder to insert a bottle, food, or spoon into the child's mouth past the tongue. If the feeder is successful in getting the food into the child's mouth, the child often forces the food back out with his or her tongue.

Tonic Bite Reflex

Tonic bite reflex is seen in children who bite down hard and then have difficulty opening the mouth or releasing the bite. It is typically observed when the child's gums or teeth are stimulated, especially in a child with a damaged central nervous system. The bite is tense and can be dangerous to the person feeding the child by hand. The bite reflex can even be dangerous to the child exploring his or her mouth with fingers and toys. It is important for the caregiver not to pull a finger or toy out of a child's mouth when the child is displaying a tonic bite but rather to flex the child's head to help break the tonic bite pattern.

Jaw Thrusting

Jaw thrusting is a forceful, sudden, exaggerated opening of the jaw. It is often seen when any stimulus is being brought toward the child's mouth, although it can occur at any time during the feeding process. It can result in difficulty with closing the mouth to take in food. In some children, the jaw may get stuck in this position, and it is very difficult for them to retain food in their mouths.

Jaw Clenching

Jaw clenching is commonly seen in the child with decreased muscle tone who is attempting to gain increased stability in the oral area. It is difficult for the child to open his or her jaw when this pattern occurs. Jaw clenching should not be mistaken for refusal of food. Improved positioning that allows for more flexion may help reduce this pattern.

ISSUES THAT AFFECT ORAL-MOTOR SKILL DEVELOPMENT

It is necessary to truly understand the cause of an atypical eating pattern before work toward improving the oral-motor skills can begin. When addressing atypical patterns, it is necessary to look at the child as a whole and not focus on just his or her mouth. It is important to examine the physical and emotional needs of the child, examine the environment, and examine the interaction between the child and the feeder. Although it is crucial to address the individual needs of each child, there are several common issues that typically affect the quality of oral-motor skills. These issues are listed and briefly discussed next.

- *Rule out medical reasons for the feeding problem.* It is critical to explore any possible connection of the feeding disorder with a potentially dangerous medical cause. The child's doctor is an important member of the feeding team and should be contacted before any significant changes are made to the child's mealtimes. For example, if a child begins school and is still using a bottle, the nutritional needs of the child should be explored before switching to a cup. Rapid transitions from one feeding method to another can result in a child's decreased caloric intake or affect an existing condition, such as FTT.

- *Identify known allergies or sensitivities.* Many children have allergies or sensitivities to foods, with reactions ranging from mild to severe. These allergies or sensitivities may be the cause of increased sensory and oral-motor problems associated with eating, such as increased drooling or respiratory congestion. Some allergic reactions may be life-threatening (e.g., a reaction to latex, which is commonly found in gloves, toys, and eating utensils). Take time to make sure that known allergies and sensitivities are identified by the entire feeding team before the child enters school.

- *Examine the environment where mealtimes take place.* A carefully planned mealtime environment can have a positive effect on the child's ability to attend to his or her meal and be an active participant in the eating process. Overstimulation from the effects of hearing, seeing, touching, and smelling can cause a negative effect on the mealtime experience. The child who is comfortable in his or her environment will be able to concentrate on the meal and demonstrate his or her true eating abilities.

- *Ensure proper positioning of the child while he or she is eating.* The position a child is in while eating can enhance or adversely affect his or her oral-motor skills. Proper positioning provides adequate stability in the trunk, which allows for adequate mobility of the muscles of the face and mouth. If the child does not feel stable and secure, compensatory postures will often be utilized, resulting in a loss of oral mobility for eating (see Chapter 5).

- *Consider the child's muscle tone.* Identifying activities that help normalize the muscle tone in the child's trunk before eating can help develop proximal stability, improve distal mobility, and address patterns of extension and retraction. Consulting a physical therapist (PT), occupational therapist (OT), or professional trained in dealing with muscle tone is strongly encouraged for learning specific techniques that can help with a child's tonal issues.

- *Provide oral/facial stimulation to the child.* Working to normalize a child's response to sensory stimulation is often at the heart of helping a child with a feeding disorder. Children often show hypersensitivity/hyposensitivity to taste, texture, temperature, and touch during mealtimes, which significantly interferes with the quality and quantity of food intake. These difficulties should be addressed before mealtimes so that the benefits of oral/facial stimulation can carry over into eating. (See Chapter 6 to learn more about oral sensitivity and stimulation techniques.)

- *Provide oral support when needed.* Some children who are unable to achieve adequate oral stability for eating may need external support for the oral structures. Methods for providing oral support include applying pressure to the cheeks, support under the chin, support to the lower lip and chin area, and pressure under the chin to the base of the tongue muscles. External oral support should only be utilized when the child is unable to achieve oral stability independently; use of these techniques should be gradually decreased over time as the child's internal oral stability increases.

- *Develop appropriate interactions between the child and the feeder.* For the child who must be fed or monitored while eating, interactions should involve mutual respect and balanced turn taking between the feeder and the child. The feeder must be able to read the child's cues/communication correctly and be in tune to the unique needs of that child. Issues such as rate of feeding, timing of feeding, and quantity of feeding will have a direct impact on the quality of the mealtime. (See Chapter 7 for more information about communication strategies for feeding.)

SPECIFIC FEEDING TECHNIQUES

There are no specific, cookbook-type ideas for improving a child's feeding problems because the problems are unique to each child. It is important to note that no feeding problem is the result of any single factor but rather combinations of factors, such as improper positioning, atypical muscle tone, sensitivity issues, behavioral concerns, structural defects/complex health care needs, sensory processing disorders, and inappropriate communication interactions. There are typical pattern variations, however, that are found in the literature. The possible causes and specific suggestions for improving these atypical patterns are discussed in Table 1. This table presents some of the most common atypical feeding patterns seen in the school-age population and provides a listing of possible causes and brief suggestions. The remainder of this book, however, is devoted to providing specific techniques related to feeding children within the educational environment for each functional area listed in Table 1.

SUMMARY

The oral musculature and structures are discussed in this chapter in terms of both individual development and how they work together in harmony for the development of smooth, coordinated, connected oral-motor skills. An intact central nervous system as well as adequate muscle tone, reflexes, and muscle strength build a foundation for the refinement of skills necessary for taking in, manipulating, and swallowing food. Oral-motor skills develop and build on previous patterns of movement in order to provide the ability for a child to eat independently. Atypical eating patterns are discussed as well as the possible causes behind these patterns, and suggestions for improving oral-motor skill development are summarized.

Kileigh

Kileigh is a 12-year-old girl with cerebral palsy and a severe tongue thrust. Kileigh has decreased muscle tone in her trunk and shoulder girdle areas, resulting in poor proximal stability. In an attempt to compensate for the decreased stability, she has learned to increase the muscle tone in her cheeks, lips, and tongue. This causes Kileigh to assume a pattern of oral and facial muscular retraction that results in poor mobility in these muscles for feeding and speech production. Kileigh must rely on an anterior/posterior pattern of movement of her tongue in an attempt to control food and liquid within her mouth. In addition, she has poor lip closure, poor cheek movement, and poor jaw control. Kileigh is typically fed while she is seated in her travel chair; however, her feet

Table 1.   Techniques for improving atypical oral-motor patterns

Atypical pattern	Functional areas[a]	Possible causes[b]	Suggestions[c]
Tongue retraction	Anatomy (see Chapter 3)	Micrognathia	Feed in prone stander or over wedge
		Cleft palate	Use slow pace
	Oral-motor (see Chapter 4)	Limited tongue mobility	Place food on side of mouth
			Build muscle tone in child's trunk
	Positioning (see Chapter 5)	Increased/decreased muscle tone	Alter child's muscle tone before feeding
		Neck hyperextension	Increase head flexion
		Poor trunk stability	Provide external trunk support
	Sensory (see Chapter 6)	Increased tongue sensitivity	Provide oral stimulation
			Keep food off tongue (use side placement of food)
	Communication (see Chapter 7)	Increased rate	Allow child to indicate readiness
			Read child's cues
Tongue protrusion	Oral-motor (see Chapter 4)	Decreased tongue mobility	Place food on side of mouth
	Positioning (see Chapter 5)	Decreased muscle tone	Build muscle tone in child's trunk
		Neck hyperextension	Increase head/trunk flexion
		Shoulder girdle retraction	Provide extension of back
	Sensory (see Chapter 6)	Decreased oral sensitivity	Provide oral stimulation
	Communication (see Chapter 7)	Increased/decreased rate	Allow child to set rate of feeding
		Increased/decreased volume	Allow child to set rate of feeding
	Behavior (see Chapter 9)	Food refusal	Give positive reinforcement for attempts to eat
Lip retraction	Anatomy (see Chapter 3)	Micrognathia	Feed in prone stander or in prone over wedge
		Cleft lip	Flex child's head
	Oral-motor (see Chapter 4)	Limited lip mobility	Provide lip stimulation
		Jaw instability	Provide external oral support
	Positioning (see Chapter 5)	Increased muscle tone in lips	Provide stimulation to cheeks/lips
		Decreased muscle tone in trunk	Build trunk muscle tone
		Neck hyperextension	Increase head/trunk flexion
	Sensory (see Chapter 6)	Oral hypersensitivity	Provide oral stimulation
	Communication (see Chapter 7)	Increased rate	Allow child to set rate of feeding
	Behavior (see Chapter 9)	Food refusal	Provide positive reinforcement

(continued)

Table 1. (continued)

Atypical pattern	Functional areas[a]	Possible causes[b]	Suggestions[c]
Low muscle tone in cheeks	Oral-motor (see Chapter 4)	Cheek instability	Teach straw drinking
	Positioning (see Chapter 5)	Decreased muscle tone	Increase trunk muscle tone Increase cheek muscle tone
	Sensory (see Chapter 6)	Poor sensory awareness	Provide sensory input in face
Jaw thrust	Anatomy (see Chapter 3)	Dental malocclusion	Consult dentist
		Temporomandibular joint dislocation	Consult dentist
	Oral-motor (see Chapter 4)	Jaw instability	Provide external oral support
	Positioning (see Chapter 5)	Increased body extension	Increase body flexion
		Neck hyperextension	Increase head flexion
	Sensory (see Chapter 6)	Oral hypersensitivity	Provide oral stimulation
Jaw clenching/ tooth grinding	Oral-motor (see Chapter 4)	Jaw instability	Provide external oral support
	Positioning (see Chapter 5)	Increased body flexion	Increase body extension
		Decreased muscle tone in trunk	Build trunk muscle tone
	Sensory (see Chapter 6)	Oral hypersensitivity	Provide oral stimulation
	Behavior (see Chapter 9)	Food refusal	Provide positive reinforcement
		Attention seeking	Provide socialization while child is eating
		Self-stimulation	Provide appropriate stimulation that is enjoyable to the child
Jaw retraction	Anatomy (see Chapter 3)	Micrognathia	Feed child in prone stander or in prone over wedge
	Oral-motor (see Chapter 4)	Jaw instability	Provide jaw stability
	Positioning (see Chapter 5)	Increased body extension	Increase body flexion
		Neck hyperextension	Increase neck flexion
	Sensory (see Chapter 6)	Oral hypersensitivity	Provide oral stimulation
Tonic bite reflex	Positioning (see Chapter 5)	Increased body flexion	Increase body extension
	Sensory (see Chapter 6)	Oral hypersensitivity	Provide oral stimulation
	Behavior (see Chapter 9)	Overstimulation	Provide appropriate environment
		Protects mouth	Provide relaxing oral movements

[a]*Functional areas* refer to specific chapter topics in this book.

[b]Refer to the corresponding chapter or the glossary at the end of this book for definitions of these terms.

[c]These suggestions or techniques are described in greater detail in the corresponding chapters.

are not resting on a surface, her hips are forward, her shoulders are elevated, her hands are clenched in fists, and her head and neck are hyperextended. She eats foods that dissolve easily with saliva, and much of her food and liquid is lost as a result of the tongue thrust. She gags easily on new foods and food that must be chewed. Kileigh must be fed by others.

Before any changes to Kileigh's feeding program can be implemented, the following questions should be addressed.

Collaboration

- Has the feeding team sat down with Kileigh's parents/caregivers to address their concerns and note their observations as well as to establish a commitment of the feeding team to carry over techniques throughout the day?

Anatomy

- What do you see in Kileigh's face or mouth structures? Are they symmetrical? Are they intact?

Positioning

- What changes occur in Kileigh's positioning when her feet are placed on a surface?
- What changes occur in Kileigh's positioning when her hips are placed back in the chair?
- What changes occur in Kileigh's positioning when her shoulders are brought down and her arms are brought forward?
- What changes occur when her hands are relaxed?
- What changes in Kileigh's positioning and the pattern of oral retraction occur when her head and neck are brought into slight flexion?

Sensitivity

- What types of sensory stimulation techniques can be utilized to help normalize the sensitivity in and around Kileigh's mouth?
- How is food currently presented to Kileigh?
- What specific foods will Kileigh eat?

Oral-Motor Skills

- What are the effects of the proximally decreased muscle tone on Kileigh's oral skills?
- What are the effects of the increased oral/facial muscle tone on her eating skills?
- What happens when food is presented to Kileigh by spoon?
- What happens when food is presented by hand?
- What happens when food is presented in smaller amounts?
- How are liquids presented to Kileigh?

Behavior

• Are any behaviors interfering with Kileigh's acceptance of food and liquid?

   Kileigh's oral pattern is limited to a tongue thrust as a result of the muscle tone issues in her trunk, shoulder girdle area, and oral/facial area. Position changes, an oral stimulation program, and changes in food placement must be addressed before the tongue thrust can be reduced. Consider the following suggestions in your feeding plan for Kileigh.

Collaboration

• Include Kileigh's parents/caregivers in the feeding plan to ensure that their concerns are being addressed and to facilitate carryover of the techniques outside the school environment.

Positioning

• Consult with a PT and/or an OT to consider techniques to help alter Kileigh's muscle tone and to provide position changes for Kileigh.

Sensitivity

• Provide consistent facial and then oral stimulation techniques to help elongate and activate Kileigh's facial and oral muscles for improved eating.
• Provide consistent toothbrushing and the use of therapy tubing throughout the day for intraoral stimulation.

Oral-Motor Skills

• Attempt to feed Kileigh with your gloved finger, rather than with a spoon, because the use of a spoon encourages the anterior/posterior tongue movement.
• Utilize side placement of food to encourage tongue lateralization, to help keep the food in the mouth, and to encourage munching skills.
• Gradually add textured foods to the food Kileigh already tolerates in order to increase the texture in her diet.
• Once munching begins, try using pieces of crackers and strips of luncheon meats, cheese, and so forth; place these foods into the side of Kileigh's mouth, directly onto the molars.
• Try to present liquids through the use of a cut-out cup containing thickened liquids. Give Kileigh only one sip at a time so that she does not resort back to sucking and so that she can work on starting and stopping the liquid flow.

Medical Issues

• Changes should be gradual with continuous monitoring of Kileigh's respiration.
• Be positive, and praise her attempts. Have fun!

REFERENCES

Alexander, R., Boehme, R., & Cupps, B. (1993). *Normal development of functional motor skills*. San Antonio, TX: Therapy Skill Builders.
Arvedson, J.C., & Brodsky, L. (Eds.). (1993). *Pediatric swallowing and feeding: Assessment and management*. San Diego, CA: Singular Publishing Group.

Morris, S.E., & Klein, M.D. (1987). *Pre-feeding skills: A comprehensive resource for feeding development.* San Antonio, TX: Therapy Skill Builders.

Vergara, E.R. (Ed.). (1993). *Foundations for practice in the neonatal intensive care unit and early intervention: A self-guided practice manual.* Rockville, MD: American Occupational Therapy Association.

chapter five

Positioning Strategies for Feeding and Eating

Patricia A. Snyder,
Darbi Breath, and Gerard J. DeMauro

An occupational therapist (OT), speech-language pathologist (SLP), and physical therapist (PT) working together on an intervention team describe to a classroom teacher the importance of body position during mealtimes. The therapists believe that "the ability to control the body's position is everything in life." When taken out of context, this statement might astonish readers. Few readers would dispute, however, the importance of being able to assume, maintain, or change positions to perform many activities of daily living.

For example, when brushing one's teeth, one usually assumes a standing position at a sink. During this activity, one alternately bends the upper body forward and toward the sink, lifts the upper body away from the sink, or moves the toothbrush around in the mouth. Obvious as well as subtle movements and postural adjustments occur during transitions toward or away from the sink and while moving the toothbrush around inside the mouth, although a standing position is maintained until the activity is completed. After completing this activity, one may change positions entirely (e.g., walk to a bed, sit on the edge, and lie down).

In order to assume, maintain, or change positions, one must have postural control, which is the ability to maintain stability of the body against the force of gravity. Many systems interact with the environment to contribute toward the goal of postural control, including musculoskeletal, sensory, and neurological systems (Horak, 1987, 1992). Virtually every task or activity in which children and adults engage requires a certain degree of postural control. Rainforth and York-Barr (1996) noted that the accomplishment of even the simplest daily activity requires a sophisticated combination of postural and movement skills.

Mealtimes are another common activity during which children and adults assume various positions and must demonstrate postural control to feed or eat successfully. As defined in Chapter 1, *eating* refers to the child's being able to actively bring food to his or her mouth independently, whereas *feeding* refers to the child's being assisted in the activity of eating (Avery-Smith, 1996). Feeding and eating are complex tasks that require dynamic postural and movement skills (Orelove & Sobsey, 1996).

Infants who have not developed sophisticated postural control and movement skills must rely on external supports to help them maintain positions against the influence of gravity while feeding. For example, a child younger than 3 months typically is supported by an adult who holds the child in a semireclined feeding position while the infant drinks from a bottle or is breast fed. This feeding position provides a stable, external support to the child's head, neck, and trunk, enabling the child to organize movements needed for oral-motor function (cf. Amiel-Tison & Griener, 1986). Similarly, a child who eats independently must be able to maintain a stable sitting position and perform a complex series of gross and fine motor skills to lift a spoon from a bowl to his or her mouth. Eating requires the ability to control posture in sitting and make minor postural adjustments throughout the feeding process.

Over time, the young child learns to control his or her posture and movements while participating in daily activities, such as mealtimes. The complex process of developing motor control against gravity frequently is unnoticed and, once learned, becomes automatic. Children perform functional tasks, such as feeding and eating, without conscious awareness of the underlying postural control mechanisms that guide movement and help maintain stability. They are able, therefore, to focus on the major goals of the eating or feeding task, such as obtaining food from a spoon.

For children who experience motor challenges, however, the complex motor and postural demands of feeding and eating do not go unrecognized by either the children or those who interact with them. A simple task, such as the ability to remove food from a spoon, may pose significant challenges for these children or for those adults who feed them. Children with motor challenges often lack the postural and movement skills needed during mealtimes. These children may benefit from external supports that adapt for their postural and movement control difficulties. Participation in mealtime activities may be enhanced by providing children with adequate external support via adaptive positioning (cf. Dunn, 1996).

In this chapter, strategies are presented for positioning during mealtimes. First, a definition of positioning is offered, and benefits of positioning for children who have motor problems are described. Next, a brief discussion of general principles of positioning and postural alignment is provided. This discussion is followed by a presentation of guidelines and a checklist for observing and analyzing postural alignment in sitting. Adaptations and strategies to address positioning challenges are outlined, and materials and equipment used for adaptive positioning are discussed. Alternative positions, including sidelying, prone, and standing, are briefly described. The chapter concludes with a discussion about the importance of working as a team to address positioning during mealtimes, and a case study is presented to demonstrate a problem-solving approach that can be used to address the positioning needs of children who have motor challenges.

WHAT IS POSITIONING?

Positioning refers to the use of adaptive techniques or equipment that provide external postural support for children who have motor challenges. These techniques and equipment assist children by adapting for postural and movement demands imposed on them by the environment. Positioning can be used to compensate for postural and movement constraints or to enhance functioning in children who experience motor challenges (Rainforth & York-Barr, 1996; Ward, 1984). The general goal of positioning during mealtimes is to provide optimal alignment and support to enhance the child's functional performance.

Although positioning strategies can help compensate for motor and postural challenges, these strategies can be combined and incorporated with "handling" techniques to promote improved postural and movement control. Before positioning a child in a chair for mealtime, adults may use handling techniques to bring the child's body into a flexed and symmetrical position. Without these preparatory techniques, the optimal position for the child may be difficult to achieve. Figure 1 illustrates the application of the interplay between handling and positioning techniques for a child with significant motor challenges.

Benefits of Positioning During Mealtimes

A major benefit of using positioning during mealtimes is to encourage postural alignment needed for the preservation of an open airway (Geyer & McGowan, 1995). Children who have difficulty maintaining postural alignment, particularly of the head, neck, and trunk, may have compromised respiratory function (Redstone, 1991); positioning can be used to enhance breathing (Morris, 1977b). Reid and Sochaniwskyj (1991) found that children with cerebral palsy who were placed in adaptive sitting positions that encouraged a more erect posture demonstrated increased tidal volume of the lungs.

A close relationship exists between a child's body position and oral-motor skills. A second benefit of positioning, therefore, is the influence on the eating sequence. An effective sequence involves 1) the ability to take in food, form a bolus, and swallow; 2) the absence of aspiration into the airway; 3) the lack of reflux of food; and 4) the normal digestion and movement of food through the intestines (Eicher, 1997).

The relationship between oral-motor abilities and overall body posture and alignment is well-acknowledged. Leslie Fay Davis, an SLP and instructor of the neurodevelopmental treatment approach, coined the phrase, "What we want at the lips, we mediate through the hips" (cited in Morris, 1982, p. 113). This statement stresses the importance of ensuring proper body positioning before tending to specific oral-motor concerns, such as lip closure on a spoon.

A third benefit of positioning for feeding is its influence on swallowing. Excessive head and neck flexion or extension affects swallowing and may increase the risk of aspiration (Bray, Beckman, & Barks, 1987). Children with motor challenges may have difficulty with controlling the position of their head, neck, and trunk against gravity, resulting in poor coordination of respiration and swallowing. People without motor challenges can inhibit res-

A

B

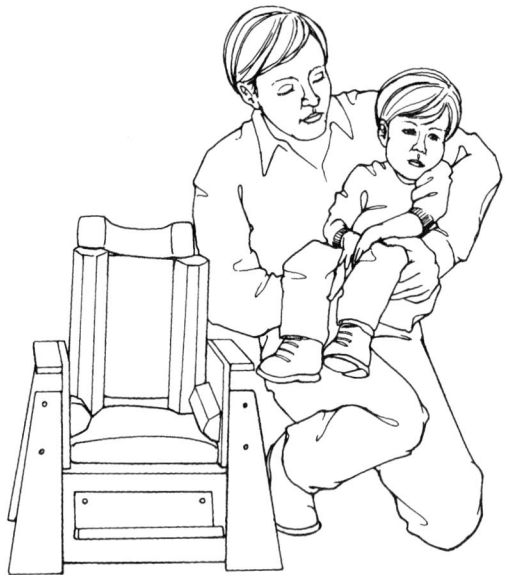

C

D

Figure 1. Application of handling and positioning techniques for a child with significant motor challenges: A) child lying on back in extension with head turned to one side, B) caregiver lifts child by using handling techniques and flexing the child's hips and knees, C) child is held by caregiver in an upright and symmetrical position, D) child's postural alignment is maintained while placed in adapted chair by caregiver.

piration to allow for more than one swallow per breath. Those people with motor challenges may lack this coordination. Figure 2 illustrates desired head and neck alignment during feeding and the influences of extreme head positions on swallowing.

Another benefit of positioning is hastened digestion, which potentially decreases the severity of gastroesophageal reflux (GER). Upright sitting, inclined prone, or sidelying positions enhance the effects of the force of gravity to hold contents in the stomach and promote normal outflow of stomach contents (Bray et al., 1987; Wolf & Glass, 1992). Positioning may also be used as an adjunct in the management of constipation experienced by some children with severe motor challenges.

Eating and feeding skills may be enhanced through adaptive positioning. Hulme and her colleagues investigated the effects of adaptive seating devices on feeding, eating, reaching, and grasping behaviors in children with multiple disabilities (Hulme, Poor, Schulein, & Pezzino, 1983; Hulme, Shaver, Acher, Mullette, & Eggert, 1987). Using survey and observational research methods, Hulme and her colleagues found that adaptive seating devices improved sitting posture, head control, and body alignment during mealtimes. Use of the devices also improved children's grasp patterns and facilitated their progressions from bottle to cup drinking and from eating blended to chopped foods.

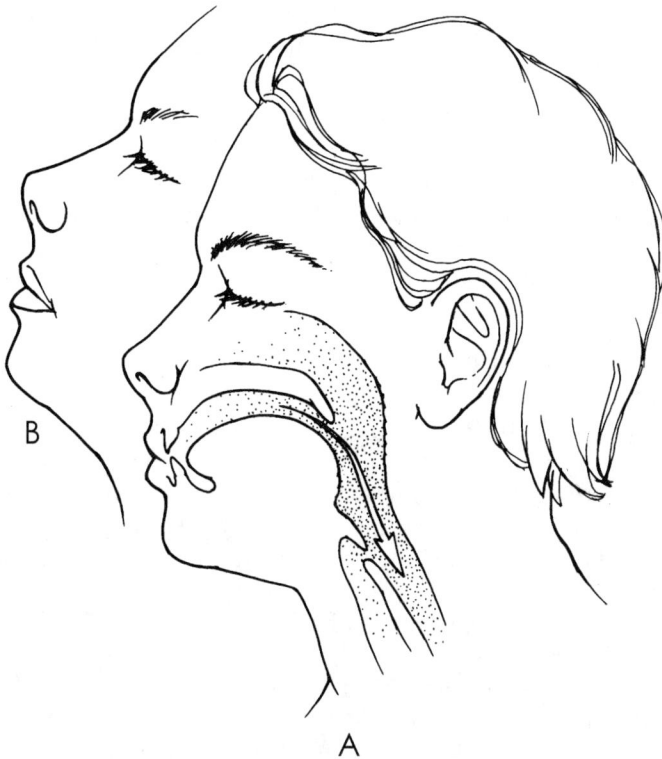

Figure 2.   Desired head and neck alignment during feeding and the influences of extreme head positions on swallowing: A) head and neck in appropriate alignment facilitates swallowing, B) head and neck in extension increases the risk for aspiration. Feeders should avoid "bird feeding" positions—the practice of feeding a child with his or her head and neck in extreme extension.

Children with motor challenges may also experience important social and communicative benefits when positioned similar to their peers without disabilities. Adaptive positioning provides external support for children, giving them the opportunity to participate in meaningful interactions during a mealtime activity. During snacktime, a preschooler with motor challenges who is positioned in an upright posture at the same height and eye level and in proximity to his or her peers will be able to engage in communicative and social interactions. A child with poor control of his or her head, neck, and trunk may be unable to meet the postural demands associated with an unsupported sitting position. When placed in a chair with inadequate support, this child may become fearful and posturally insecure. The child may spend his or her time and energy trying to maintain an upright position in order to avoid falling out of the chair, rather than participating in social exchanges with peers.

Positioning strategies can help address many interpersonal aspects of the feeding process. Children who have motor challenges may exhibit behaviors that are difficult to interpret or that may be misinterpreted during mealtimes (Morris, 1977a). Parents who observe children arching their body may be uncertain whether this behavior is an attempt to withdraw from the interaction or an uncontrolled movement. If the child is positioned so that uncontrolled movements are less likely to occur, the caregiver may be able to assess communicative signals more accurately. Positioning can enhance parent–child relationships by providing the child with necessary supports to engage in communicative and social interactions during mealtimes.

Advantages of positioning usually are described with respect to children with motor challenges. Feeders should be aware, however, of how their own positions benefit mealtime activities. The position of the adult can influence the child's posture. The relationship between the location of the feeder and the child should be carefully considered when food or drink is presented during feedings. Attempts should be made to present the food at, or slightly below, the child's eye level (Finnie, 1974; Orelove & Sobsey, 1991). Figure 3 shows how the position of the adult and the level of food presentation can benefit the child's postural alignment.

General Principles of Positioning

The optimum position for feeding or eating varies from child to child, but certain general principles should be considered when positioning decisions are made. An understanding of these general principles is important for at least three reasons. First, these principles are used as a guiding framework while considering children's individual needs. Second, because children may eat or be fed in more than one position, an understanding of how the general principles apply across different feeding positions is important. Third, these principles may be applied to enhance children's participation in activities other than mealtimes.

Table 1 shows the general principles of positioning. Stability can be provided through the use of external supports, which compensate for or enhance the individual's level of postural control and provide an adequate base of support. The external supports should provide stability but not be overly restrictive. For example, use of numerous straps across the trunk may restrict a child's ability to move forward and grasp a spoon.

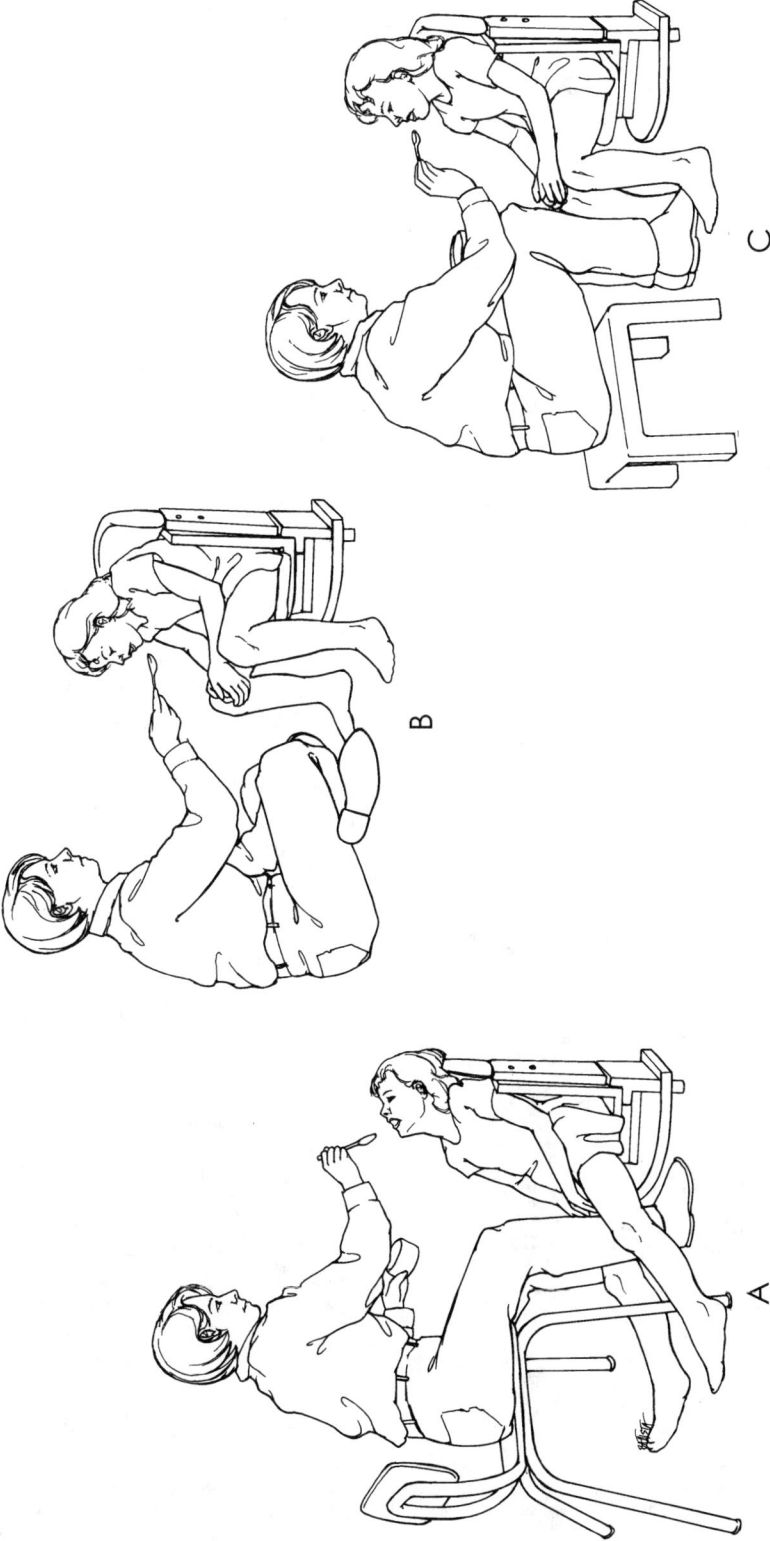

Figure 3. How the position of feeder and level of food presentation affects eating and feeding: A) feeder's position and presentation of food above child's eye level leads to extension and negatively influences alignment of the child's head, neck, and body; B) feeder's position and presentation of food too far below child's eye level leads to excessive flexion of the child's head and neck (positions A and B may interfere with eating and feeding); C) feeder's position and presentation of food at or slightly below child's eye level promotes desired head and neck alignment.

Table 1.   General principles of positioning

When positioning children for feeding and eating
- Provide support to ensure stability, using the least amount of adaptation necessary.
- Foster postural alignment and symmetry of the body.
- Consider the practical and motor requirements of the task.
- Use positions that promote function and active participation.
- Use positions that minimize the deleterious effects of specific motor challenges (e.g., tonal deviations, primitive reflexes, muscle imbalances, limited joint mobility).
- Facilitate comfort, and ensure the safety of the child and feeder.
- Use positions that keep the child as upright as possible.
- Choose positions that are useful for and acceptable to the child, parent, or caregiver.

Postural alignment refers to the relationship of body parts to one another and the position of the body with reference to gravity and the base of support (Shumway-Cook & Woollacott, 1995). Children with motor challenges frequently have difficulty independently achieving or maintaining postural alignment. Attempts should be made to ensure symmetrical alignment. Figure 4 illustrates how alignment and symmetry can be enhanced through the use of adaptive positioning.

Rainforth and York-Barr (1996) suggested selecting positions, whenever possible, that match the practical and motor aspects of the task. For example, sitting is the typical position used for finger feeding, as opposed to prone or sidelying. The sitting position "sets the stage" for efficient self-feeding skills. In order to meet the practical and motor aspects of self-feeding tasks in a sitting position, however, some children will need additional external supports.

Achievement of stability, postural alignment, and symmetry must be continually assessed in relation to the promotion of independent functioning and participation. If a child is unable to bring his or her arms forward and

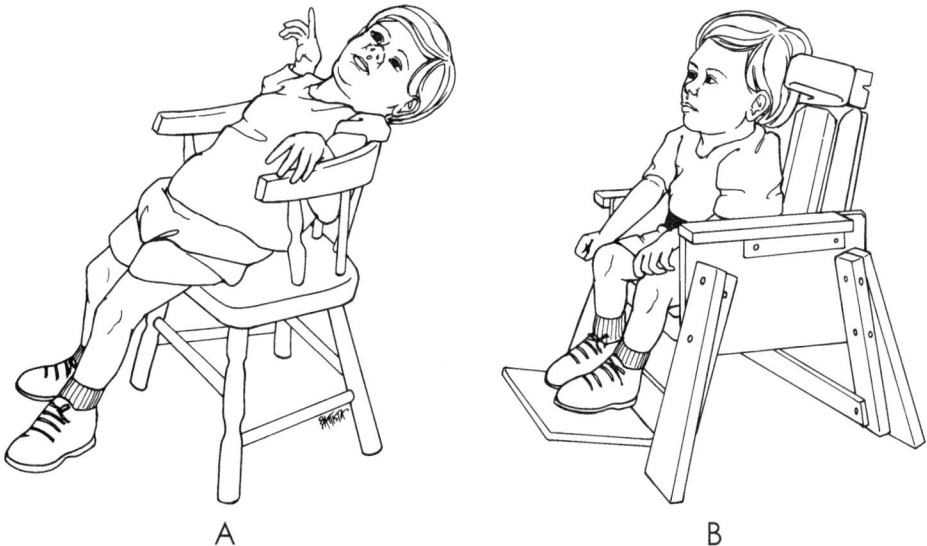

A   B

Figure 4.   How the type of chair that the child uses affects postural alignment: A) child sits in chair that does not promote symmetry and alignment; B) child sits in an adapted chair, and symmetry and alignment are improved.

hands to mid-line, he or she will have difficulty reaching for and holding a cup, even though his or her body may be stable, aligned, and symmetrical. Figure 5 shows how adaptive positioning strategies can be used to achieve stability, alignment, and symmetry and help the child hold a utensil and bring food to his or her mouth.

The deleterious effects of motor challenges can be minimized through the use of adaptive positioning strategies. A child who exhibits a persistent asymmetric tonic neck reflex (ATNR), in which the position of the child's head influences the position and control of the child's arms, may have difficulty with self-feeding. Figure 6 illustrates use of adaptive positioning to lessen the influence of ATNR and to promote eating.

Comfort and safety are critical considerations when using positioning strategies. A position that is uncomfortable for the child, regardless of potential benefits, will not be tolerated and may make mealtimes less pleasant. Children with motor challenges often learn to feed and eat in postures that may be viewed as contradictory to the basic principles outlined in Table 1. Those involved in making positioning decisions should acknowledge that these postures may feel "normal" to the child, and positioning changes will need to be introduced slowly and with caution. The primary purpose of eating and feeding is to satisfy hunger; therefore, children should be given time to adjust to positions so that both their hunger and positioning needs are met. New positions might be introduced during activities other than mealtimes until the child appears comfortable with the new positions.

An additional basic principle of positioning is to use an upright feeding position whenever possible. There are many benefits associated with upright

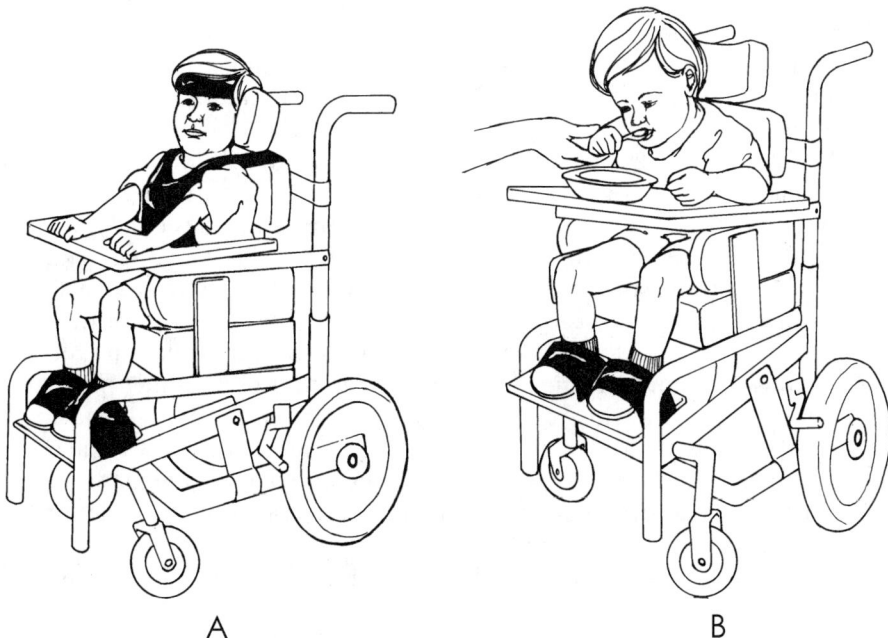

A   B

Figure 5.   How positioning strategies affect eating: A) positioning strategies that promote stability, alignment, and symmetry but not active participation by the child; B) positioning strategies that promote stability, alignment, symmetry, and active participation in eating.

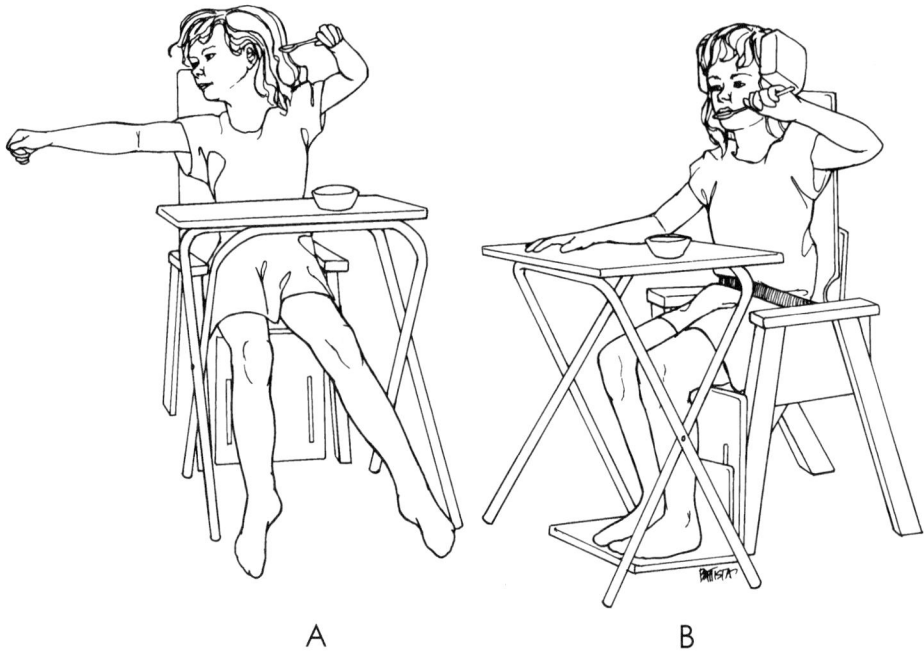

Figure 6.   How the use of adaptive positioning can lessen the influence of ATNR and promote independent eating: A) child attempts to feed self, but ATNR interferes with the child's ability to feed self; B) child positioned in adapted chair with external supports. The influence of the ATNR is lessened.

positions, such as enhanced respiratory function, oral-motor control, digestion, and use of arms for self-feeding. Upright positioning also decreases the risk of aspiration.

A final, but perhaps most important, positioning principle relates to usefulness and acceptability of the position for the family or caregiver. These individuals implement and evaluate recommended positions on an ongoing basis because they spend the most time with the child during meals. Their feedback about usefulness is vital when making positioning decisions. For example, if recommended adaptive positioning strategies or supports cannot be used in a restaurant, alternative suggestions will be necessary.

Positioning strategies must be acceptable to the family. Acceptability may involve weighing cost–benefit factors, discussing family priorities, and remaining sensitive to the social-emotional aspects of positioning recommendations. Recommendations involving significant investments of time to position the child in expensive equipment may not be acceptable to the child's family. For example, the family may prefer to adapt a kitchen chair for their child who has motor challenges rather than purchase a commercially available seating system that would never be used by children who do not have motor challenges. Family members should be involved in all aspects of decision making related to positioning and making adaptations for their child.

General Components of Postural Alignment

In order to achieve stability, alignment, and symmetry, specific parts of the body that contribute to postural alignment must be considered. The alignment of the head, neck, shoulders, trunk, pelvis, and hips is considered in all feeding and eating positions because these parts of the body are important contributors to postural stability. Table 2 shows general components of postural alignment.

The hips and pelvis are considered to be symmetrical when they rest equally and evenly on a supporting surface. Neutral pelvic alignment is characterized by a lack of excessive forward or backward tilting of the pelvis. Forward pelvic tilting is known as an *anterior pelvic tilt*, and backward pelvic tipping is referred to as *posterior pelvic tilt*. The position of the pelvis can affect many other regions of the body. Hip and trunk positions, in particular, are influenced by pelvic alignment. Figures 7 and 8 illustrate the effects of pelvic position on the hips and trunk.

An aligned, symmetrical, and stable trunk is important for maintaining alignment of the shoulders, neck, and head. Malalignment, asymmetry, and instability of the trunk leads to postural compensations in other areas of the body, such as the shoulders and head (see Figure 8).

The legs contribute to postural stability in most positions and contribute directly to the base of support in sitting positions. Support should be available for the legs in all positions and to the feet in sitting positions.

The shoulders, neck, and head need a stable and aligned trunk to serve as the base of support. The shoulders should be level and relaxed. If the shoulders are pulled back (i.e., *retracted*), rolled forward (i.e., *protracted*), or elevated, the position of the neck and head are affected. Shoulder position directly influences arm position. For example, retracted shoulders may prevent forward movement of the arms, which is a movement needed for self-feeding.

The positional stability and alignment of the head and neck will directly affect oral-motor control. For example, if the head falls backward into an extended position, then the mouth opens widely, and lip closure is difficult. A head and neck positioned in extreme flexion (i.e., chin to chest) presents chewing and swallowing challenges.

How Can Teachers and Caregivers Observe and Analyze Postural Alignment?

Children with a variety of disabilities, including those with cerebral palsy of various types (i.e., spastic, athetoid, ataxic), Down syndrome, spina bifida, and other conditions characterized by motor and postural delays may benefit from adaptive positioning strategies. The underlying aspects of these children's motor challenges frequently result in a delay or disorder in their postural control. These children often are unable to assume and maintain the

Table 2.   General components of postural alignment

- Pelvis and hips symmetrical
- Pelvis in a neutral position
- Trunk symmetrical and stable
- Shoulders level and relaxed
- Head in a neutral and mid-line position
- Arms forward with hands in mid-line
- Legs supported

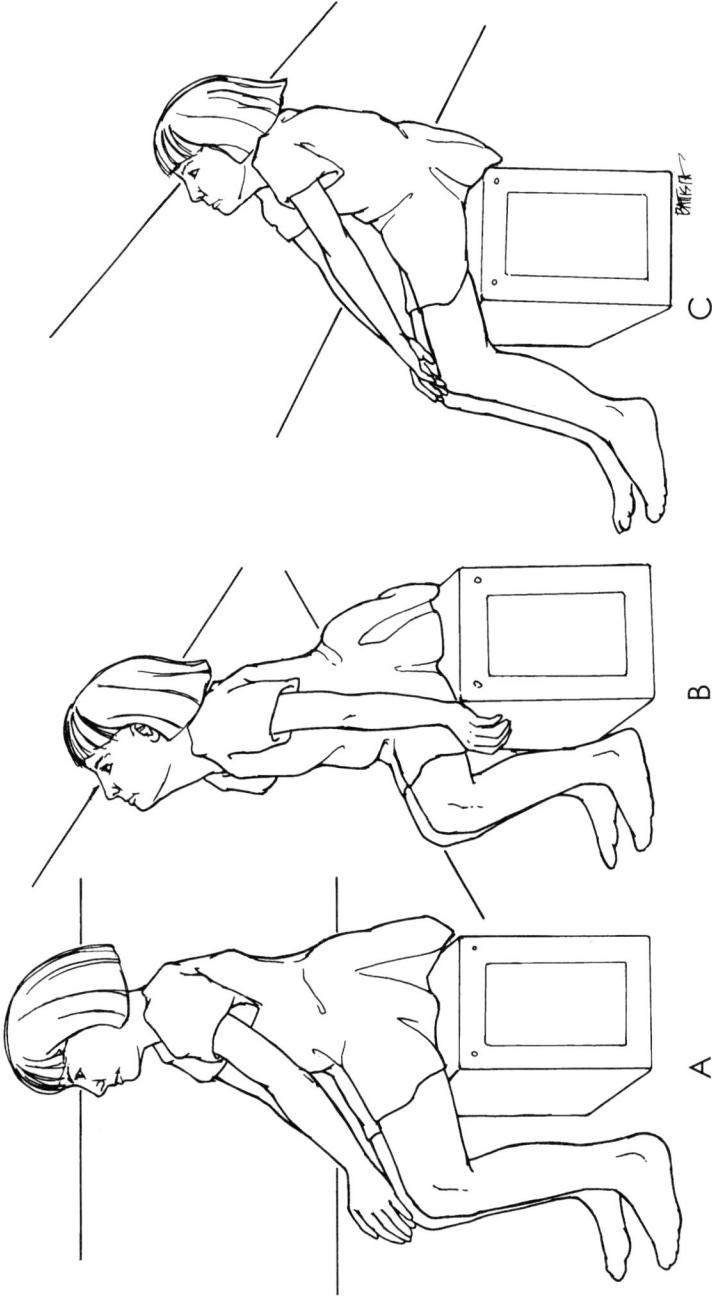

Figure 7. The effects of pelvic position on the hips, trunk, neck, and head alignment: A) effects of a neutral or slight anterior pelvic tilt, which is a desired position; B) effects of excessive anterior pelvic tilt—trunk is forward and arms and shoulders may be pulled back; C) effects of excessive posterior pelvic tilt—trunk is rounded, and head and neck may be in excessive extension or flexion.

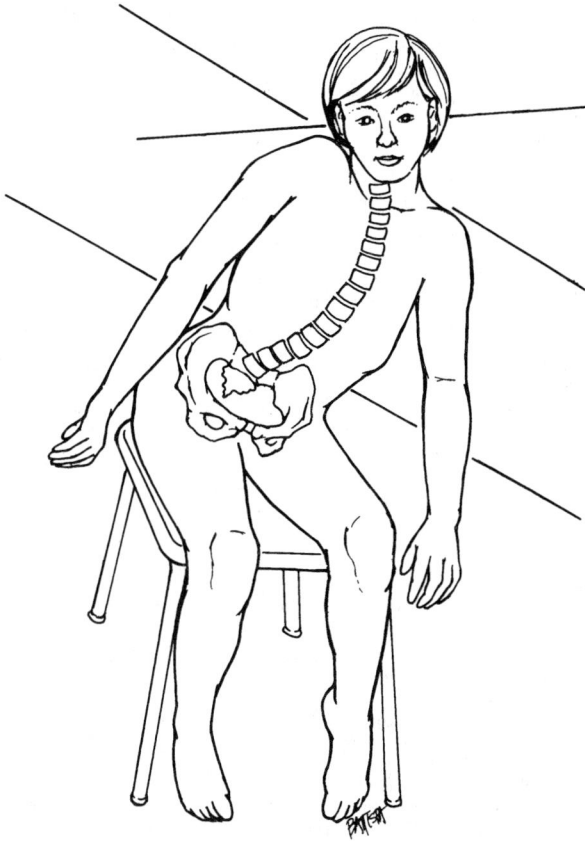

Figure 8.   The pelvis is a key point of control. Note how malalignment of the pelvis leads to asymmetry of the trunk, uneven shoulders, and compensatory head and neck positions.

postural alignment described in Table 2 without the use of positioning strategies, which include the provision of external supports.

The specific underlying motor impairments that contribute to postural alignment are multiple and complex and may be difficult to differentiate. For the purpose of this chapter, the specific underlying motor impairments that affect posture are recognized to be associated with limitations in joint range of motion, muscle/postural tonal abnormalities, decreased muscle strength, decreased force production in functional muscle groups, faulty timing and firing of muscular contractions, balance disorders, and related sensory and cognitive components that contribute to motor and postural control. Regardless of which impairments contribute to children's postural alignment, observation and analysis of posture in various positions will assist in identifying mealtime positioning needs and strategies.

Observations should be conducted in the position(s) planned to be used during mealtimes. Whenever possible, children's postural alignment should be observed first without the use of adaptive supports. Changes in breathing patterns; muscle tone; reflex activities; sensory, perceptual, and cognitive skills; and functional abilities should be noted as different positions are observed.

Figure 9 is a checklist that teachers or caregivers may use to observe a child's postural alignment in the seated position. Observing how the child's body is aligned in this position is an important first step in the problem-solving process used to make positioning decisions.

Initial emphasis on the checklist is directed to the pelvis because it is considered a key point of control (Cook & Hussey, 1995). As illustrated in Figure 7, the position of the pelvis often affects postural alignment in other areas of the body (Bergen, Presperin, & Tallman, 1990). Alignment of central regions of the body (i.e., the pelvis, hips, and trunk) often is considered prior to observing alignment of the head, neck, shoulders, and limbs.

Although alignment considerations are listed separately for the various body parts, malalignment in one area will adversely affect other parts of the

Child's Name: _____   Age: _____

Date: _____

| Body part | Lower half of the body | | | |
	Alignment considerations	Yes	No	Comments
Pelvis and hips	a. Is the pelvis upright in a neutral or slightly anterior tipped position?	☐	☐	
	b. Are the pelvis and hips symmetrical with equal distribution of weight on the "sit bones" (i.e., ischial tuberosities) and the knees facing forward?[a]	☐	☐	
	c. Are the hips flexed to approximately 90°?[b]	☐	☐	
	If no to a, b, or c:			
	Does the pelvis tip too far backward with excessive hip extension with or without asymmetry?	☐	☐	
	Does the pelvis tip too far forward with excessive hip flexion with or without asymmetry?	☐	☐	

(continued)

Figure 9.   Postural alignment checklist for sitting positions. ([a]If the pelvis and hips cannot be moved easily into neutral positions, therapists should be consulted. Children with pelvic and hip malalignments may have a variety of conditions that warrant therapeutic expertise to address positioning needs. These malalignments may include hip subluxation and dislocation, pelvic obliquity [i.e., one side of the pelvis is higher than the other], and pelvic rotation [i.e., one side of the pelvis is more forward than the other]. Other malalignments may include "windswept" hips [i.e., one hip is internally rotated and the other hip is externally rotated] and scoliosis [i.e., curvature of the spine]. For more complete descriptions of these malalignments and positioning considerations, consult Cook and Hussey [1995] and Bergen et al. [1990]. [b]When individuals are positioned in chairs, the hips, knees, and feet are commonly placed at 90° angles. These angles, however, often are difficult to maintain when performing functional tasks [Radell, 1997], and not all therapists agree about the importance of promoting a 90°–90°–90° position during sitting. For example, some therapists believe a forward inclination [approximately 5°–10°] of the seat back promotes a slight anterior pelvic tilt and a more upright and stable sitting posture, which can improve upper limb function and head position [McClenaghan, Thombs, & Milner, 1992; Miedaner, 1990; Sochaniwskyj, Koheil, Bablich, Milner, & Lotto, 1991]. In other situations, particularly when children exhibit severe extensor thrusting in the lower half of their bodies, their hips may need to be flexed to greater than 90°.)

Figure 9.   (*continued*)

Lower half of the body				
Body part	Alignment considerations	Yes	No	Comments
Thighs and legs	a. Are the thighs well-supported in slight abduction with the seat surface 1–2 inches behind the knees?	☐	☐	
	b. Are the knees flexed to at least 90°?	☐	☐	
	If no to a or b:			
	Do the legs press tightly together?	☐	☐	
	Do the legs spread apart excessively?	☐	☐	
	Are the knees extended excessively?	☐	☐	
	Are the knees flexed excessively?	☐	☐	
Feet and ankles	a. Are feet and ankles well-supported and ankles positioned under or slightly behind the knees?	☐	☐	
	b. Are ankles flexed to 90°?	☐	☐	
	c. Are feet and toes facing forward?	☐	☐	
	If no to a, b, or c:			
	Are feet not flat and not resting on a supporting surface?	☐	☐	

Upper half of the body				
Body part	Alignment considerations	Yes	No	Comments
Trunk	a. Is the trunk upright?	☐	☐	
	b. Is the trunk symmetrical?	☐	☐	
	If no to a or b:			
	Is the trunk rounded excessively?	☐	☐	
	Does the trunk fall forward?	☐	☐	
	Does the trunk arch backward?	☐	☐	
	Does the trunk fall to one side?	☐	☐	
Shoulders and arms	a. Are shoulders level and relaxed?	☐	☐	
	b. Are the arms forward and in mid-line?	☐	☐	
	If no to a or b:			
	Do the shoulders elevate?	☐	☐	
	Are the shoulders asymmetrical?	☐	☐	
	Are the shoulders excessively protracted with arms turned inward?	☐	☐	
	Are the shoulders excessively retracted with arms pulling back?	☐	☐	

(*continued*)

Figure 9.   (*continued*)

Body part	Alignment considerations	Yes	No	Comments
	Upper half of the body			
Head and neck	Is head in mid-line with a slight chin tuck?	☐	☐	
	If no:			
	Do the head and neck extend excessively with or without asymmetry?	☐	☐	
	Do the head and neck flex excessively with or without asymmetry?	☐	☐	

body. For example, the child in Figure 4A exhibits a posterior pelvic tilt. As a result, he shows excessive rounding of his trunk with legs extended. When this child's hips and pelvis are repositioned in an appropriate adapted chair, as shown in Figure 4B, overall postural alignment is improved.

Addressing Postural Alignment Challenges: Strategies and Adaptations

Once the child's general postural alignment is observed and the checklist is completed, the next step in the problem-solving process involves considering strategies and adaptations that can be used to address identified alignment challenges. Appendix A of this chapter illustrates various positioning difficulties in sitting that may have been observed in various regions of the body and offers general and specific strategies and adaptations to address these challenges.

Appendix A continually directs attention back to the key points of control because of the importance of proper pelvic and hip alignment, symmetry, and stability. For example, when the legs are pressed tightly together, the first strategy suggested is to review pelvic and hip alignment before considering other strategies such as using a pommel. The organization of the suggested strategies and adaptations serves as a constant reminder that the most noticeable malalignment(s) may not be where the challenge originates. Use of a pommel to separate legs that press tightly together is likely to be ineffective unless the pelvis and hips are positioned appropriately.

MATERIALS AND EQUIPMENT FOR ADAPTIVE POSITIONING

Positioning challenges can be addressed by adapting standard chairs or chairs designed for children with special needs. The types of adaptations made to chairs will change, depending on the positioning needs that are encountered. Different chairs may elicit different challenges, depending on the seat depth and width, height, shape, firmness, or amount of back and lateral supports provided (Breath, DeMauro, & Snyder, 1997). When adapting chairs, family members and interventionists should use the least intrusive and most natural adaptations to address positioning challenges.

Many of the adaptations and strategies shown in Appendix A require the selection and use of materials or equipment. These items may be made or purchased for a low to high cost. Use of some of these materials or equipment requires specialized training or advanced construction skills. Durability, availability, and acceptability are also important considerations when choosing materials and equipment (Oren, 1994). Appendix B of this chapter lists materials and equipment commonly used to address positioning challenges.

The materials and equipment listed in Appendix B typically are used as temporary adaptations to address positioning challenges encountered with young children. As children grow, their positioning challenges may need to be addressed through the use of commercially available or customized seating systems. Decisions about whether these systems should be used for positioning during mealtimes and other functional activities or as mobility aids should be based on comprehensive, interdisciplinary assessments (Cook & Hussey, 1995). The basic alignment considerations shown in Figure 9 can be used during the process of a seating assessment, and the selection of system adaptations can be based on considerations similar to those listed in Appendix A. Commercial seating systems typically are more costly, but they are more durable and can be used for longer periods of time. Options for these seating systems include stationary and mobile chairs (see, e.g., Bergen et al., 1990; Deitz-Curry, 1996). Figure 10 shows a commercially available stationary chair, and Figure 11 illustrates a customized, mobile seating system. These figures depict many commonly used adaptations to support alignment, promote symmetry, and enhance function. Specific adaptations selected for use with a particular chair will vary with each child.

Teachers and caregivers should ensure that specialized equipment is used properly during mealtimes to address alignment challenges. Their observa-

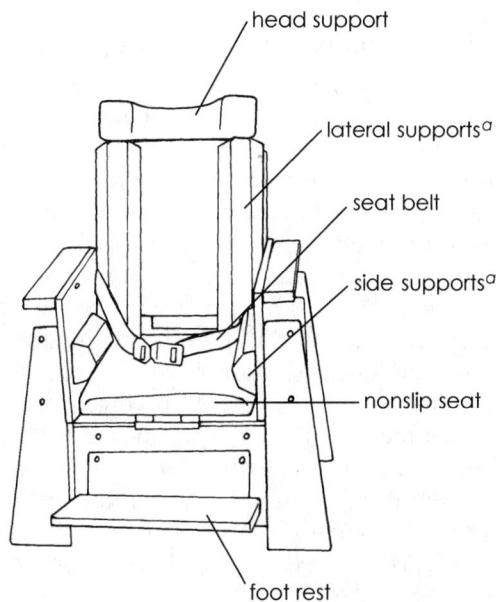

Figure 10.   A commercially available stationary chair manufactured by Rifton Corporation. Note the multiple "low-tech" adaptations included on this seating system. ([a]Supports are made from foam tubing.)

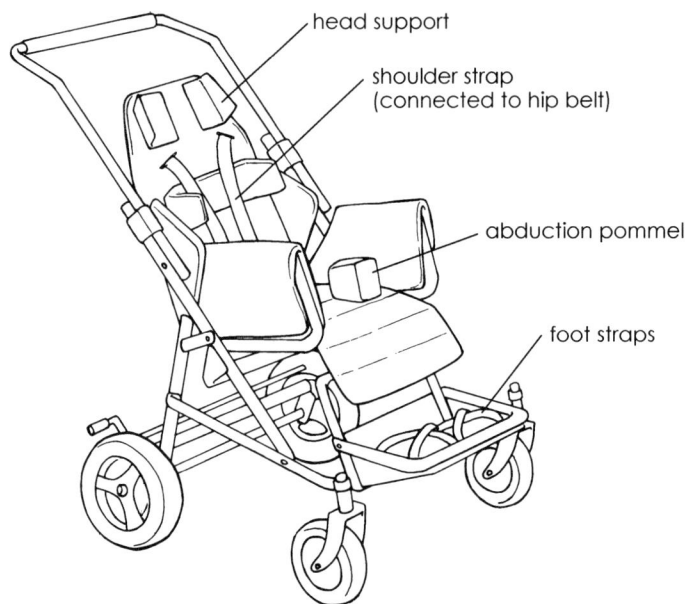

Figure 11. A commercially available, customized mobile seating system. Note that this system allows for slight backward tilting in space. The desired angle between the chair back and seat are maintained even when the chair is tilted.

tions about how the system influences feeding and eating skills are crucial for ongoing assessment of the usefulness and appropriateness of the equipment.

ALTERNATIVE POSITIONS USED DURING MEALTIMES

Occasionally, alternative positions to sitting will be recommended for use during mealtimes. Inclined sidelying, inclined prone, or supported standing may be used as optional mealtime positions or, in prescribed circumstances, may be the primary position used for feeding or eating. The decision to use these alternative positions for mealtimes should be made in collaboration with therapists, other medical personnel, and families.

The sidelying position can provide a stable base of support and may promote symmetry. The effects of gravity are altered in this position and may be used advantageously to influence the feeding sequence. Children who are fed via a gastrostomy tube, for example, may be positioned in inclined sidelying on their right side to facilitate emptying of the stomach (Bray et al., 1987). Proper alignment in the sidelying position may be accomplished by making sidelyers, using some of the adaptive equipment and materials described in Appendix B, or by purchasing commercially available sidelyers.

Inclined prone is sometimes used as a feeding position for infants, particularly those infants who exhibit excessive flexion of the head, neck, and trunk. A wedge can be used to achieve the appropriate incline. Illustrations of the inclined prone position can be found in Morris and Klein (1987). This position provides support for the trunk, encourages weight bearing through the shoulders and forearms, and places the head and neck higher than the hips and pelvis. This position may be recommended for use with children who have micrognathia (i.e., a retruted jaw) because this position alters the effects of gravity on the oral cavity (Wolf & Glass, 1992).

Supported standing may be used as an optional position during mealtimes for children who spend excessive amounts of time in a sitting position. These children frequently have extremely poor trunk control and do not walk independently. The standing position places the child upright, yielding mealtime benefits similar to those described for sitting. Supported standing equipment options include prone boards, supine standers, parapodiums, and flexi-standers (see Morris & Klein, 1987). The angle of the prone stander should be assessed by team members to determine the optimal incline to achieve alignment and stability of the head, neck, trunk, pelvis, and legs. The angle at which the arms can be used functionally also should be noted. Ward (1984) reported that angles commonly range between 45° and 70°; 60° of inclination is most common.

The height of the prone stander should be assessed carefully. The top of the stander should be just above the level of the breastbone (i.e., sternum) and should not interfere with arm movements needed for eating. If the stander does not have a tray, it should be placed adjacent to a table of appropriate height to maintain desired angles and promote the child's participation in mealtime activities.

IMPORTANCE OF WORKING AS A TEAM TO ADDRESS POSITIONING

This chapter presents a problem-solving process for addressing mealtime positioning by 1) focusing on the delineation of general considerations related to positioning children in sitting for feeding and eating, 2) describing how to observe and assess postural alignment in the sitting position, and 3) offering strategies and adaptations that might be used to address identified positioning challenges. Various team members can be involved in this problem-solving process, including the child, family members, teachers, therapists, nurses, nutritionists, physicians, equipment vendors, and social workers. Each team member may have unique and overlapping roles to play in the dynamic and ongoing decisions that are made to address positioning challenges.

Involving children in the problem-solving process requires attention to their verbal and nonverbal expressions. Older children may be able to play an active role in decision making by selecting from a menu of possible positioning alternatives. They might choose the color of their seating system and the types of accessories used or express whether particular adaptations are comfortable and enhance their ability to eat. Younger children may not be able to indicate verbally their choices about positioning alternatives, but they often communicate their acceptance or rejection of various positioning strategies or adaptations by using nonverbal gestures or vocalizations. Adults should carefully monitor the communicative signals of young children during mealtimes. Changes in facial expression, crying, or other avoidance gestures should cause reconsideration of positioning approaches.

The roles family members and teachers play in this problem-solving process, individually and collectively, are important for many reasons. First, these individuals spend the majority of time with the child and are keen observers and recorders of positioning needs. Second, they are individuals who primarily will implement positioning strategies identified by the positioning team. Third, these individuals are in the best position to evaluate the effectiveness, the appropriateness, and the acceptability of the recommended strategies and adaptations.

OTs, PTs, and SLPs often participate on the positioning team. These individuals collaborate to address the interrelationships among positioning, oral-motor control, communication, and self-feeding through detailed assessments. Therapists often are called on to address complex positioning challenges, and many positioning decisions should be made only after consulting these team members. Examples may include children who have fixed contractures or deformities, children with compromised respiratory or cardiovascular systems, children who are at risk for skin breakdown, and children who are tube fed. Physicians, nurses, and nutritionists may join the positioning team to address challenges presented by these children as well as children who exhibit GER and metabolic disorders and those who have significant swallowing dysfunctions. Videofluoroscopic studies may be recommended to assess swallowing function and the impact of positions on swallowing efficiency (Geyer & McGowan, 1995). Physicians often write prescriptions for positioning equipment based on decisions made by the positioning team, particularly for expensive, customized systems.

Equipment vendors become involved in team decision making when commercial or customized equipment is needed. Well-trained and experienced vendors provide team members with an up-to-date menu of appropriate equipment options. Vendors supply equipment and are sometimes able to lend the equipment for trial and long-term periods (Angelo, 1997).

Social workers are critical members of the positioning team. These individuals help locate potential funding sources for equipment and consult with team members about financial implications associated with positioning decisions.

Team members work together to address the child's current positioning needs, discuss potential future needs, and assess needs across different environments. A child's positioning needs are unlikely to remain static over time. Positioning will be viewed as a process, rather than as a product, only when team members engage in collaborative problem solving and decision making.

Cassie

Cassie was born on May 25, 1993, at 28 weeks' gestation. She remained in the neonatal intensive care unit for approximately 12 weeks. Cassie's medical history includes a Grade III intraventricular hemorrhage, respiratory distress syndrome, and neonatal seizures. She required oxygen for 7 days and had a difficult time making the transition to oral feeding. After discharge from the hospital, she was reported to be seizure-free and was referred to the high-risk follow-up clinic.

At 9 months of age, the neurologist who worked in the clinic diagnosed Cassie as having spastic diplegia, a type of cerebral palsy commonly associated with prematurity. Cassie was referred to an early intervention program for services. She and her family received a variety of services and supports during the time she was enrolled in the program, including special instruction and integrated occupational, physical, and speech-language therapies.

At 3 years of age, Cassie was enrolled in a preschool program in the local community, where she receives "specialized" services from therapists who work in the public school system. The therapists visit the preschool on a regular basis to deliver integrated therapy and consult with Cassie's teachers. Currently, Cassie is described as having no major health problems, although she experiences recurrent upper-respiratory infections.

Cassie is an only child who lives with both of her parents. Her father, Larry, is a 30-year-old self-employed painter. He spends most of the day at jobsites throughout the community. He leaves home early in the morning (around 5 A.M.) and returns home at about 6 P.M. During the summer months, Larry leaves home earlier and arrives home from work later in the day. Cassie's mother, Debbie, is 30 years old. She completed 2 years of college and currently is not working. Debbie is attending beauty school daily from 8 A.M. to 5 P.M. Cassie is often cared for by her maternal grandmother after preschool and occasionally on weekends.

Cassie's teachers and parents describe her as a loving, happy child who enjoys playing and talking with other children. She is beginning to walk with the aid of a posterior walker and wears ankle-foot orthoses while standing and walking. Cassie is able to sit independently; but her back is rounded, her pelvis is tipped backward, and her legs are extended. Cassie does not exhibit cognitive delays, but her speech is sometimes difficult to understand. Her language abilities are commensurate with her chronological age. Cassie has difficulty during fine-motor activities, particularly when she has to use both hands together to manipulate small objects. She feeds herself, using a spoon and fork, although she frequently spills food and seems to tire during the course of the meal or snack. Her teachers and parents describe her self-feeding skills as slow, uncoordinated, and immature.

At the present time, Larry and Debbie's major concerns related to Cassie's eating and feeding include the amount of time Cassie takes to eat, the "messiness" at mealtimes, and her "slumping" in the chair. Her teachers and therapists want to address these concerns. Cassie's teachers have asked the therapists to help them problem-solve and determine the best ways to position Cassie during snacks and mealtimes in the classroom. A major goal of the teachers is to keep Cassie seated at the table with the other children—they do not want to use equipment for positioning that would prevent Cassie from sitting at the table with her peers.

At the individualized education program meeting, these and other priorities and concerns were discussed. Everyone agreed that the therapists and teachers would further assess Cassie's mealtime positioning needs and make recommendations that could be used at school and home.

The therapists and teachers completed the Postural Alignment Checklist for Sitting Positions (shown in Figure 9) while observing Cassie on several occasions during classroom mealtimes. During these observations, Cassie was seated in a child-size chair without any supports or adaptations. A completed checklist based on these observations is shown in Figure 12.

A review of the checklist shows that Cassie sits in a child-size chair with her pelvis tipped too far backward. This position results in decreased hip flexion, a rounded back, legs pressed together, extended knees, and unsupported feet. Her shoulders are elevated; and, at times, she retracts and pulls her arms back-

Child's Name: _Cassie_ Age: _3 years_

Date: _5/96_

Lower half of the body

Body part	Alignment considerations	Yes	No	Comments
Pelvis and hips	a. Is the pelvis upright in a neutral or slightly anterior tipped position?	☐	■	
	b. Are the pelvis and hips symmetrical with equal distribution of weight on the "sit bones" (i.e., ischial tuberosities) and the knees facing forward?	■	☐	
	c. Are the hips flexed to approximately 90°?	☐	■	
	If no to a, b, or c:			
	Does the pelvis tip too far backward with excessive hip extension with or without asymmetry?	■	☐	Posterior pelvic tilt, when seated in chair without adaptations, contributes to "slumping" reported by parents
	Does the pelvis tip too far forward with excessive hip flexion with or without asymmetry?	☐	■	

Thighs and legs			
a.	Are the thighs well-supported in slight abduction with the seat surface 1–2 inches behind the knees?	☐ ■	Seat surface is even with knees
b.	Are the knees flexed to at least 90°?	☐ ■	Flexed to only about 40°
If no to a or b:			
	Do the legs press tightly together?	☐ ■	
	Do the legs spread apart excessively?	☐ ■	
	Are the knees extended excessively?	■ ☐	
	Are the knees flexed excessively?	☐ ■	
Feet and ankles			
a.	Are feet and ankles well-supported and ankles positioned under or slightly behind the knees?	☐ ■	
b.	Are ankles flexed to 90°?	☐ ■	
c.	Are feet and toes facing forward?	■ ☐	
If no to a, b, or c:			
	Are feet not flat and not resting on a supporting surface?	☐ ■	Feet not supported on any surface

Figure 12. Completed postural alignment checklist for Cassie.

(continued)

Figure 12. (continued)

Upper half of the body				
Body part	Alignment considerations	Yes	No	Comments
Trunk	a. Is the trunk upright?	□	■	
	b. Is the trunk symmetrical?	■	□	
	If no to a or b:			
	Is the trunk rounded excessively?	■	□	*Trunk rounding contributes to poor arm control?*
	Does the trunk fall forward?	□	■	
	Does the trunk arch backward?	□	■	
	Does the trunk fall to one side?	□	■	
Shoulders and arms	a. Are shoulders level and relaxed?	□	■	
	b. Are the arms forward and in mid-line?	■	□	*Difficult to maintain this position, particularly during activities*
	If no to a or b:			
	Do the shoulders elevate?	■	□	
	Are the shoulders asymmetrical?	■	□	
	Are the shoulders excessively protracted with arms turned inward?	□	■	
	Are the shoulders excessively retracted with arms pulling back?	■	□	*Occasionally*
Head and neck	Is head in mid-line with a slight chin tuck?	□	■	*Associated with pelvic and trunk misalignment?*
	If no:			
	Do the head and neck extend excessively with or without asymmetry?	■	□	*Not always excessive, depends on the "task demand"*
	Do the head and neck flex excessively with or without asymmetry?	□	■	

ward. Cassie's head is slightly extended in association with the malalignment of her pelvis and trunk.

After the checklist was completed and reviewed, the team consulted Appendix A of this chapter for possible sitting adaptations. Keeping in mind the priorities of the parents and the goals of the teachers, the team began to address positioning, using the least-intrusive strategies that would address the challenges identified in Figure 12. Adaptations were made to the chair in which Cassie was observed—the same chair also used by her peers.

Adaptations were made that resulted in changes in Cassie's postural alignment. First, the seat depth was decreased by securing a 2-inch block of Constructa Foam to the back of the chair with adhesive-backed Velcro. Cassie's pelvis became slightly more upright, and her hip flexion increased to approximately 90° after placement of the foam; but additional adaptations were needed to maintain this position. Dycem (a nonslip material) was placed on the chair seat to decrease forward sliding. When Cassie attempted to self-feed, however, her hips extended. To prevent hip extension, a seat belt was constructed from 2-inch strapping and a plastic buckle. This seat belt was attached at a 45° angle to the underside of the chair with rivets. Collectively, these strategies improved Cassie's pelvic and hip position, resulting in a more upright alignment of her trunk and decreased extension of her knees. After these adaptations were implemented, Cassie's feet rested firmly on the floor. Cassie's base of support was increased as a result of the strategies used to address pelvic and hip alignment. She no longer pressed her legs together.

The adaptations enabled Cassie to use both hands during mealtimes more effectively. She exhibited a decreased tendency to retract her shoulders and pull her arms backward during rest and feeding. The stability and realignment of her pelvis, hips, and trunk resulted in decreased shoulder elevation and allowed Cassie to use and maintain a slight chin tuck during mealtimes.

Cassie has been using her adaptive chair for approximately 1 month, and her teacher and therapists have noticed a decrease in spillage and fatigue when self-feeding. Having observed these changes, the therapists and teachers contacted Cassie's parents, Larry and Debbie, to discuss Cassie's progress and further develop positioning options for use at home. A home visit was suggested by the therapists and teachers; however, this option was not possible because of Larry's and Debbie's schedules. Instead, Larry suggested that he bring the chair and booster seat from home to Cassie's school, where he could work with the team to make adaptations.

Larry brought an adult-size kitchen chair and Cassie's booster seat to school. At home, Cassie sits in the booster chair, which is placed on the adult-size chair. The team observed Cassie and found that the booster seat provided stability for her pelvis and hips, and the seat depth was appropriate; but Cassie continued to slide forward and extend her legs, and she had no support for her feet. Dycem was placed on the seat surface to prevent slipping. Given the supporting base of the booster chair, a seat belt was not needed. Because of the height of the adult-size chair, a foot rest was required and constructed from plywood. Larry attached the foot rest to the front legs of the chair by using basic hardware. Additional holes were drilled in the chair to allow for adjustments to the foot rest position as Cassie grows. Larry varnished the foot rest to match the chair color, and he plans to adapt an additional chair at Cassie's grandmother's house.

Another option considered by the team was the purchase of a commercially available chair specially adapted to fit Cassie. This option was not chosen, however, because Cassie continues to demonstrate improvement in her postural control, and her family did not want to spend money on expensive equipment that Cassie might not need in a few years. The team reached the consensus that the temporary adaptations were sufficient at this time.

PRACTICE EXERCISE

....

After reading this chapter, complete the Postural Alignment Checklist for Sitting Positions (see Appendix C at the end of this book) by observing a child in your class who has motor challenges as he or she sits in a chair that is not adapted. Ensure the child's comfort and safety in the chair throughout the observation session.

Once you have completed the Postural Alignment Checklist for Sitting Positions, consult the Adaptations and Strategies for Positioning in Sitting form listed in Appendix A of this chapter. Try to identify adaptations or strategies that might be appropriate to address the postural alignment challenges you noted on the checklist. Note why you believe the adaptations or strategies are appropriate for the child.

In order to confirm the accuracy of your observations and checklist ratings, consult with a therapist. How do your observations and ratings compare with those of the therapist? Ask the therapist to confirm your "recommended" adaptations or strategies. Does the therapist agree with your adaptations or strategies? Why or why not?

REFERENCES

Amiel-Tison, C., & Griener, A. (1986). *Neurological assessment during the first year of life.* New York: Oxford University Press.

Angelo, J. (1997). A guide for assistive technology therapists. In S. Lane (Ed.), *Assistive technology for rehabilitation therapists* (pp. 1–14). Philadelphia: F.A. Davis.

Avery-Smith, W. (1996). Eating dysfunction position paper. *American Journal of Occupational Therapy, 50*(10), 846–847.

Bergen, A.F., Presperin, J., & Tallman, T. (1990). *Positioning for function: Wheelchairs and other assistive technologies.* Valhalla, NY: Valhalla Rehabilitation Publications.

Bray, M., Beckman, D., & Barks, L. (1987). Mealtime interventions for persons with compromised oral-motor function. In Developmental Disabilities Special Interest Section of American Occupational Therapy Association (Eds.), *Problems with eating: Interventions for children and adults with developmental disabilities* (pp. 85–107). Rockville, MD: American Occupational Therapy Association.

Breath, D., DeMauro, G., & Snyder, P. (1997). Adaptive sitting for young children with mild to moderate motor challenges: Basic guidelines. *Young Exceptional Children, 1*(1), 10–16.

Cook, A.M., & Hussey, S.M. (1995). *Assistive technologies: Principles and practice.* St. Louis: Mosby.

Deitz-Curry, J.E. (1996). Wheelchair selection and maintenance. In L.A. Kurtz, P.W. Dowrick, S.E. Levy, & M.L. Batshaw (Eds.), *Handbook of developmental disabilities: Resources for interdisciplinary care* (pp. 294–310). Gaithersburg, MD: Aspen Publishers.

Dunn, W. (1996). Occupational therapy. In R.A. McWilliam (Ed.), *Rethinking pull-out services in early intervention* (pp. 267–313). Baltimore: Paul H. Brookes Publishing Co.

Eicher, P.S. (1997). Feeding. In M.L. Batshaw (Ed.), *Children with disabilities* (4th ed., pp. 621–641). Baltimore: Paul H. Brookes Publishing Co.

Finnie, N.R. (1974). *Handling the young cerebral palsied child at home.* New York: E.P. Dutton.

Geyer, L.A., & McGowan, J.S. (1995). Positioning infants and children for videofluoroscopic swallowing function studies. *Infants and Young Children, 8*(2), 58–64.

Horak, F. (1987). Clinical measurement of postural control in adults. *Physical Therapy, 67,* 1881–1885.

Horak, F. (1992). Motor control models underlying neurologic rehabilitation of posture in children. In H. Forssberg & H. Hirschfeld (Eds.), *Movement disorders in children: Medicine and sport science* (Vol. 36, pp. 21–30). Basel, Switzerland: Karger.

Hulme, J.B., Poor, R., Schulein, M., & Pezzino, J. (1983). Perceived behavioral changes observed with adaptive seating devices and training programs for multiple handicapped developmentally disabled individuals. *Physical Therapy, 63,* 204–208.

Hulme, J.B., Shaver, J., Acher, S., Mullette, L., & Eggert, C. (1987). Effects of adaptive seating devices on the eating and drinking of children with multiple handicaps. *American Journal of Occupational Therapy, 41,* 81–89.

McClenaghan, B.A., Thombs, L., & Milner, M. (1992). Effects of seat-surface inclination on postural stability and function of the upper extremities of children with cerebral palsy. *Developmental Medicine and Child Neurology, 34,* 40–48.

Miedaner, J.A. (1990). The effects of sitting positions on trunk extension for children with motor impairment. *Pediatric Physical Therapy, 2*(1), 11–14.

Morris, S. (1977a). Interpersonal aspects of feeding problems. In J. Wilson (Ed.), *Oral-motor function and dysfunction in children* (pp. 103–113). Chapel Hill: University of North Carolina.

Morris, S. (1977b). Sensorimotor prerequisites for speech and the influence of cerebral palsy. In J. Wilson (Ed.), *Oral-motor function and dysfunction in children* (pp. 123–128). Chapel Hill: University of North Carolina.

Morris, S. (1982). Interacting frameworks in the treatment program. In M.M. Palmer (Ed.), *The normal acquisition of oral feeding skills: Implications for assessment and treatment* (pp. 105–141). New York: Therapeutic Media.

Morris, S.E., & Klein, M.D. (1987). *Pre-feeding skills: A comprehensive resource for feeding development.* San Antonio, TX: Therapy Skill Builders.

Orelove, F.P., & Sobsey, D. (1996). Mealtime skills. In *Educating children with multiple disabilities: A transdisciplinary approach* (3rd ed., pp. 301–338). Baltimore: Paul H. Brookes Publishing Co.

Oren, J.B. (1994). Adaptive equipment for handicapped children. In J.S. Tecklin (Ed.), *Pediatric physical therapy* (pp. 412–445). Philadelphia: Lippincott-Raven Publishers.

Radell, U. (1997). Augmentative and alternative communication assessment strategies: Seating and positioning. In S.L. Glennen & D.C. DeCoste (Eds.), *The handbook of augmentative and alternative communication* (pp. 193–241). San Diego, CA: Singular Publishing Group.

Rainforth, B., & York-Barr, J. (1996). Handling and positioning. In F.P. Orelove & D. Sobsey, *Educating children with multiple disabilities: A transdisciplinary approach* (3rd ed., pp. 79–118). Baltimore: Paul H. Brookes Publishing Co.

Redstone, F. (1991). Respiratory components of communication. In M.B. Langley & L.J. Lombardino (Eds.), *Neurodevelopmental strategies for managing communication disorders in children with severe motor dysfunction* (pp. 29–48). Austin, TX: PRO-ED.

Reid, D.T., & Sochaniwskyj, A. (1991). Effects of anterior-tipped seating on respiratory functions of normal children and children with cerebral palsy. *International Journal of Rehabilitation Research, 14,* 203–212.

Shumway-Cook, A., & Woollacott, M. (1995). *Motor control: Theory and practical applications.* Baltimore: Williams & Wilkins.

Sochaniwskyj, A., Koheil, R., Bablich, K., Milner, M., & Lotto, W. (1991). Dynamic monitoring of sitting posture for children with spastic cerebral palsy. *Clinical Biomechanics, 6,* 161–167.

Ward, D.E. (1984). *Positioning the handicapped for function* (2nd ed.). St. Louis: Phoenix Press.

Wolf, L.S., & Glass, R.P. (1992). *Feeding and swallowing disorders in infancy: Assessment and management.* San Antonio, TX: Therapy Skill Builders.

Appendix A
Adaptations and
Strategies for Positioning in Sitting

Body part	Chair sitting challenges	General (★) and specific (☞) strategies and adaptations to consider	Illustrations of strategies and adaptations
Pelvis and Hips		★ Child is in as upright a position as possible with an adequate base of support for the pelvis, hips, thighs, and feet. Trunk and pelvis are upright and resting against chair back. Feet are flat and well-supported. Shoulders are level and relaxed. Head is in mid-line with chin slightly tucked	See Figure 9
	Pelvis tilts too far backward with excessive hip extension with or without asymmetry	☞ Be certain that the seat of the chair is not too deep. Child's knees should be 1–2 inches beyond the edge of the seat. If seat depth is too long, child's pelvis will tip backward and child will slide forward in chair. To decrease seat depth, secure foam inserts or other solid materials against the back of the chair with Velcro, straps, or other permanent attachments. Dycem or other nonslip materials may be used to reduce forward sliding.	See Figure 7C and Figure 10
		☞ Position pelvis in an upright position against back of chair to increase hip flexion to approximately 90°	

	☞ Stabilize pelvis by using a seat belt affixed at a 45° angle to the chair back or seat.	See Figure 4B
	☞ Place wedge on chair seat to promote forward inclination of pelvis.	
Pelvis tilts too far forward with excessive hip flexion with or without asymmetry	☞ Position the pelvis and trunk upright and against the back of chair.	See Figure 7B
	☞ Dycem or other nonslip materials may be used to stabilize an upright position of the pelvis.	
	☞ Stabilize pelvis by using a seat belt affixed at a 45° angle to the chair back or seat.	
Thighs and Legs Legs press tightly together	☞ First, consider strategies and adaptations for the pelvis and hips and be certain knees are flexed to 90°.	
	☞ Check chair seat to ensure adequate width (1–1½ inches between legs and side of chair).	
	☞ Be certain chair seat is firm; if not, place firm pad on seat.	

Body part	Chair sitting challenges	General (★) and specific (☞) strategies and adaptations to consider	Illustrations of strategies and adaptations
		☞ Use a knee spacer (i.e., pommel) at edge of seat to increase space between thighs to promote slight abduction. Do not use a pommel to prevent a child from sliding forward.	See Figure 11
	Legs spread apart excessively ("frog legs")	☞ First, consider strategies and adaptations for the pelvis and hips.	
		☞ Be certain that the seat of the chair is not too short. If the seat is too short, the thighs may spread apart and roll outward because of lack of support. To increase seat depth, remove back insert, if present, or use chair with a deeper seat.	
		☞ Pad sides of seat, if appropriate, with foam, small pillows, or Noodles.	See Figure 10
	Knees extend excessively	☞ First, consider strategies and adaptations for the pelvis and hips.	
		☞ Be certain hips are flexed to 90°.	
		☞ Increase hip and knee flexion by placing a towel roll, small bolster, or reverse wedge under thighs.	

Knees in excessive flexion

☞ First, consider strategies and adaptations for the pelvis and hips.

☞ Position feet under knees and, if necessary, secure feet in position by using nonslip materials.

☞ Attach or use lower leg supports on the chair.

☞ As a last resort, consider use of ankle straps; consult therapist before using.

Feet and Ankles

Feet not flat or not resting on supporting surface

☞ First, consider strategies and adaptations for pelvis, hips, thighs, and legs.

☞ Reassess seat depth and adjust, if necessary, so feet reach floor.

☞ Assess chair height. If chair is too high and feet do not contact floor evenly, use a lower chair, place a footrest on the chair, or use phone books or other hard materials to provide a support surface for the feet. Dycem can be used to secure placement of supports.

See Figures 10 and 11

Body part	Chair sitting challenges	General (★) and specific (☞) strategies and adaptations to consider	Illustrations of strategies and adaptations
		☞ As a last resort, consider use of ankle straps, but consult therapist before use.	
Trunk	Trunk is rounded excessively	☞ First, consider strategies and adaptations for pelvis and hips, especially if pelvis tips too far backward with excessive extension.	
		☞ Be certain seat back is high enough, providing adequate support for spine. Typical height for seat back is mid-scapular level. Children with rounded trunks may require seat backs extending above mid-scapular level.	
		☞ As a last resort, consider the use of an "H" or "butterfly" harness, but consult a therapist before use.	See Figure 5A
	Trunk falls forward	☞ First, consider strategies and adaptations for pelvis and hips.	
		☞ Be certain seat back is high enough to provide adequate support for spine. Typical height for seat back is at the mid-scapular level. Children with rounded trunks may require seat backs that extend beyond the mid-scapular level.	

Trunk arches backward

☞ As a last resort, consider the use of an "H" or "butterfly" harness, but consult therapist before use. | See Figure 5A

☞ Consult therapist for assistance with tilting seat backward in space. If this adaptation is used, be sure hip angle is maintained.

☞ First, consider strategies and adaptations for pelvis and hips.

☞ Be certain seat back is high enough to provide adequate support for spine. Typical height for seat back is at the mid-scapular level. Children who arch their trunks may require seat backs that extend beyond the mid-scapular level.

☞ As a last resort, consider the use of an "H" or "butterfly" harness, but consult therapist before use. | See Figure 5A

☞ Consult therapist for assistance with tilting seat backward in space. If this adaptation is used, be sure hip angle is maintained.

99

Body part	Chair sitting challenges	General (★) and specific (☞) strategies and adaptations to consider	Illustrations of strategies and adaptations
	Trunk falls to one side	☞ First, consider strategies and adaptations for pelvis and hips.	
		☞ Be certain seat back is high enough to provide adequate support for spine. Typical height for seat back is at the mid-scapular level. Children with rounded trunks may require seat backs that extend beyond the mid-scapular level.	
		☞ Consider use of lateral trunk supports made from towel rolls, small pieces of foam, or more durable or commercially available materials attached to back of chair.	See Figure 10
		☞ Consult therapist for assistance with tilting seat backward in space. If this adaptation is used, be sure hip angle is maintained.	
Shoulders and Arms	Shoulders are elevated	☞ First, consider strategies and adaptations for pelvis, hips, and trunk.	
		☞ Be certain seat back is high enough to provide adequate support for spine.	

☞ Shoulder elevation may be used by the child to compensate for lack of head, neck, and trunk control. Strategies related to increasing support for these areas should be considered first.

☞ Be sure lap tray or tabletop surface is not too high, causing shoulder elevation.

Shoulders are asymmetrical

☞ First, consider strategies and adaptations for pelvis and hips. Next, consider strategies for trunk falling to one side. Be certain head is positioned and supported in mid-line.

Shoulders are excessively protracted with arms turning inward

☞ First, consider strategies and adaptations for pelvis, hips, and trunk; especially consider those related to backward tipping of the pelvis and rounding of the trunk.

☞ Be sure arms rest comfortably on lap tray, with elbows slightly bent.

☞ Vertical or horizontal dowels can be attached to the lap tray or tabletop surface to promote proper arm alignment.

See Figure 5B

Body part	Chair sitting challenges	General (★) and specific (☞) strategies and adaptations to consider	Illustrations of strategies and adaptations
	Shoulders are excessively retracted, with arms pulling backward	☞ Consider use of shoulder harness, but consult therapist prior to use.	See Figure 11
		☞ Consider the use of an "H" or "butterfly" harness, but consult therapist before use.	See Figure 5A
		☞ First, consider strategies and adaptations for pelvis, hips, and trunk; especially consider those related to arching of trunk.	
		☞ Be certain seat back is high enough to provide adequate support for spine.	
		☞ Place a small towel roll behind shoulder girdle to promote forward movement of the shoulder.	
		☞ Attach small, firm, permanent protraction blocks to seat back.	See Figure 5B
		☞ Provide a lap tray or tabletop surface.	See Figure 5B
		☞ Vertical or horizontal dowels can be attached to the lap tray or tabletop surface to promote proper arm alignment.	
		☞ Attach lateral supports to lap tray to promote forward arm movement.	

Head and Neck

Head and neck extend excessively with or without asymmetry

- ☞ Be sure alignment challenges in all other regions of the body have been addressed.
- ☞ Place small pillow behind head.
- ☞ Extend seat back height to support head and neck. If this intervention results in further extension of head and neck, discontinue use and consult a therapist.
- ☞ Consider use of contoured head and neck support.
- ☞ Feeder uses jaw control technique while applying gentle pressure on child's chest.

See Figure 10

Head and neck flex excessively

- ☞ Be sure alignment challenges in all other regions of the body have been addressed.
- ☞ Use hand on top of child's head as an external support to promote a more upright and mid-line position.

Body part	Chair sitting challenges	General (★) and specific (☞) strategies and adaptations to consider	Illustrations of strategies and adaptations
		☞ Use a jaw control technique to support the head.	
		☞ A "tilted in space" feeding position may need to be used with children who continue to show excessive head and neck flexion when all other alignment challenges have been addressed. Consult a therapist to assist with this adaptation.	
		☞ Specialized and customized head rests and supports may be required. Consult a therapist to assist with these adaptations.	

Appendix B
Materials and Equipment Commonly
Used to Address Positioning Challenges

Materials	Brief description	General cost	Advantages and disadvantages	Uses	Source(s)
Nonslip sheets	Dycem, plastic place mats, shelving liner (see Figure 10)	Low	✂ Machine washable ✂ Available in a variety of colors	✂ Stabilize pelvis, hips, or feet ✂ Stabilize bowls, cups, and so forth on table surface	AliMed 297 High Street Dedham, MA 02026-9135 Local discount stores
Strapping	Velcro, webbing (see Figure 10)	Low to medium	✂ Available with adhesive back ✂ Washable	✂ Make chest/trunk "harness," ankle straps, seat belts to position pelvis ✂ Secure other temporary adaptations	AliMed 297 High Street Dedham, MA 02026-9135 Fabric stores Local discount stores
Padding and Supports	Pillows, towels, open-cell foams (i.e., foam rubber), foam tubing sold for pool use (e.g., Noodles), contact paper–covered telephone books (see Figure 10)	Low	✂ Readily available ✂ Temporary ✂ May become soiled ✂ Easily removed	✂ Fabricate foot supports and lateral trunk supports ✂ Adapt width, depth, and height of chair	Local discount stores Cushion/fabric stores

Closed-Cell Foam	ConstructaFoam, AdaptaFoam	High	✂ Durable ✂ Must be purchased in large sheets ✂ Requires electric knife to cut ✂ Can be covered with fabric or special paint ✂ Able to be sculpted ✂ Available in a variety of densities and widths ✂ Need glue or heat gun to bond pieces together	✂ Fabricate wedges, back supports, bolsters, and foot supports ✂ Adapt width, depth, and height of chair	AliMed 297 High Street Dedham, MA 02026-9135

Materials	Brief description	General cost	Advantages and disadvantages	Uses	Source(s)
TriWall	3-ply corrugated cardboard ½–¾ inch thick	Medium	✂ Lightweight ✂ Adjustable sizes and shapes ✂ Serves as a good template prior to purchasing a customized chair or chair pieces ✂ Easily covered with contact paper, latex paint, or vinyl tape	✂ Fabricate seat inserts, back supports, head and neck supports, lateral trunk supports, and temporary chair inserts ✂ Fabricate chair	Cardboard manufacturers Local container and packaging companies Rehabilitation vendors
Acrylic	Plexiglas, polycarbonate, polyethylene (high temperature plastic)	High	✂ Requires heavy carpentry tools to cut ✂ Can crack ✂ Easily scratched ✂ Requires acrylic cleaner for maintenance	✂ Construct lap trays	Local home improvement centers Glass and window suppliers

Material	Examples	Cost	Considerations	Uses	Sources
Wood	Plywood, pine	Medium	✂ Requires carpentry tools and skills to cut ✂ Needs to be well-finished to avoid splintering ✂ Can cover with contact paper, varnish, padded vinyl, or paint ✂ Not water resistant unless sealed	✂ Fabricate chair inserts and dowels ✂ Adapt lap trays ✂ Adapt standard chairs (e.g., add back rest, add foot rest, extend back height)	Lumber yards Local home improvement centers

chapter six

Sensory Aspects of Feeding

Suzanne McKeever Murphy and Vanessa Caretto

One of the most important aspects of feeding is the understanding of sensory processing and its effects on oral feeding. The ability to perceive, process, and interpret sensory stimuli, as it pertains to feeding, is the very foundation of a successful feeding program. As a result, difficulties with the ability to process accurately sensory information are all too often at the core of the majority of feeding problems in school-age children. This chapter helps educators understand the sensory system and its correlation to skills necessary for eating. Abnormal sensory reactions often associated with atypical feeding patterns are explored. Sensory stimulation techniques are provided, along with experiential activities to help educators get a feeling for what the child with a feeding difficulty may be experiencing. A discussion on how to apply these techniques during meals is presented, along with a vignette for problem solving and an opportunity to apply the information gained from the material presented in this chapter.

CENTRAL NERVOUS SYSTEM FUNCTIONING

The sensory system and the motor system work together harmoniously within the central nervous system (Orelove & Sobsey, 1996). Information from the environment and the internal state of the body is collected and brought to the central nervous system through the senses. This information is collected by microscopic structures, called *receptors,* throughout the body. These receptors are found in the skin, muscles, joints, internal organs, blood vessels, and sense organs. The receptors send electrical signals to the brain or the spinal cord or both. In addition, the brain and spinal cord are responsible for sending information to the joints and muscles throughout the body to control movements. These two pathways work as an interrelated loop that enables a person to appropriately function within his or her environment. The nervous system works in a manner known as *crossed representation.* In other words, the right side of the brain controls the motor skills and receives sensory information from the left side of the body and vice versa.

Sensory feedback from motor activities is interpreted by the central nervous system and is used to plan, organize, and execute further movements. Not all sensory information is processed, however. The central nervous system filters the information, disregards some sensations, and processes others. The system then interprets the information to help the child discern whether the stimulus is pleasant or threatening. Stimuli that are pleasant and nonthreatening can help calm the child, improve attention to a task, and organize the entire central nervous system, thus allowing the child to participate more fully in an activity. Stimuli that are unpleasant or threatening will typically result in a protective response (e.g., gagging) or withdrawal from the stimuli. Each child responds to his or her own level of stimulus (i.e., threshold) and has a range in which he or she will be aware of the stimulus. Difficulties can occur when the central nervous system does not control and process an appropriate amount of sensory information at a level comfortable to the child (Morris & Klein, 1987).

The child who has difficulty perceiving and interpreting sensory stimuli will typically show a hyperreaction or a hyporeaction to the stimuli (Morris & Klein, 1987). Neurological damage is often at the center of a dysfunctional sensory system. Specifically, a damaged central nervous system can lower the threshold and result in an excessive reaction to stimuli. Other possible causes of a dysfunctional sensory system are increased or decreased postural muscle tone, an absence of appropriate sensory stimulation in the past (e.g., nonoral feedings), previous negative oral stimulation (e.g., nasogastric feedings), or an overactive gag reflex.

SENSORY SYSTEMS

Children receive information from many sensory systems: visual, auditory, olfactory, gustatory, tactile, and proprioceptive. The brain typically integrates all of this information and uses it to interpret the world. All of these sensory systems play an integral part in the feeding experience. The senses that affect feeding are discussed briefly next; the most common atypical sensory reactions are discussed later in this chapter.

Visual

The visual presentation of food provides a sensory expectation for the feeding experience of a child. The color of the food, the placement of the food on the serving dish, and the amount of food offered to a child can produce positive or negative responses. The visual stimulation within the room as well as the color of clothing worn by the feeder can also elicit a response from the child.

Auditory

The sounds within the feeding environment can play a major role in the feeding process. Auditory input cannot be ignored or shut out by those who have difficulty filtering out unwanted stimuli. The environment in which a child is fed must be carefully monitored for auditory volume and distractibility. Once a more comforting sound level is achieved, sound can be used to soothe and organize the child as well as to establish appropriate feeding rhythms.

Olfactory

The sense of smell is closely linked to taste. Smells are interpreted in the brain and are part of the *limbic system* (a system that regulates body functions, emotions, and the sense of smell). Smell has a strong emotional component and is strongly attached to memory storage (Morris & Klein, 1987). Therefore, both positive and negative experiences are associated with feeding and the sense of smell. Odors from food, the environment, or even the perfume of the feeder can have a dramatic effect on a feeding session.

Gustatory

Gustatory information is received by way of the taste buds in the mouth. Taste buds are found on specific areas of the tongue. Feedback is interpreted as bitter, sweet, salty, sour, or a combination of these tastes. Taste varies with each individual. Sweet tastes are detected on the anterior third of the tongue. Salty tastes are detected on the anterior lateral borders. Sour tastes are detected on the posterior lateral borders, whereas bitter tastes are detected on the posterior portion of the tongue. Children who are hyperreactive will often respond to more bland foods, whereas those children who are hyporeactive often respond better to spicy foods. Children who have received tube feedings or who have had tracheostomies will often prefer spicy foods that have more sensory input. Sweet tastes have been linked to increased drooling and are thought to be one of the most powerful tastes. Taste sensation changes with age as taste buds are lost.

Tactile

The sense of touch is very complex and is received through receptors on the skin. The various types of touch are classified by pressure (e.g., light touch, deep touch), temperature (e.g., hot, cold), and pain. There are many touch receptors in the face and mouth (Orelove & Sobsey, 1996). These help to establish awareness of the oral muscles while eating. Some touch stimuli are arousing and can put a child on alert, whereas other stimuli help the child to organize and calm him- or herself.

Proprioceptive

The perception of joint or body movement, or position of the body that is received through the muscles, tendons, and soft tissue, is known as *proprioception*. The proprioceptive input provides the central nervous system with feedback that tells what the muscles and limbs are doing at any time. Necessary adjustments in posture are then made as movement and activities are carried out. Children with proprioception problems appear clumsy and may have trouble sitting in a chair or using eating utensils correctly (Case-Smith, Allen, & Pratt, 1996).

Although each of these systems has been addressed separately, all of the systems actually overlap to help provide a rich sensory experience throughout mealtimes. These sensory experiences will either assist the feeding process or be detrimental to it.

The four sensory processes with which the educator will most likely be challenged during feeding are 1) touch, 2) taste, 3) temperature, and 4) texture. These are the sensations most often encountered in and around the mouth. Parents often report that their child does not like the taste of a particular food. After further examination, however, it is often discovered that touch in and around the mouth, the texture of the food, and the temperature of the food are the causes of the adverse reaction.

During mealtimes, the child who has difficulty interpreting sensory information typically shows negative reactions that often interfere with his or her food intake. A list and discussion of these reactions follows. Further examination of behaviorally based sensory reactions can be found in Chapter 9.

ABNORMAL SENSORY REACTIONS DURING FEEDING

Sensory-based feeding problems can be seen in many different types of reactions during feeding. The following are examples of these reactions: The child may have difficulty with textures, but not liquids; the child may tolerate his or her own fingers in his or her mouth, but not others' fingers; the child's tongue may retract to touch; the child's mouth may remain open when food is placed inside; or the child may hold food under his or her tongue to avoid swallowing (Palmer & Heyman, 1993). The reactions vary from individual to individual and may be mild to severe. The most common sensory reactions observed during feeding are discussed next.

Refusing Food

Refusal of food is one of the more common signs of hyperreaction to oral stimuli. The child will often refuse food because of the effects of touch, taste, temperature, and texture; he or she may be responding to one or more of these sensations. It is important to be aware of the sensations to which the child is reacting and then provide the necessary stimulation. Refusal of food can lead to nutritional concerns. It is often difficult to maintain a child's balanced diet when the child with a hyperreactive sensory response has limited food preferences. Children who refuse to eat will often make up for the lack of food by getting most of their caloric needs through bottle feeding. The refusal of food is also closely linked to a condition called *failure to thrive* (FTT), in which the child has weight gain and growth below normal limits for his or her age. A child who has difficulty accepting food should be closely followed by a physician and a nutritionist.

Picky Eating

The child who is a picky eater is also often hyperreactive to oral stimuli. The parents often learn what their child will accept and stick to their child's preferred menu. Typical foods on the list for a picky eater are round noodles in sauce, cheese puffs, cookies, crackers, chips, and so forth. The common factor in these foods is that they all dissolve easily when entering the mouth and mixing with saliva.

Gagging

Gagging is a more serious symptom of hyperreaction. The tongue and palate are the most sensitive areas in the mouth. For some children, when food touches the tongue, it elicits a gag reflex. The gag reflex is present for survival because it protects the trachea. At birth, the gag reflex is in the anterior portion of the mouth and then gradually moves back to the posterior portion of the tongue with age, oral stimulation, and eating. In some children, the gag reflex is hyperreactive and is brought about through smell, sight, taste, temperature, and/or texture.

The absence of a gag reflex is often the result of significant damage in the central nervous system. This hyporeaction to stimuli is extremely dangerous. Without the gag reflex, the child is at risk for aspiration because the airway is unprotected. This child should not be fed orally until a gag reflex can be consistently elicited.

Vomiting

Vomiting is the most severe hyperreaction in feeding. It can lead to FTT and should be taken very seriously. When continual vomiting is first discovered, a medical referral should be made to rule out gastroesophageal reflux, aspiration, and/or behavioral components. If vomiting is allowed to continue, serious complications may arise. For this reason, it is recommended that a physician be an integral team member in the intervention of this problem. In addition, other team members, such as a psychologist and a nutritionist, should be consulted in order to address emotional factors and dietary concerns.

Stuffing Food into the Mouth

The child who stuffs food into his or her mouth is often thought to have a problem with the rate of eating. In fact, many of these children pack their mouths with food because it leaves less room for the food to move around in the oral cavity and touch sensitive parts of their mouths. It takes less oral mobility and skill to control a large amount of food than a small piece of food. Other children stuff their mouths for a different reason. They have decreased awareness in their mouths and often need more sensory input to activate their oral-motor skills. Therefore, by overloading their mouths, these children are increasing the sensory input and are able to perceive the input more effectively.

Sucking Food

Most children prefer to suck their food, rather than chew, because sucking allows the food to soften in their mouths before it is swallowed. Children who suck their food often have difficulties with sensory processing, oral-motor skills, and/or swallowing. With careful observation, it is often possible to hear and see the child swallow the food because it has not broken down well in the child's mouth.

The child who has difficulty interpreting and tolerating various sensory information will most likely benefit from a consistent sensory stimulation program. This will typically allow the child to learn tolerance of sensory input, thus improving his or her overall dietary intake.

SENSORY STIMULATION PROGRAMS

The goal of a sensory stimulation program is to help "normalize" the sensitivity in and around the child's mouth, rather than "desensitize" the sensitivity. It is important to remember that a certain amount of sensitivity is what allows individuals to enjoy eating, control food in their mouths, and protect their airways.

There are a few techniques for providing oral/facial sensory stimulation that help ensure greater success at feeding time. These techniques are discussed next and should be experienced by the educator before attempting to utilize the techniques on a child. These experiential activities help the educator by providing a greater understanding of the sensory effects resulting from the stimulation techniques.

Distal to Proximal

Whenever stimulation is provided to another person, it is desirable to attempt to work more distal to proximal. In other words, stimulation should begin away from the face (i.e., on the hands or trunk) and gradually move toward the face. The areas farthest from the face are more familiar to touch from the environment and are not considered to be as intimate as the facial area. It is very natural to touch a person on the arm or hand during everyday activities, yet touch to the face is reserved for those with whom intimate contact is typical. It is necessary to show respect to those children needing feeding intervention, and respectful touch should always be considered. Children who have oral/facial hyperreactions will also often show increased sensitivity to tactile stimulation on their hands. Thus, stimulation that begins on the hands will often help the child prepare for self-feeding later. It may take several days or even weeks for a feeder to work up to stimulating the face and inside of the mouth, so the progression should be slow, and the child should not be rushed. Patience will pay off in the end.

Deep, Firm Pressure

The use of deep, firm pressure is typically the technique best tolerated by most children. Light touch is arousing to the central nervous system and can put a child on alert. Imagine driving down the highway with the wind blowing in your hair, music playing loudly, and your thoughts far away. Suddenly. . . you feel a spider crawling up your leg! Your typical response would be "alert, alert!" Many people would wreck the car! If a book fell off of the dashboard into your lap, however, it could briefly startle you, but the reaction would not be as dramatic. Deep, firm pressure works best to activate the sensory system and allow input into the joint and muscle receptors.

Symmetrical Input

Stimulation to the body should be done in a symmetrical fashion. A deep touch is very powerful, and the resulting reactions are strong and often last for several minutes. Educators should always be aware of how and where they touch a child so that they do not cause a different reaction than the one they are expecting. To feel the effect of symmetrical input, take the palm of your right hand and place it on your right cheek. Using firm, deep pressure, slowly bring your palm down in a diagonal direction toward your mouth. Stop. Slowly count to 5. Do you feel the heat and a type of burning sensation that your stimulation caused? Do you feel asymmetrical? (Go ahead and do the same exercise to your other cheek to regain your symmetry!) This is very powerful when it is considered that most of us have an intact sensory system, and this reaction was achieved after only one stroke. Symmetrical stimulation works best using only a small amount.

Types of Sensory Input

It is very important to be aware of the type of stimulation that is being provided. On the cheeks, it is best to use the palm instead of the fingertips. Around the lips, it is best to use the sides of the finger, rather than the fingertip. Smooth, continual input is best for the sensory system to interpret and helps organize the child. Children who have decreased muscle tone in the cheeks benefit from the use of quick strokes to help increase the muscle tone. Those children who have increased muscle tone in the cheeks benefit from slower strokes to help decrease the muscle tone.

It is important to note that it is necessary to always use gloves whenever providing stimulation in and around a child's mouth. Not all gloves are the same. Some gloves leave a bad taste or have an odor that is unpleasant to the child. They are often covered with a powder residue. Some children have latex allergies, and the use of latex gloves can be life-threatening. Because glove-to-skin contact is often irritating, it may be helpful to wrap the gloved hand or finger in a washcloth, towel, or diaper. These materials should always be soft and dry because wet material turns very cold quickly, and the cold temperature may become another source of negative stimulation.

Use of Distraction

Imagine that you are a child who is fearful of touch and watching as a towel or hand slowly approaches your face. How scary that must be! It is necessary to make stimulation as pleasant and enjoyable as possible in order to have it be a successful part of the child's daily feeding intervention. Singing, talking soothingly, and playing games are wonderful ways to distract the child and remove the focus from the stimulation. The child often gets so caught up in the activity that he or she is unaware that sensory stimulation has been provided. For example, an educator takes a small towel and puts it on the child's head. As the towel is slowly pulled down symmetrically on the child's cheeks, the educator plays Peekaboo (e.g., "Where's Suzie?"). The child gets so caught up in the game that he or she is frequently unaware that facial stimulation has been provided to his or her cheeks. The educator can sing a song with a specific beat or count the child's teeth while providing stimulation inside the child's mouth. Many children also enjoy pretending to be the teacher and pretending to provide the stimulation to the educator. This can work on a turn-taking basis so that the child gets the maximum amount of stimulation while having fun. It is important to always remember that *when a child feels in control, he or she will cooperate more willingly.*

TECHNIQUES FOR PROVIDING STIMULATION

There are actual techniques for providing stimulation in and around the child's mouth. Many of the most common sensory stimulation techniques are discussed next. Unless the educator has a complete understanding of the sensory system, caution is extended to try only touch input and leave techniques such as icing, brushing, and vibration to those professionals who are trained in these techniques. The educator should consult with other team members (e.g., the occupational therapist [OT], speech-language pathologist, and/or the physical therapist [PT]), as discussed in Chapter 2, before attempting to use these techniques. Some forms of stimulation can actually elicit seizures in children if caution is not taken. When considering what types of stimulation techniques to utilize, the educator should be careful not to overload the child with too many sensory experiences at once. Instead, sensory techniques should be introduced gradually, prioritizing them developmentally or according to the child's greatest functional needs. Based on observations of the child's reactions to the stimuli, techniques should be modified or changed in order to increase the benefits of the stimulation program.

Facial Stimulation

Stimulation on the face can have significant effects on muscle length, muscle activity, and sensory awareness of the facial musculature. The result of the stimulation is often evident at mealtimes because it helps prepare the muscles for activation during eating. The techniques that are discussed are gentle and not overly invasive to the sensory system. When working on the musculature of the cheeks and lips, it is important to work toward the mouth. A typical method of facial stimulation is shown in the following steps:

- Stroke downward on the cheeks toward the corners of the lips.
- Stroke downward from the nose toward the upper lip with the side of one finger.
- Stroke upward from the chin to the bottom lip with the side of one finger.
- Stroke around the lips in a circular motion with a finger pad to stimulate the "pucker" muscle.

Oral Stimulation

When working inside the mouth, more caution is advised. Educators should be careful of a child's teeth, especially when working with a child with a tonic bite reflex; and educators should exercise caution when working inside the mouth of a child with a history of vomiting. There are several different options available for providing stimulation to the gums, the internal cheek muscles, and the tongue, depending on the degree of oral sensitivity. The most common techniques of oral stimulation are

- Digital stimulation (i.e., with fingers)
- Massage brush (e.g., beginning toothbrush)
- Finger cots (i.e., glove-like material for fingertips only)
- Toothbrush (without toothpaste)
- Therapy tubing (i.e., cylinder-shape piece of rubber tubing)

Providing stimulation inside the mouth with these techniques helps organize the child's sensory system and encourages the development of mature oral-motor skills without the use of food. Therefore, the child can work on cheek and lip activation, tongue mobility, and munching and/or chewing without having to control and swallow food in his or her mouth. These techniques also provide touch input without the interference of taste, temperature, and texture.

Stimulation inside the mouth should be provided to the gums, teeth, cheeks, lateral borders, anterior third of the tongue, and occasionally the hard palate. Wrapping a gloved hand in a towel or using finger cots allows stimulation to occur in these areas while gauging the amount of input being provided. The massage brush and toothbrush allow for stimulation without having to put hands or fingers inside the child's mouth. These are also tools that children can learn to use independently, with supervision, to provide their own stimulation. Perhaps one of the most beneficial forms of oral stimulation is the use of therapy tubing. The tubing is cut into a 5- to 6-inch piece and tied into a knot at both ends. The child is given the tube on which to chew. The use of therapy tubing has been found to improve lip closure, cheek activation, tongue lateralization, and chewing skills without the need for food stimulus. In addition, therapy tubing has been found to have a calming, organizing, and focusing effect on the child (Scheerer, 1991). It is important not to leave the child unattended with the therapy tubing.

Oral stimulation is an effective method to help normalize oral and facial sensitivity, if exercised consistently and appropriately. Oral stimulation is often the foundation from which improved feeding skills are built. Stimulation that is provided before meals will often carry over into improved oral-motor skills, increased food intake, increase in variety of foods tolerated, and decreased eating time.

INCORPORATING SENSORY STIMULATION INTO A FEEDING PLAN

Sensory stimulation techniques should become a consistent part of daily classroom experiences. They are often incorporated only into the mealtime routine when, in fact, there are numerous situations throughout the day that might be enhanced with an overall stimulation program.

Oral/Facial Stimulation

Many children within a classroom may benefit from an oral/facial stimulation program, and all children will benefit from improved oral hygiene. Therefore, making oral stimulation a part of the daily routine for all children may have a positive effect on the classroom as a whole. It is best when the child does not have to be singled out for the oral stimulation, if this is possible in the classroom. For example, as children are preparing to go to lunch, they can get their mouths ready by brushing their teeth. This is a good time to provide the stimulation to those children in the classroom who need it in a less embarrassing way. For the younger child, by giving him or her the therapy tubing before meals, stimulation can be provided without taking away time from the other children. For the child who frequently puts nonedible objects in his or her mouth throughout the day, sensory stimulation materials, such as therapy tubing or a toothbrush, may need to be conveniently located within the classroom where the educator or the child can gain access to them easily. For the child who has difficulty getting organized, calm, or focused, oral stimulation may be the catalyst for acquiring these behaviors.

INTEGRATING TOUCH, TASTE, TEMPERATURE, AND TEXTURE INTO THE MEAL

There are specific techniques available that allow touch, taste, temperature, and texture to be addressed more effectively during each meal. Next is a look at each of these sensory processes.

Touch

Tactile stimulation in and around the mouth helps elongate musculature, activate musculature, and prepare the muscles for the sensory effects of feeding. If facial/oral stimulation is done effectively, it can minimize the effects of the other sensory stimuli of taste, temperature, and texture.

Incorporating techniques discussed previously allows the opportunity to work on the sensory issues associated with tactile sensitivity. It should be noted that hypersensitivity will be found often on the palms and feet as well as in the mouth. Stimulation of the palms helps with self-feeding skills. As discussed in Chapter 5, some younger children or those with more severe mental and/or physical disabilities may benefit from positioning that provides them with more stability and more security, thus allowing them to tolerate stimulation to the face and oral areas.

Taste

It is important to determine which tastes cause difficulty for the child. Bland foods are often preferred by the young child, especially if he or she is on a diet of commercial baby food. Once the child's diet consists of mostly table foods prepared by the feeder, the child will often prefer richer flavors. Children who have a hyporeaction to taste will often respond better to foods prepared with herbs and spices (Morris & Klein, 1987). The child who has difficulty integrating sensory information will often respond better when sour or bitter tastes are removed from his or her diet (Morris & Klein, 1987). Sweet tastes are often preferred by many children, and, therefore, caution should be taken not to overuse these tastes in the feeding program because the child can become dependent on these foods. Food tastes can have a significant effect on the mealtime and can be a motivational tool if used correctly.

Temperature

Many children have a preference to food temperature, which can be a difficult variable to control. Hot, warm, room temperature, cool, and cold are just a few variations of temperature that may be encountered. Parents are usually the best advisors on temperature preferences for their children. The difficulty arises when a child likes his or her food warm, and it gradually cools down as the meal progresses. Some children will actually stop eating and refuse to accept more food, which may be interpreted as a sign that they are full. In fact, the temperature change may have been enough of a stimulus to interrupt the entire meal, in which case the cause of the refusal of food may not be clear to the feeder. It is also important for the feeder to be aware that certain feeding utensils used will conduct the temperature of the food being served. A metal spoon or fork will stay hot or cold for a long time; and the child may be reacting to the utensil, rather than to the actual food.

Cold foods and utensils can be utilized to stimulate oral musculature and get more oral activation if used appropriately. For example, a pacifier dipped into ice-cold water can actually help stimulate a suck. Cold liquids given to a child a little at a time can actually be used to help stimulate a swallow. Extreme caution should be taken, however, if there is a known or suspected underlying medical cause for a reduced suck and swallow. (See Chapter 2 for additional information on the subject of medical collaboration.)

Texture

The child who has difficulty accepting a variety of textures can be very challenging to feed. As discussed previously, the reactions can range from picky eating to gagging and vomiting. Textured foods are extremely important in a child's diet because chewing these foods helps promote bone and muscle growth in the oral/facial structures. A diet rich in a variety of textures also provides a child with good oral stimulation on which the sensory system depends. The child who lacks a textured diet will often put inappropriate materials in his or her mouth and chew on inappropriate materials because the child's sensory system craves the sensory input in the muscles and joints. Therefore, introducing more texture into a child's diet, in combination with an adequate oral stimulation program, can help decrease biting, chewing on nonedibles, and mouthing objects in the child's environment. The rule for increasing texture in a child's diet is to do so gradually. The child is dependent on a gradual increase because he or she will not switch from eating pudding-like textures one day and wake up requesting a hamburger the next day. If children are not challenged with new textures, they can survive on soft foods indefinitely. It is also important to remember that the older a child gets, the more difficult it becomes to change his or her diet.

It is possible to change the texture of a child's diet in many ways. Several of the most common techniques are discussed next.

- Adding a new texture to an already preferred texture is a very popular practice. If the child accepts soft foods such as pudding, small broken-up pieces of graham cracker can be added to the pudding. The cracker will dissolve easily with saliva if the child has difficulty accepting it. The graham cracker changes the feel and the consistency of the pudding without challenging the child excessively.

- Combining two preferred foods into one new food can be a texture change, too. This is often more effective if the child is not allowed to observe food preparation. The combination of smashed, steamed carrots and mashed potatoes will be new to the child but not too difficult for the child to accept.

- The use of a commercially available food grinder is a more objective way to gradually increase textures. Perhaps a food that was ground 10 times and accepted easily by a child can be offered to the child later after being ground only 9 times. The decrease in the need to grind the food can be charted, and the texture increase can be observed over time. Food grinders can be kept in the classroom or cafeteria and cleaned easily. This method is preferred over blenderized food, which becomes a mixture of "moosh" that is neither very challenging nor age appropriate.

- When moving from soft foods to those with more texture, the feeder should remember to use foods that are easily dissolved with saliva, such as graham crackers. Easily dissolved foods begin to break down as they enter the mouth, and the child does not need to work as hard to manipulate them. It is a good idea to start with a list and determine through trial and error which foods break down and which foods need to be chewed.

- A good rule to remember is that whenever a new food or texture is introduced to a child, side placement should be utilized. By placing the food directly onto the chewing surface, food can be kept off the child's sensitive tongue, allowing the child more oral-motor control with which to manipulate the food within his or her mouth. This technique can be done by the educator, or the child can be taught to do it on his or her own.

As first discussed in Chapter 2, it is crucial to the success of the feeding program that changes in oral stimulation, food variety, and food presentation be done consistently and with the cooperation of the entire feeding team, especially the parent or caregiver. Without the cooperation of all people involved in the feeding process, the educator risks the chance for feeding to become a negative experience for the child. Unless the child is accepting of the changes in the feeding routine, the success of the entire feeding plan is in jeopardy.

SUMMARY

This chapter includes a brief look at the central nervous system and how it can interpret the effects of basic sensory stimuli. The entire sensory system, as a whole, has a part to play in the success of each mealtime. The most common sensory reactions observed in feeding are reviewed, and the importance of a consistent and thorough sensory stimulation program is presented. Ground rules for providing sensory stimulation are addressed as well as specific techniques on how to utilize sensory stimulation within the school environment. Another piece of the feeding plan is now in place to ensure successful feeding intervention.

Killian

Killian is a 3-year-old girl with Down syndrome. Killian has decreased facial and oral muscle tone. She is referred to as a "picky eater" who only eats round noodles in sauce, chips, cookies, and pudding. All foods must be served at room temperature. Killian's mother packs her lunch for her every day with these same four foods. When offered other foods, Killian refuses to eat and often throws her food. Killian packs large amounts of food into her mouth if allowed and sucks her food, rather than chews it. Killian feeds herself by spoon and puts the food straight into her mouth. She gets upset when her face is washed with a wet washcloth after she eats, and she refuses to brush her own teeth.

P R A C T I C E   E X E R C I S E

Before a sensory and feeding program for Killian can begin, the following questions must be addressed.

Collaboration

- Has the feeding team sat down with Killian's parents and/or caregivers to get a feel for their concerns and observations as well as to form a team commitment to carry over techniques throughout Killian's day?

Anatomy

- Are there any structural anomalies that would interfere with eating?
- Are Killian's face and oral areas symmetrical?

Positioning

- How is Killian positioned when she eats?
- Do changes in Killian's positioning provide her with more stability in her trunk?

Sensitivity

- What type of sensory stimulation program needs to be initiated in order to help normalize the sensitivity in and around Killian's mouth?
- What will Killian eat?
- What are the effects of touch, texture, temperature, and taste?
- What tools might work best for providing sensory stimulation to Killian?
- How could sensory stimulation be incorporated into Killian's mealtimes and her day?

Oral-Motor Skills

- How does Killian control the food in her mouth?
- What happens when small amounts of food are given to her?
- What happens when she finger feeds?
- What are the effects of low muscle tone on Killian's oral-motor skills?

Communication

- Is the feeder able to read Killian's cues?
- Is the feeder adjusting the rate and volume of feeding to Killian's needs?
- Is the feeder sensitive to when Killian is ready for more food or when she is finished?

Behavior

- What reactions does Killian get from others when she refuses to eat?
- What types of reinforcement are being used when Killian does attempt to eat new foods?

Killian has increased sensitivity (i.e., hyperreaction) to tactile stimulation, food texture, and food temperature. She has learned to compensate by accepting only the type of foods that dissolve easily with saliva. Consider the following suggestions in your feeding plan for Killian.

Collaboration

- Include Killian's parents in the feeding plan to ensure that their concerns are being addressed and to facilitate carryover of the techniques at home in order to more effectively improve Killian's feeding skills.

Positioning

- Consult with the PT and/or OT for suggestions on proper positioning.
- Consult with the PT and/or OT to learn techniques for altering muscle tone to help improve positioning for feeding.

Sensitivity

- Provide consistent facial stimulation with a dry cloth before meals, utilizing quick strokes to increase Killian's muscle tone.
- Use a toothbrush (without toothpaste) before meals, and use therapy tubing throughout the day for oral stimulation and improved oral-motor skills.
- Gradually change the temperature of the foods that Killian accepts, or try mixing a warm food with a food that is at room temperature.
- When washing Killian's face, use a dry cloth first to get as much muscle stimulation as you can, remembering to use firm, deep pressure. Make sure that it is fun and that she enjoys the interaction.

Oral-Motor Skills

- Offer Killian small, bite-size portions of food to eat so that she must chew the food and not be allowed to stuff the food into her mouth.
- Place pieces of food (e.g., crackers, luncheon meats, cheese, and so forth) into Killian's mouth, directly onto her molars from the side so that the food stays away from her tongue and is already on the chewing surface. This will encourage tongue lateralization and chewing. It will also encourage more success with a variety of textures because food will not be placed on Killian's tongue.

Communication

- The educator should make sure that time is spent learning to read Killian's communication attempts and that the speed and volume of feeding matches Killian's needs.

Behavior

* Try not to make feeding a struggle because behavioral issues will arise as a result.
* Be positive, praise Killian's attempts, and have fun!

REFERENCES

Case-Smith, J., Allen, A.S., & Pratt, P.N. (1996). *Occupational therapy for children* (3rd ed.). St. Louis: Mosby.

Morris, S.E., & Klein, M.D. (1987). *Pre-feeding skills: A comprehensive resource for feeding development.* San Antonio, TX: Therapy Skill Builders.

Orelove, F.P., & Sobsey, D. (1996). *Educating children with multiple disabilities: A transdisciplinary approach* (3rd ed.). Baltimore: Paul H. Brookes Publishing Co.

Palmer, M.M., & Heyman, M.B. (1993). Assessment and treatment of sensory versus motor-based feeding problems in very young children. *Infants and Young Children, 6*(2), 67–73.

Scheerer, C.R. (1991). Perspectives on an oral motor activity: The use of rubber tubing as a "chewy." *American Journal of Occupational Therapy, 46*(4), 344–352.

chapter seven

Communication Strategies for Feeding

Suzanne McKeever Murphy and Dianne Koontz Lowman

At the heart of every successful feeding session lies a respectful interaction between the child and the feeder. This interaction can only come about through adequate *communication,* or the exchange of ideas and information between a speaker and a receiver (McCormick & Schiefelbusch, 1990). This chapter includes a brief discussion on communication development and various modes of communication commonly used by children. The importance of reading the child's cues, establishing trust, and allowing the child to feel in control during feedings is stressed. Strategies for enhancing socializing during mealtimes as well as encouraging verbal skill development through feeding are provided. The need for augmentative and alternative communication (AAC) is explored, and a brief overview of augmentative options is given.

COMMUNICATION

It is nearly impossible not to communicate. Messages are constantly being sent and received through almost everything that an individual does. Communication takes place through the use of sounds, words, gestures, facial expressions, body language, writing, physical contact, and many other types of behaviors (Orelove & Sobsey, 1996). Communication can be vocal, verbal, or nonverbal but is most often a combination of all of these means. Language, speech, pragmatics, and paralinguistic features all are found under the umbrella of communication. *Language* is the knowledge and use of specific symbols that represent ideas about the world (McCormick & Schiefelbusch, 1990). *Receptive language* is the understanding and interpretation of communication, and *expressive language* is the utilization of the symbols. *Speech* is the use of specific combinations of sounds produced together to carry meaning. Speech production involves great complexity but is the most effective and specific method of expression. In order to produce speech, an individual must have adequate respiration (i.e., breathing), phonation (i.e., voicing), resonation (i.e., the prolongation and intensity of sound), and articulation (i.e., use of the oral structures to form speech sounds). The term *pragmatics* refers to the rules that apply to the way that language is used in specific situations. Individuals must learn how to use language for specific functions (e.g., requesting information). They must determine the appropriate form of message to accomplish the desired communication goal (by learning what the listener knows and does not know). They must also learn the rules for appropriate social exchanges (e.g., initiating, turn taking, and ending conversations). *Paralinguistic* features of language include various speech modifications (e.g., intonation, pitch, stress, pausing, rate) that change the meaning of the message (McCormick & Schiefelbusch, 1990). Understanding these terms and concepts allows the educator to maximize the success of communication during mealtimes. Within a typical classroom, a wide range of communication modes may be experienced, ranging from verbal communication to the use of body language to only a change in respiration and breathing rate. It is crucial to the success of the child's eating abilities that the educator knows the complexities of communication and the variety of modes in which the child can communicate.

Normal Development of Speech as it Relates to Feeding During the First Year of Life

By 1 year of age, most children are eating table foods and using words to communicate. These skills have been intertwined since the child was in utero. Their progression goes hand in hand, with feeding being the foundation for more complex speech development as the child matures. An interruption in the feeding process will most likely lead to delayed or disordered speech development. A brief look at the development of feeding as it relates to speech will give the educator an opportunity to see the relationship between these two skills.

- At birth, the infant's oral-motor skills are controlled primarily by reflexes. The sucking pattern is a "total pattern" that involves the cheeks, jaw, tongue, and lips working together to allow the infant to breast- or bottle-feed. Sound production is also reflexive and is produced through total body movement. The infant's cry is very high-pitched and monotonous.

- At 2 months of age, the infant uses a "suckle" pattern. Drooling increases as the tongue moves in and out of the mouth more often, and the child loses the natural stability of the head and neck, which was previously provided by physiological flexion. The infant's cry is more varied, and the caregiver begins to attach meaning to the different types of cries. A greater variety of vowel sounds (i.e., vocalizations) are heard with body movements.

- From 3 to 5 months of age, the infant has more control of the head, neck, and upper body. As a result, the infant also has improved liquid intake because of increased lip control and a more coordinated suck, swallow, and breathe sequence. Spoon feeding is typically introduced, which involves use of the infant's developing lip closure. The infant's sound production relates directly to lip closure in feeding because babbling sounds at this age are most often produced by placing the lips together (e.g., mama, baba).

- The 6-month-old infant has sufficient abdominal control, proximal stability, and oral mobility to allow for significant changes in feeding and speech production. True sucking begins to emerge, which enables the infant's tongue tip to elevate slightly. Longer sequences of sucking, swallowing, and breathing allow for an increase in liquid intake. Spoon feeding is also more efficient. Sounds produced by the infant consist of consonants that are produced in the front or the back of the mouth by the increased tongue and lip mobility and control (e.g., dadadada, mamamama, gagagaga). The sounds are strung together in long chains until the infant gains the control to start and stop phonation.

- By 7–9 months of age, the infant is able to take long sips from a bottle, drink from a stabilized cup, lateralize the tongue to control more textured foods, and munch on some solid foods. Feeding movements are independent of body movements as is sound production. Long chains of babbling sounds are produced (e.g., dadadadada) as well as some consonant vowel combinations that begin to sound more like real words (e.g., mama, dada).

- The 10- to 11-month-old is a very efficient bottle or breast feeder. Cup drinking continues to improve. Spoon feeding is also very efficient. Food is scraped off of the lower lip by the upper teeth. More solid foods are introduced with successful munching and emerging chewing ability. Sound production changes as feeding improves. The /f/ sound emerges, along with many more consonants that allow the child to approximate a few words (e.g., bye-bye, hi, no).

- By 12 months of age, the child is typically eating most table foods (with the exception of meats and some vegetables) and is using many single words and word approximations. The development of stability in the body allows for increased mobility in the mouth for both feeding and speech development. Feeding and speech skills will continue to be refined during the next few years of the child's development.

ESTABLISHING RAPPORT DURING FEEDING

For the child who has had a difficult time with eating, developing a trusting relationship with the feeder is of utmost importance. Many children have endured oral surgeries, invasive procedures, and frustrating attempts at oral feeding and have learned to be wary of adults attempting to feed them. The first step in rectifying this is for the educator to acknowledge the past feeding history of the child. Time spent building trust with the child as well as with the parents will be more than beneficial later. Trust is something that is earned and takes time to develop. It involves reading the child's communication cues effectively, acknowledging the child's feelings, and allowing the child to have some control over the feeding session. Once trust is established and maintained over time, the child is well on his or her way to being a more successful eater.

Reading the Child's Communication Attempts Successfully

The educator must first familiarize him- or herself with the variety of communication modes that the child is able to use. It is very important to make sure that the child is allowed to initiate communication throughout meal-times, rather than just assume the role of responder. The child needs to be able to communicate ideas such as hunger, fullness, wanting more, not want-ing more, wanting something different, changing the pace of eating, and finishing the meal. In addition, the child may attempt to communicate that he or she is uncomfortable with his or her positioning, is uncomfortable with sensory stimuli, or perhaps is fearful of a particular situation. Whenever pos-sible, a child's attempt to communicate should be acknowledged and given a response. If the child's intent is not easily read, behaviors used most often by the child may need to be shaped to have meaning. Shaping meanings for a child's behaviors often can be developed over time by the educator's re-sponding consistently to the child's behaviors. The educator may find it nec-essary to sit back between spoonfuls of food and observe the child to see whether the feeding methods used are allowing the child to handle the food adequately and be an active participant in the interaction. By waiting for the child to signal readiness before the next bite or spoonful of food, the feeder provides opportunities for the child's increased initiation. Body movement or quieting may be the only communication attempt that indicates readiness. Some communication attempts, such as refusal, cannot be reinforced every time; however, these signals should be acknowledged while other commu-nication options are provided for the child. (See Chapters 2 and 9 for more information about a child's behaviors during feeding.)

Improving Communication During Mealtimes

The natural turn taking that occurs during mealtimes provides a wonderful opportunity for improving a child's communication. Receptive language skills are often stimulated through new feeding vocabulary, new concepts associ-ated with eating, and natural interaction. Verbal skills can be stimulated through verbal modeling of sounds and words. It is important to choose sounds that correspond to the oral-motor skill that the child is learning in feeding. Through consistent repetition of sounds and words associated with feeding, the child has the opportunity to hear sounds multiple times and store them in his or her memory so the sounds can be matched to feeding activities in the future. Some children prefer to listen to a speaker, rather than make sounds themselves, so the educator must ensure adequate pauses that allow the child to practice sounds and/or words. Reinforcing any at-tempts that the child initially makes is important in encouraging the child to make more attempts. Words used should be consistent with the activity, and a core vocabulary should be built. For example, the educator should try not to say *drink* one time, then *juice* the next time, *sip* the next time, and so forth. A word should be chosen for an activity, and the educator should use the word consistently so that the child is not confused by too many labels. Action words or words paired with actions are often the first words to be used by the child. It is important that the educator makes sure there are plenty of opportunities to use the new vocabulary. Although there is a lot of thought behind the communication stimulation at mealtimes, it is still a time to enjoy the child and have fun!

Helping the Child Feel in Control

A child with eating difficulties often feels out of control during mealtimes as well as in other parts of his or her life. There may be times during the day when the child must have medications, be fed by gastrostomy tube, or attend therapies or doctor visits. There is no room for compromising in these situations. The one thing that the child can control is what goes into his or her mouth. If the educator makes feeding a struggle by setting firm limits and by taking control of the meal, it is likely to end in failure. By having clear goals in mind and allowing the child to take part in the decision of how the goals will be carried out, the mealtime will most likely be successful. Suggestions for increasing the child's feelings of control include allowing the child to choose between two foods or two liquids. Choice making typically gives the child a feeling of control, but the educator should be careful not to provide too many choices because this can overstimulate the child. The educator can ask the child how many bites of a particular food he or she wants or give the child choices. For example, the educator could ask, "Do you want three bites or five bites?" The child's answer can be surprising. Many children will choose the higher number of bites as they get caught up in the game and competition. It is crucial that the educator always keeps his or her word so that the child's trust is not betrayed. The child can also help decide where he or she wants to eat or what utensils he or she would like to use. Allowing the child to hold a utensil while the educator feeds him or her may also give the child control. The child can feed him- or herself one bite of food, and then the educator can provide the next bite of food. The idea is to give the child the *feeling* of control while still working toward the established goals. When the child feels in control and is a partner in the feeding process, he or she is typically more willing to try new techniques and new foods, will have greater food intake, and will generally recover quicker if he or she becomes stressed by something new.

Making Mealtimes Enjoyable

Each mealtime should be a pleasant experience for both the educator and the child. When there is a trusting and respectful relationship between the educator and the child, the feeding interaction becomes a dance that is carefully orchestrated and choreographed. The social and communicative opportunities that exist at mealtimes are often unequaled in their natural motivation and reinforcement. Most children enjoy eating because the reinforcement is immediate, and they get to partake in one-to-one interaction with the educator. Orelove and Sobsey (1996) discussed some important guidelines for "cooperative feeding" that help ensure a more enjoyable meal:

1. The feeder should watch and listen to the child and coordinate the presentation of food with the child's breathing and movement.

2. The feeder should ensure appropriate positioning and lighting so that the child has a clear view of the food.

3. The feeder should use a smooth and predictable pace while feeding.

4. A verbal or tactile "ready" signal from the feeder should be utilized.

5. The feeder should wait, observe, and reinforce any signal of readiness.

6. Any distractions and interruptions should be minimized.

Another technique for making mealtimes more enjoyable is the inclusion of peers at meals. Often, when a child has difficulty with the sensory and control issues of eating, becoming interested in the interactions of another child can provide a distraction that allows the child who is experiencing difficulties with feeding to gain greater food intake. Peer pressure is also a common motivation for improved eating. It provides the child who has a feeding difficulty with a role model who is his or her own age. The desire to be like others is often the catalyst that encourages the child to eat more food or to try eating new foods.

Because eating is often a time for socializing, the educator must decide if it is in the child's best interest to address specific feeding goals during a main meal. If possible, it is often preferable to allow the child to eat with his or her peers without interruption from the educator. This allows the child to focus on the social aspects of feeding and to minimize attention being drawn to him or her while eating. In some instances, the use of specific feeding techniques are more appropriate during a snacktime or a one-to-one feeding session. For the child who can eat independently, feeding techniques are typically used to improve the quality of oral-motor skills and can often slow the child down. When worked on individually or in smaller groups, targeted goals can be addressed in shorter intervals with less attention drawn to the child. For the child who needs a lot of assistance, perhaps most of the meal can be fed to the child before the class goes to the cafeteria, allowing the child to socialize and explore food while in the group situation. This is a decision best addressed by the entire feeding team, once all of the information regarding the child's overall needs has been gathered.

COMMON DIFFICULTIES AFFECTING COMMUNICATION DURING MEALTIMES AND STRATEGIES FOR ADDRESSING THESE CONCERNS

There are numerous causes for communication breakdown during mealtimes. The causes may relate to problems associated with the child, problems associated with the feeder, or problems within the environment. Difficulty in one of these areas will most likely lead to a breakdown in the other areas because feeding is interactive and dynamic.

Problems Involving the Child

Problems associated with the child are typically caused by physical or behavioral concerns. Although some examples of these problems are discussed next, much of this information is provided in the various chapters throughout this book. A summary of how these difficulties relate to communication failure is provided in this section.

- *Muscle tone*—The child who does not have adequate muscle tone often has difficulty providing adequate cues to the feeder. Inadequate muscle tone may affect the child's ability to produce words; vocalizations; and consistent gestures, consistent facial expressions, and/or body language. This inconsistency makes the message difficult to interpret; therefore, a communication breakdown typically occurs. An example of affected ability to communicate would be a child who has significant spasticity (i.e., increased muscle tone) in the muscles of his mouth and throughout his body that makes smooth, controlled movements necessary for sending messages a challenge.

- *Anatomical structure abnormalities*—For the child with abnormal structures of the oral area, communication can be difficult. Depending on the extent of the abnormality, the child's ability to produce speech may be significantly affected. Some common abnormalities include cleft lip, cleft palate, missing or malaligned teeth, small jaw (i.e., micrognathia), and defects of the trachea and/or larynx. The results of these abnormalities can range from impaired speech production to the inability to produce speech. In more severe cases, the child may have had a tracheostomy, which further complicates speech production as well as feeding.

- *Impaired interactions*—Some children have difficulties with interactive communication because of mental disabilities and/or impaired learning skills. Their ability to send and/or receive messages is affected. The problem may stem from the inability to interpret symbolic communication or from an inability to use socially accepted forms of communication. An example of a child with impaired interaction is a child with autism. Children with autism often use idiosyncratic modes of communication (i.e., communication unique to that individual), such as humming or flapping hands. It is up to the educator to spend ample time observing the child and gathering information from significant others in order to attach meaning to these behaviors and begin to shape the behaviors toward more acceptable and conventional modes of communication. All too often, the child is communicating to the best of his or her ability, but the child's attempts go unnoticed or punished and are, therefore, not reinforced. As stated previously, it is almost impossible for people not to communicate; every opportunity should be taken to discern a child's methods of communicating.

Problems Involving the Feeder

Although effective feeding intervention incorporates a team approach, an actual feeding session typically involves two people. Therefore, it is important to examine the role that the feeder assumes during mealtime interactions. The ability to give and read cues effectively has a positive impact on each feeding session. Even if the child can eat independently, it is often up to the educator to ensure that the child is able to communicate his or her needs throughout the meal.

- *Isolating feeding from the child's global development*—It is not uncommon for the educator to focus more on the amount of food a child eats than on the process of eating because of the continually increasing demands in the child's schedule. Unfortunately, a lot of valuable interactions are missed as a result. If feeding is viewed as a way of addressing the child as a whole, the opportunity exists for improvement in socialization, communication, sensory processing, motor stimulation, and so forth. The educator can make a list of all of the skills incorporated into mealtimes and begin to expand the goals being addressed during this time.

- *Missed opportunities for reading the child's cues*—If the feeder gets too concerned about the skill of eating, it is easy to miss the very important messages that the child is providing. It is important to allow time for the child to initiate interactions with each spoonful or bite of food. Allowing the child to take control of the exchange typically increases the child's need and desire to communicate. This also helps ensure that the rate and rhythm of the feeding is appropriate for the child. By observing what the child does before each bite, while the food is in his or her mouth, and then after the child has swallowed the food, the educator will have numerous opportunities to receive and interpret the cues that the child is using.

- *Taking control*—The educator always wants to keep in mind that the goal of feeding is independence. Feeding the child initially will help develop the child's oral-motor skills to their highest potential. Once these skills are mastered to the child's best ability, the educator needs to begin addressing self-feeding. Improved feeding independence goes hand-in-hand with the goal of independence in communicating feeding needs. Requesting more, requesting help, and communicating the need for a different food item or utensil are some of the functions that allow the child to eat independently. These skills need to be addressed while continuing to monitor the child's oral-motor skills. A good tool in deciding what communication needs the child will require during meals throughout the day is an Ecological Inventory. This tool examines each situation throughout the child's day in order to determine the communication skills necessary for that situation. (An Ecological Inventory is discussed in more detail in Chapter 2.) Because the child typically eats two of the three main meals at home, this is a tool that should be addressed with the child's caregiver. This will ensure that appropriate and functional vocabulary can be addressed.

Problems Involving the Environment

Difficulties for the child in the feeding environment should be identified so that distractions are minimized. By observing the child and reading his or her cues effectively, the educator should be able to identify areas of concern that the child has and make changes that will improve the mealtime. Some of the more common problem areas are positioning, visual / auditory distractions, and insufficient opportunities for communication to occur. It is not uncommon for problems in these areas to result in a refusal by the child to eat or an increased length of feeding time and a decreased amount of food eaten. Enabling the child to effectively communicate his or her feeling of comfort throughout the meal helps ensure a more cooperative attitude from the child.

- *Improper positioning*—The importance of appropriate positioning on the effect of eating skills cannot be overemphasized (Orelove & Sobsey, 1996). The subject of proper positioning is best addressed by the feeding team as a whole. The child needs adequate stability while allowing for adequate mobility in the muscles of the head, neck, and mouth for eating. Improper positioning will most likely have a negative impact on the child's ability to communicate effectively. The result is a significant limitation in the ability to use a variety of communication modes adequately. Children who are positioned appropriately at the beginning of a meal should be monitored frequently to ensure that the position is maintained or that any changes have not limited their eating and communication skills. (See Chapter 5 for more complete information on positioning.)

- *Visual/auditory distractions*—For the child who is easily distracted, an environment that is overstimulating often has an adverse effect on communication interactions. Some children may shut down and not communicate at all, whereas others may become agitated. The disturbing stimuli should be identified and minimized whenever possible. Appropriate stimuli, however, can often encourage communication attempts by the child.

- *Insufficient opportunities for communication*—When looking at a typical mealtime for a child in the educational environment, it is important to look at the opportunities for communication. By completing an Ecological Inventory, opportunities in the child's day to communicate about feeding can be explored. Situations to consider involve the selection of food for a grocery list, choosing food for a particular meal, choosing materials to be used for eating, choosing the order in which the food will be eaten, choosing food or drink, and so forth. For the child who is verbal, expanding the understanding and use of concepts can be built into the mealtime situation.

- *Poor communication between school and home*—As previously stated, the child typically eats at least two meals at home. It is often crucial to the success of feeding goals that communication between the child's school and home be consistent and frequent. The quality of feeding at home has a direct impact on the quality of feeding at school. If at all possible, the parents and educators should meet and discuss as well as demonstrate feeding techniques being used with the child. Any changes in diet, medications, positioning, behavioral expectations, and communication strategies need to be discussed. A monthly or quarterly home visit by the educator is strongly suggested in order to observe the child's mealtime environment and make any necessary changes to the feeding program.

Some children who have difficulties with interactive communication are unable to speak or to use speech effectively. For those children, an AAC system may be appropriate.

AUGMENTATIVE AND ALTERNATIVE COMMUNICATION

AAC can be described as any form of communication that requires something other than the child's own body (Cook & Hussey, 1995). *Augmentative communication* refers to the use of aids or techniques that supplement existing vocal or verbal communication. *Alternative communication* refers to communication used by a person without vocal ability (Mustonen, Locke, Reichle, Solbrack, & Lindgren, 1991). There are two categories of AAC. *Aided systems* require the use of a device, such as a picture, communication book, or computerized aid. *Unaided systems* are those AAC systems for which the child uses only hand or body movements to communicate (Miller, 1993). The purpose of AAC is to help the child become more communicative and, ultimately, more independent during mealtimes.

If the child does not have a communication system that is understood by others, challenging behaviors may become the child's only means of "communicating." (See Chapter 9 for a discussion of the communicative intent of challenging behaviors.) It is important that the feeding team find the best way for the child to communicate needs and desires as soon as possible. For young children, critical time is lost while waiting to see whether speech will develop. There is no evidence that teaching nonspeech communication interferes with speech development (Cook, Tessier, & Klein, 1996). In fact, there is evidence that children may begin to speak after beginning to use some form of AAC (Miller, 1993).

Table 1 highlights a sample of the numerous AAC systems that are available. AAC systems range from those involving low technology to those involving high technology (e.g., electronic systems). Generally, it is preferable to begin with the most "low-tech" options that are effective and move to more "high-tech" systems only as needed. Making the decision about the type of AAC system(s) that would be most appropriate for the child requires the collaborative efforts of all feeding team members, including the family and child. When discussing the various AAC systems, team members need to consider two important points. First, the team should choose a system that does not lock the child into only one way of communication. It is important to teach communication in more than one mode (Mustonen et al., 1991). Many children who use AAC vary their means of communicating according to purpose, partner, activity, or environment (Allaire, Gressare, Blackman, & Hostler, 1991). For this reason, it is important to give the child a repertoire

Table 1.   Examples of augmentative and alternative communication options

Unaided Systems
- Nonsymbolic behaviors
    Vocalizations
    Facial and body expressions
        Eye gaze (e.g., looking at food desired)
        Head nod
- Gestures
    Pointing to food desired
- Signing
    American Sign Language
    Signing Exact English
- Speech

Aided Systems
- Communication boards (e.g., vocabulary displays)
    Single-sheet displays
    Multiple-sheet displays (e.g., notebook, flipchart, card sets, wallet, vest)
    Picture Exchange Communication System
- Switch-activated devices
    Activating switches, toys, tape recorder
        Talking Rocker Plate Switch, Cheap Talk
- Personal Computer
    Operated by keyboard, mouse, trackball, touch screen, switch, joystick
- Commercial AAC systems[a]
    Single-switch scanning
        Dial Scan, Zygo
    Simple voice output
        Alpha Talker, Speakeasy, Wolfe, Cheap Talk
    Direct selection, spelling only
        Canon communicator
    Direct selection with rate enhancement
        Dynavox, Liberator, Touch Talker
    Multiple selection method with rate enhancement
        Dynavox, Liberator, Light Talker, Light Writer

Adapted from Cook & Hussey (1995) and Miller (1993).
[a]This list represents a small sample of the numerous commerical systems that are available.

of ways of communicating that can be varied as needed. Second, the team should match the characteristics, preferences, and needs of the individual child with aspects of the chosen AAC system(s). For example, signing can be valuable for some children because this system is portable, the message can be sent quickly, and the act of signing enhances eye contact and personal interactions. Signing, however, involves good motor control and is unintelligible to people who do not know how to sign. If the child has significant motor problems or if the family does not prefer to learn sign language, then this system is not the best match for this child and family (Miller, 1993; Musselwhite & St. Louis, 1988).

The following steps can aid the feeding team with determining which AAC system would be the most appropriate for the individual child (Baumgart, Johnson, & Helmstetter, 1990; Cook et al., 1996). Examples of questions are included with each step; the team needs to conduct an extensive discussion of all components.

1. *Determine the child's communicative needs and opportunities.* Based on the Ecological Inventory conducted earlier with the family, determine how many times during the day the child eats. Where does the child eat meals? Who is the feeder? Is the menu set, or does the child have a choice of foods?

2. *Determine the child's current communication repertoire.* How does the child currently indicate hunger, a choice of food or liquid, the need for a change of pace or pause in eating, readiness for more food, and when he or she is finished? Which of the child's current communication behaviors are effective? Which of the child's behaviors can be shaped into communication that is more conventional?

3. *What are the barriers to successful communication?* Determine the reasons communication is not successful. Also, determine any potential barriers, such as resistance to signing at home or in the community, time demands of various environments, or limited portability of the potential system.

4. *Determine the best "indicating response" to be used.* Does the child respond best by vocalizing, looking at or touching the object, nodding his or her head, pointing, or hitting a switch?

5. *Determine the best "symbol system."* Is it most appropriate for the child to use actual food, miniature foods, photographs, color pictures, picture symbols, line drawings of food, or words?

6. *Design the "display."* How many items can be displayed at one time? Can the child use a single sheet or multiple sheets? Should the food be arranged by category or use color codes?

7. *Design the training steps.* How will the child learn to use the AAC system? Will training be conducted during mealtimes or snacks or at another time? How will this training be coordinated between the child's school and home?

Numerous resources on AAC systems are available. The previous discussion has highlighted only a portion of the components that need to be considered by the feeding team.

SUMMARY

This chapter focuses on communication strategies as they relate to feeding. Common definitions associated with communication are provided. A brief summary of the parallel between feeding and communication skill development during the first year of life is presented. Suggestions for establishing rapport between the educator and the child are discussed. Common difficulties associated with feeding and communication are pointed out, and strategies for improving communication during mealtimes are given. Adequate feeding skills are the very foundation for later speech development; working to help the child achieve independence in both feeding and communication will most likely have a direct impact on the child's quality of life.

Megan

Megan is a 5-year-old girl who has autism. She has good receptive language skills and is able to point to 25 pictures when named. Megan's primary means of communication is *echolalia* (i.e., the immediate echoing back of a spoken word or phrase), followed by communication through facial expressions, body language, and occasional screaming. Megan is becoming increasingly more frustrated by her lack of ability to communicate her wants and needs during mealtimes, as evidenced by an increase in her screaming.

Before a communication program can begin at mealtimes, the following questions should be addressed.

Collaboration

- Has the feeding team sat down with Megan's parents/caregivers to discuss their concerns about her change in behavior during mealtimes?
- Has the team discussed any previous attempts at using AAC?
- Has the feeding team completed an Ecological Inventory with Megan's caregivers to determine Megan's daily routine?

Anatomy

- Are there any structural causes for Megan's lack of functional verbalizations?

Sensitivity

- Are there any sensory causes for the increase in screaming during mealtimes?

Positioning

- How is Megan positioned while she is eating?
- Does the positioning allow for freedom of communication?
- How does Megan's positioning affect her eating skills?

Oral-Motor Considerations

- Is Megan able to control the food in her mouth?
- Are Megan's oral-motor skills adequate for verbal speech production?

Communication

- How does Megan communicate now?
- Does she initiate communication? If so, how?
- Does Megan combine gestures with her vocalizations or words?

Behavior

- What reactions does Megan get when she attempts to communicate?
- What reactions does Megan get when she uses echolalia? What reactions does she get when she screams?
- What does Megan do when her communication is understood? What does Megan do when her communication is not understood?

Medical Issues

- Has the possibility of a medical cause for Megan's screaming during mealtimes been ruled out?

Hearing

- Has Megan had an audiological exam?

The feeding team met and observed Megan throughout the day and found that the screaming occurred during mealtimes when she was frustrated because she could not communicate her wants and needs. The team decided that it needed to explore options in order to augment Megan's existing repertoire of communication methods. The team looked at the fact that Megan had good receptive language skills, could identify 25 pictures, was not initiating communication, and did possess the ability to be verbal. The feeding team decided to explore using an AAC system known as the Picture Exchange Communication System (PECS) (Frost & Bondy, 1994). The PECS program was designed to be utilized with children who have autism or other disabilities. It requires minimal materials, can be used in a variety of settings, and uses a step-by-step approach to functional communication (Frost & Bondy, 1994). The PECS program involves having the child choose a picture of a desired object or action and giving the picture to another person in order to initiate a request for the item or action.

The PECS program was used with Megan during meals because the food was an immediate reinforcement. Megan would choose a picture corresponding to an item she wanted, and the educator would respond by saying, "You told me you want a cookie." Then the educator would give Megan the cookie. Megan quickly learned to initiate communication with this program. In addition to the pictures, the verbal label of the item was emphasized so that verbal speech was also a primary focus of the training. Soon Megan was attempting to verbalize along with her picture request.

REFERENCES

Allaire, J., Gressare, R., Blackman, J., & Hostler, S. (1991). Children with severe speech impairments: Caregiver survey of AAC use. *Augmentative and Alternative Communication, 7,* 248–255.

Baumgart, D., Johnson, J., & Helmstetter, E. (1990). *Augmentative and alternative communication systems for persons with moderate and severe disabilities.* Baltimore: Paul H. Brookes Publishing Co.

Cook, A.M., & Hussey, S.M. (1995). *Assistive technologies: Principles and practice.* St. Louis: Mosby.

Cook, R.E., Tessier, A., & Klein, M.D. (1996). *Adapting early childhood curricula for children in inclusive settings.* New York: Merrill.

Frost, L.A., & Bondy, A.S. (1994). *The picture exchange communication system training manual.* Cherry Hill, NJ: Pyramid Educational Consultants, Inc.

McCormick, L., & Schiefelbusch, R.L. (1990). *Early language intervention: An introduction.* New York: Merrill.

Miller, J. (1993). Augmentative and alternative communication. In M.E. Snell (Ed.), *Instruction of students with severe disabilities* (4th ed., pp. 319–346). New York: Merrill.

Musselwhite, C., & St. Louis, K. (1988). *Communication programming for persons with severe disabilities: Vocal and augmentative strategies* (2nd ed.). Boston: College-Hill Press.

Mustonen, T., Locke, P., Reichle, J., Solbrack, M., & Lindgren, A. (1991). An overview of augmentative and alternative communication systems. In J. Reichle, J. York, & J. Sigafoos, *Implementing augmentative and alternative communication: Strategies for learners with severe disabilities* (pp. 1-37). Baltimore: Paul H. Brookes Publishing Co.

Orelove, F.P., & Sobsey, D. (1996). *Educating children with multiple disabilities: A transdisciplinary approach* (3rd ed.). Baltimore: Paul H. Brookes Publishing Co.

chapter eight

Adapted Equipment for Feeding

Dianne Koontz Lowman

Throughout this book, a number of intervention techniques to assist children with feeding difficulties have been discussed, including providing physical assistance, modifying positioning, modifying foods, modifying food presentation, and modifying the mealtime environment. Modifying equipment is another method of assisting with feeding and eating (Orelove & Sobsey, 1996). This chapter explores different ways of modifying equipment, ranging from simple changes to more complex changes involving technology. Adaptations that take into consideration the needs and wishes of the child and family and that promote the principle of normalization (i.e., the child eating as "normally as possible") are stressed.

WHAT IS ADAPTIVE EQUIPMENT?

Adaptive equipment includes all of the tools used during the feeding process, including adapted tables, chairs, spoons, plates, and cups. An adaptation is any device, material, or technique that is used to accomplish a task more efficiently (York-Barr, Rainforth, & Locke, 1996). The term *adapted equipment* refers to equipment that has been modified or changed to meet the needs of a specific child. Adapted equipment can be used to support or maintain the feeding process (Heller, Alberto, Forney, & Schwartzman, 1996; Morris & Klein, 1987; Orelove & Sobsey, 1996). Adapted equipment also can be used to develop independent eating skills (Campbell, 1993). Table 1 lists all of the different types of adapted feeding equipment available.

Adapted equipment can be an effective means to assist children with feeding problems. It is important, however, to emphasize that not all children need adapted equipment. Many children with disabilities eat well with regular household utensils (Orelove & Sobsey, 1996). A divided Tupperware plate has a raised edge for scooping. Some commercially available spoons decorated with cartoon characters have enlarged handles. Adapted equipment should facilitate mealtimes rather than prevent the child from eating in a normalized manner in school, at home, or in the community. It is important to consider the environments in which the child will typically eat

Table 1.   Types of adapted equipment used during the feeding process

---

Seating or positioning
  Various types of seats (e.g., corner, Rifton)
  Prone stander
  Travel chair
  Bolster chair

Oral stimulation
  NUK toothbrush
  Infa-Dent finger toothbrush
  Toothette disposable oral swabs
  Massagers
  Chew toys
  Therapy tubing

Food preparation
  Food grinder
  Blender

Cups
  Infa-Trainer cup
  Cut-out cups (e.g., flex cups, nose cups)
  Cups with one or two handles

Utensils
  Adapted utensils (e.g., spoons, forks, knives)
  Universal cuff

Plates and bowls
  Scooper dish
  Plate guard
  Nonslip pad (e.g., Dycem)
  Suction cups

Sandwich holder

  "High-tech" adaptations
  Ball-bearing feeder
  Friction feeder
  Suspension feeder
  Electric feeder

---

meals (e.g., at school, at home, in the community) and use specialized equipment only when necessary. When deciding whether equipment should be adapted, several criteria should be considered (Inge, 1992; York-Barr et al., 1996):

- An adaptation should not be used if the child has the potential to learn the skill without one.

- The decision to use adapted equipment should always be made by a team that includes the educator, the therapists, the child, and the parents.

- It is important always to select the least intrusive design that allows the child to be as independent as possible.

Criteria for selecting the specific adapted equipment include considering the wishes of the child and family, the durability and ease of cleaning the equipment, and the developmental appropriateness of the equipment (Case-Smith, 1994; Case-Smith & Humphry, 1996).

IMPORTANCE OF THE TEAM

It is always important to work with team members while adapting or selecting specialized feeding equipment. The occupational therapist (OT) should be consulted before modifying any equipment. It is especially important to include the child in this discussion. The child indicates which equipment "feels" right, works, or is appropriate to use in school. Sometimes when a student reaches the teenage years, equipment that appears "different" to peers is not desirable. The family can help to identify which equipment is appropriate for the student's specific mealtime arrangements, types of foods prepared, and time available. Once the feeding team has decided that an adaptation is necessary, the first priority is to look at the position of the child during mealtimes.

POSITIONING PROPS AND SEATING DEVICES

Before a child can use any piece of equipment, that child must be seated properly and securely. (Detailed information about appropriate positioning and seating equipment is presented in Chapter 5.) It is important to match appropriate seating devices with the environment in which the child will be eating. For example, eating in a prone stander may be appropriate at home but may not be appropriate in a busy school cafeteria.

PREPARATION FOR MEALTIMES

In order to ensure that the feeding process and mealtimes are as successful as possible, it is important to plan and prepare. In addition to special preparations of food, it is important to prepare the child to orally receive food.

Oral Stimulation

Activities that provide oral stimulation can prepare the child for mealtimes. (See Chapter 6 for a complete discussion of oral stimulation.) Oral stimulation can help "normalize" the sensitivity in and around the child's mouth, thus making eating and mealtimes more pleasant experiences. Equipment for toothbrushing, both before and after the meal, includes a regular toothbrush, the NUK toothbrushes, Infa-Dent Finger Toothbrush, the feeder's finger inside a nipple, or Toothette disposable oral swabs (see Figures 1A–C). A variety of therapy tubing, chew toys, blow toys, and massagers are also available (see Appendix D at the end of this book). The educator should always consult with other team members, such as the OT or the speech-language pathologist, before attempting to use any oral stimulation techniques. These therapists will help identify which techniques or equipment are safe and appropriate for each individual child.

Food

As discussed in Chapter 6, introducing more texture into a child's diet, in combination with an oral stimulation program, is extremely important for children with oral-motor feeding problems. It is always important to work with team members to develop a plan to move from puréed or ground food to regular table food. The use of a commercially available food grinder (see Figure 1D) is one way to gradually increase textures of food. Hand or crank food grinders are preferable over electric blenders. With the hand grinder,

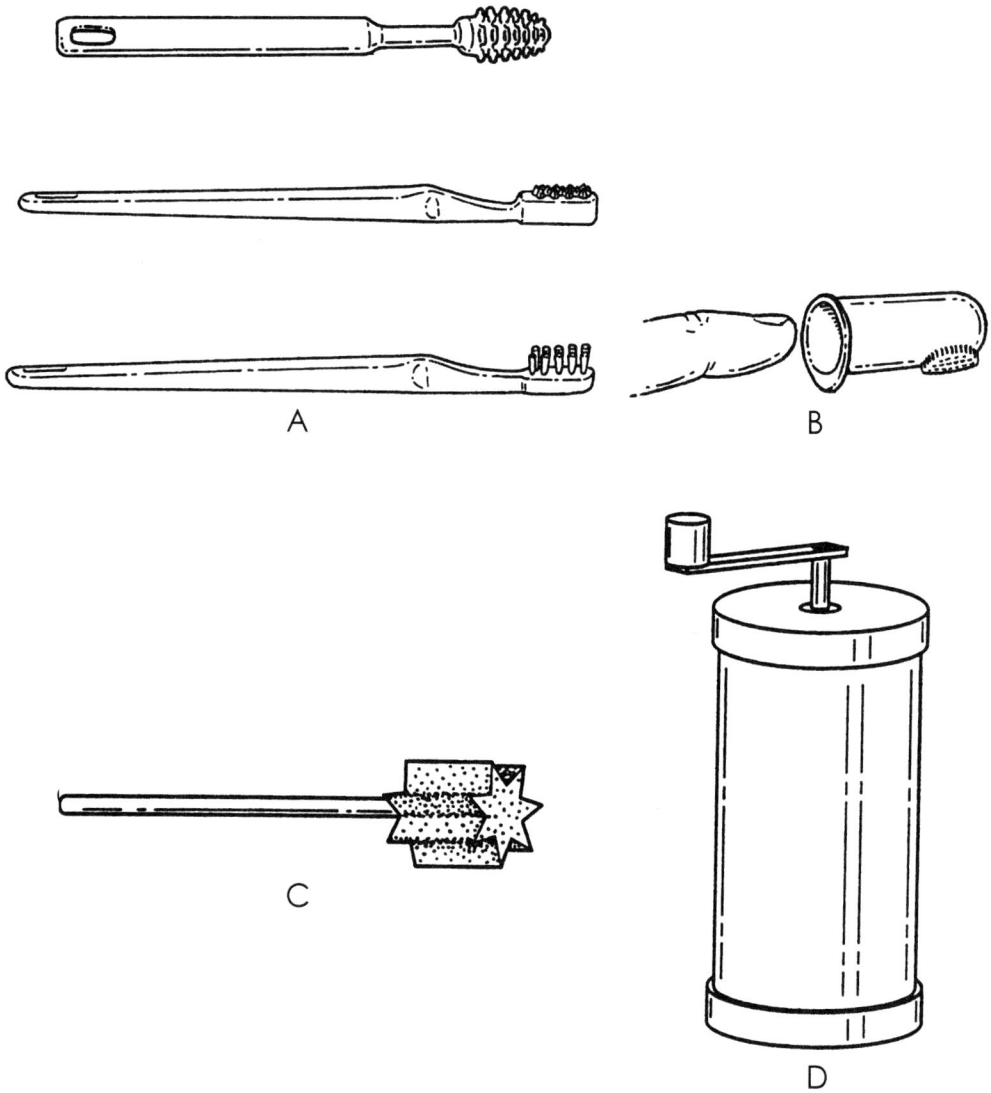

Figure 1.   Equipment to be used before and after a meal: A) NUK toothbrush trainer set, B) Infa-Dent finger toothbrush, C) Toothette disposable oral swab, D) food grinder.

food texture can be progressively altered by changing the food grinder setting (e.g., moving from food that was ground 10 times to food ground 9 times) (Case-Smith & Humphry, 1996). Food grinders can be used easily in the school cafeteria or when eating out at a restaurant. Electric blenders are more difficult to use in school; blenderized food tends to become a mixture of "moosh" that is not challenging or age appropriate. It is very important to grind foods separately; feeders should never blend or mix different foods together. It is neither appealing nor respectful to the child with disabilities to blend together hot dogs, french fries, and peaches.

ADAPTATIONS OF EQUIPMENT

The types of adaptations that can be made range from low technology ("low-tech" adaptations) to high technology ("high-tech" adaptations). A low-tech adaptation may be as simple as placing a nonslip pad under the child's plate or enlarging the handle of the spoon. High-tech adaptations may be as complicated as an electrical self-feeder. The type of adaptation needed should be based on the individual needs of the child. Some general guidelines for adaptations related to types of motor challenges are presented in Table 2.

Cups

The transition from drinking from a nipple to drinking from a cup can be difficult for many children with oral-motor difficulties. Figure 2 shows some of the different types of cups available, including cups with or without a lid, with or without handles, and with a regular or controlled flow (Morris & Klein, 1987). The therapist can discuss with the feeding team the advantages and disadvantages of each type of cup.

The cut-out (or cut-away, flex, or nose) cup shown in Figure 2A is used to facilitate drinking without hyperextension of the neck (Morris & Klein, 1987). Cutting away part of the rim of the cup allows the cup to be tipped up without hitting the child's nose or requiring the child's head to be tipped back (Orelove & Sobsey, 1996). Cut-away cups can be purchased commercially or homemade by cutting out a soft, plastic cup.

The child's physical abilities determine whether to use a cup with or without handles, as illustrated in Figure 2B. A child with a limited grasp may find it easier to grasp a glass with a very small diameter. Some children with muscle control problems may prefer cups with one or two handles because they have difficulty holding a cup without handles (Klein & Delaney, 1994). Handles provide more security for the child so his or her grasp will not be lost while holding the cup to drink (Morris & Klein, 1987).

Table 2.   General guidelines for adaptations related to motor challenges

- Enlarge or build up handles for easier grasp.
- Extend or lengthen the handle for children with restricted range of motion.
- Use bent handles for children with limited motion patterns.
- Use swivel utensils that stay level regardless of the position of the hand for children with restricted motions.
- Use a rocker spoon or fork for a child with only one functioning hand.
- Use a utensil cuff for a child with limited or no grasp.
- Use small-diameter glasses for children with limited grasp.
- Use cups with handles large enough to insert fingers (or hand) through for children with poor grasp.
- Use long straw for children with limited range of motion.
- Use a friction or nonskid surface for a child using only one hand or for children who have uncontrolled movements.
- Use a plate guard for a child using only one hand or for children who have uncontrolled movements to keep food on the plate and aid in picking up food with eating utensils.
- Use a sandwich holder for children with uncontrolled movement or high-level paralysis.

From Reed, K.L. (1991). *Quick reference to occupational therapy* (p. 523). Gaithersburg, MD: Aspen Publishers; adapted by permission.

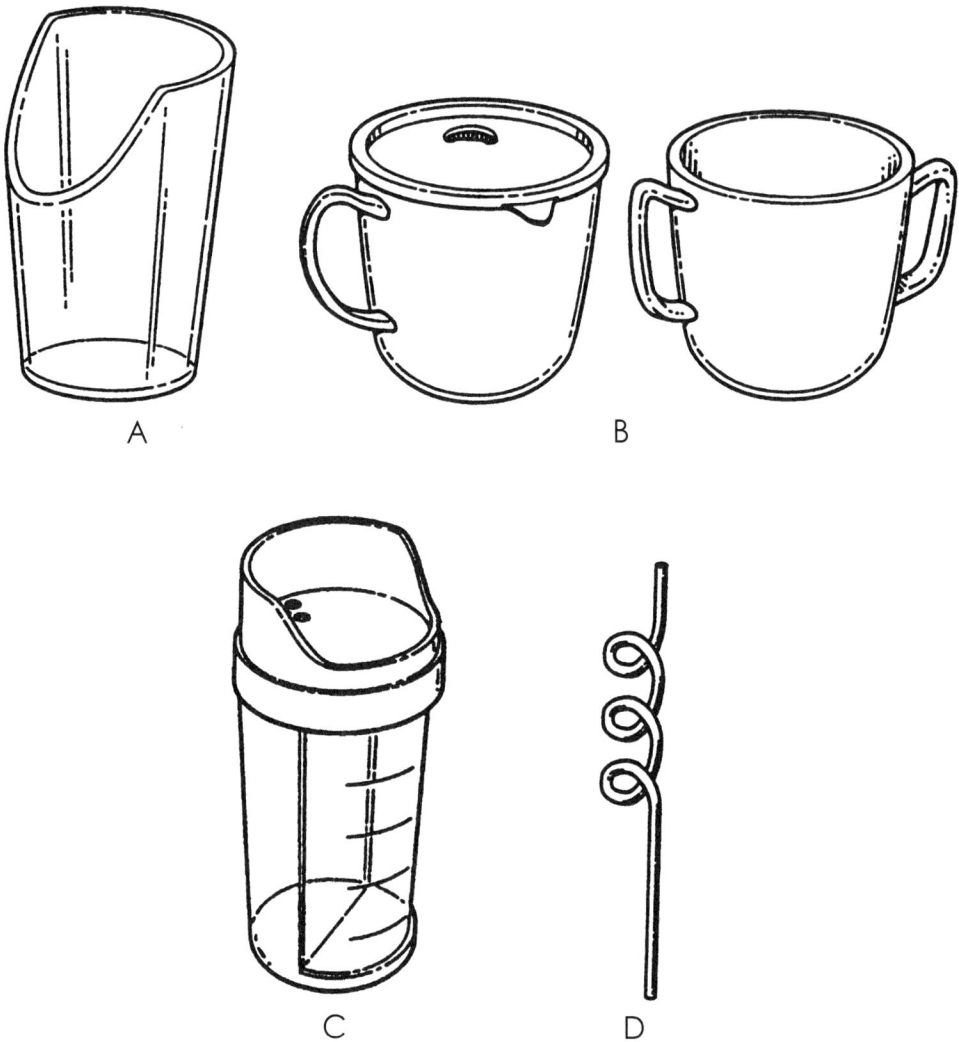

Figure 2.   Different types of cups and a drinking straw: A) cut-out, flex, or nose cup; B) cups with regular rims and one or two handles; C) Infa-Trainer cup; D) Krazy Straw.

Lids can assist the child who has lots of spillage problems by controlling the flow of liquid into the child's mouth (Case-Smith & Humphry, 1996). The feeding team should decide whether to use a lid with or without a spout. A spout can be helpful for the child who needs to bite on the cup edge for support, but a spout can interfere with the maturation of jaw, lip, and tongue control (Klein & Delaney, 1994). Some children with disabilities also become "stuck" at the stage of using the spout and have difficulty moving to using the regular cup rim (Morris & Klein, 1987). In addition, spouts should not be used when the child exhibits a suckling tongue movement pattern (Case-Smith & Humphry, 1996). For these reasons, many therapists recommend choosing covered cups that have a regular shaped cup edge (see the cups with lids shown in Figures 2B and 2C). Lids such as the one on the Infa-

Trainer in Figure 2C are adjustable, allowing the feeder to control the flow of liquid (Klein & Delaney, 1994).

Straws

Drinking from a straw can promote the child's ability to suck and improve lip closure, strength, and control (Klein & Delaney, 1994). Straw drinking can also promote a chin tuck position because the child leans forward to reach the straw (Case-Smith & Humphry, 1996). Straw drinking facilitates independence; the child can drink without moving the cup from the table (Case-Smith & Humphry, 1996). Some parents prefer drinking from a straw when eating in restaurants. Shown in Figure 2D is a Krazy Straw, available from party stores, which not only looks fun but also provides oral-motor practice (Morris, 1997).

Spoons

Children with a hypersensitive bite or gag reflex may do better with adapted spoons (Orelove & Sobsey, 1996). As illustrated in Figure 3, there are a number of factors to consider when choosing a spoon; these factors include the size of the bowl, the plastic material covering the bowl, the shape of the handle, and the length of the handle. The size of the bowl of the spoon must be in proportion to the child's mouth (Klein & Delaney, 1994). In addition, the shape of the bowl of the spoon affects feeding difficulty. If the bowl is deeper, the food is more difficult to remove (see Figure 3B). If the bowl is more shallow, the food is easier to remove (see Figure 3A). The material covering the spoon is also important to consider. Plastic spoons must be sturdy enough not to break when bitten. Cold, metal spoons might irritate some children; nylon, plastic, or rubber-coated spoons work well for children who are hypersensitive to hot or cold stimuli (Orelove & Sobsey, 1996). Small, disposable plastic spoons are good for some children because they minimize stimulation; however, these spoons cannot be used with a child who may bite because these spoons could easily break and splinter as a result (Orelove & Sobsey, 1996).

As illustrated in the three examples in Figure 3C, spoon handles can be adapted to aid in the development of independent spoon-to-mouth skills. The handle of the spoon can be "built up" to make it easier for the child to grasp; a variety of textures, weights, and shapes of spoons can be used. The weight of the spoon can affect control; heavier spoons sometimes help a child control the movement of the spoon (Klein & Delaney, 1994). The bent-handle spoon, which is shown in Figure 3D, can be helpful for children with limited movement. A variety of aids can be used to assist the child with holding the handle of the spoon. The universal cuff, which is shown in Figure 3E, can be purchased to help the child hold the handle. Elastic and hook-and-pile Velcro closures can also be useful. In Figure 3F, an elastic ponytail holder is used to help the child hold the spoon.

Plates and Bowls

When learning to self-feed, one difficulty encountered may be learning to scoop food onto the spoon. A dish or tray with a raised edge or a plate guard fastened on the edge of the plate gives the child a surface against which to

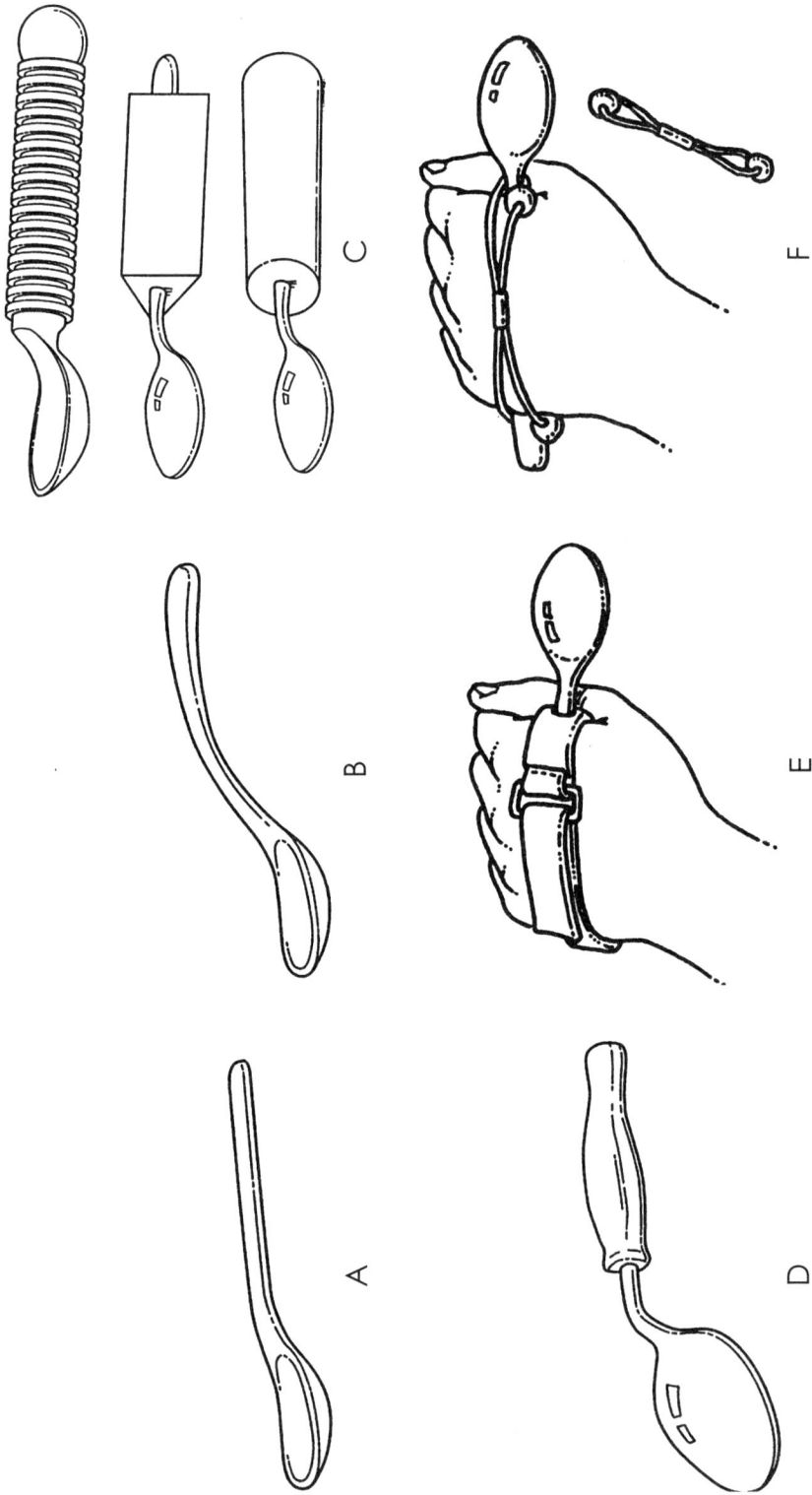

Figure 3. Different types of spoons and adaptations to aid in holding spoons: A) spoon with a flat bowl, B) spoon with a deep bowl, C) spoons with large handles, D) spoon with a bent handle, E) universal cuff, F) elastic handle made from a ponytail holder.

scoop food. If needed, a plate guard can also give the child a surface to hold onto for support. The "scoop dishes" illustrated in Figure 4 have suction cups underneath to stabilize them on the table (Case-Smith & Humphry, 1996). Nonskid pressure-sensitive pads, such as Dycem, can also be placed under the plate to prevent it from sliding around the table.

It is important to choose adaptive equipment that is appropriate for the child's environment. Putting a plate guard on a regular lunch tray may be more desirable than using a brightly colored adapted plate that is different from the ones used by the other children.

Sandwich Holder

A *sandwich holder* is a plastic holder that grips a sandwich; this unit can be inserted into a utensil holder that a child holds (Sammons Preston, 1997). A child will need assistance with placing the sandwich in the holder, but he or she can independently eat the sandwich once it has been placed in the holder.

HIGH-TECH ADAPTATIONS

A number of different types of mechanical feeders are commercially available: a ball-bearing feeder, a friction feeder, and a suspension feeder (Case-Smith, 1994; Case-Smith & Humphry, 1996; Erhardt & Merrill, 1998; Heller et al., 1996; Sammons Preston, 1997). Each of these feeders is appropriate for children with different needs. For example, a ball-bearing feeder may assist a child with hypotonia (i.e., low muscle tone) (Erhardt & Merrill, 1998). A ball-bearing feeder supports the weight of the child's arm, and ball bearings allow easier movement of the arm. A friction feeder is appropriate for students with spasticity, mild tremors, or ataxia. Friction bands at joints help control extraneous motion (Sammons Preston, 1997).

More sophisticated adapted equipment, such as the electric feeder shown in Figure 5, may enable a child to self-feed without using his or her arms (Case-Smith & Humphry, 1996; Garber, Gregorio, Pumphrey, & Lathem, 1994; Heller et al., 1996). Slight head motion on a chin switch activates a motorized pusher that fills the spoon and automatically moves the spoon toward the child's mouth.

ADAPTATIONS TO PROMOTE INDEPENDENT EATING

Next are two examples of simple adaptations that promote the child's ability to eat independently. In both of these cases, the feeding team problem-solved to determine the child's need, determined that appropriate equipment was not available commercially, and used handmade equipment that was just right for the individual child's need. Figure 6 shows a plate and glass holder used by a high school student who had difficulty coordinating hand-to-mouth movements. After many attempts to teach this student to bring the glass to his mouth were unsuccessful, the feeding team developed this adaptation that allowed the student to lean forward and drink from a straw. The surface of the holder was covered with a nonslip mat, and the glass was placed in the cutout hole. The student was able to lean forward and drink independently from a straw (York-Barr et al., 1996). Figure 7 illustrates a spoon splint and plate wedge adaptation used by a 4-year-old boy with lim-

A

B

Figure 4.   Scooper tableware: A) scooper plate and scooper bowl, B) scooper bowl. (Photographs courtesy of Sammons Preston.)

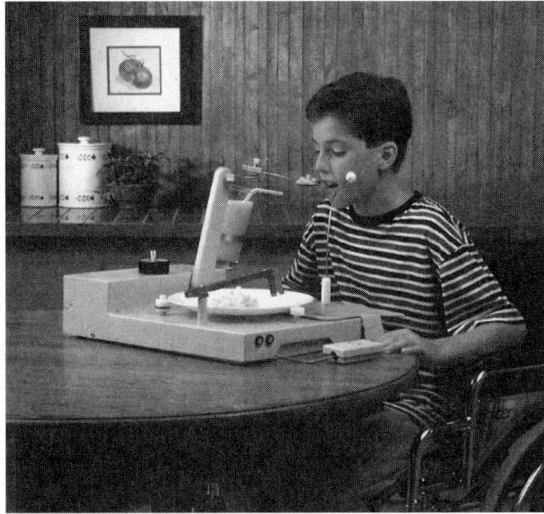

Figure 5.   Electric self-feeder. (Photograph courtesy of Sammons Preston.)

ited range of motion. A spoon was molded into the splint by the OT. The bent spoon protruded between the child's thumb and index finger. The plate wedge was made from cardboard and covered with nonslip material. The wedge was angled steeply enough for the child to use vertical arm movements. The child was independently able to scoop food that was thick enough or sticky enough to stay in the plate (York-Barr et al., 1996).

Figure 6.   Plate and glass holder. (Developed by Nancy Caldwell; From York-Barr, J., Rainforth, B., & Locke, P. [1996]. Developing instructional adaptations. In F.P. Orelove & D. Sobsey, *Educating children with multiple disabilities: A transdisciplinary approach* [3rd ed., p. 134]. Baltimore: Paul H. Brookes Publishing Co.; reprinted by permission.)

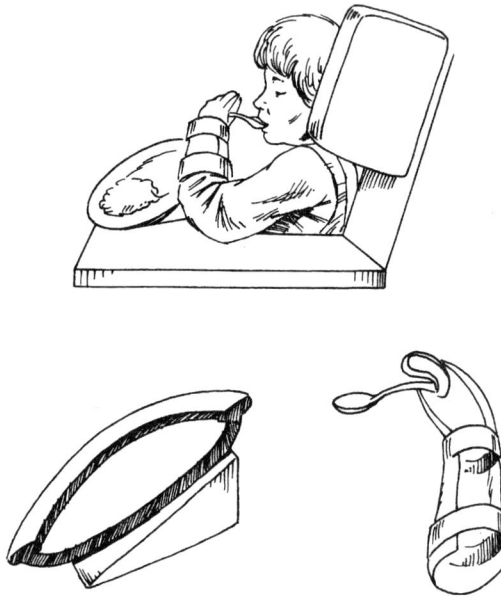

Figure 7.   Spoon splint and plate wedge adaptations (Developed by Jennifer York-Barr; From York-Barr, J., Rainforth, B., & Locke, P. [1996]. Developing instructional adaptations. In F.P. Orelove & D. Sobsey, *Educating children with multiple disabilities: A transdisciplinary approach* [3rd ed., p. 135]. Baltimore: Paul H. Brookes Publishing Co.; reprinted by permission.)

SUMMARY

This chapter presents a brief overview of the types of adapted equipment available to assist children with feeding and eating difficulties. It is important to remember that not all children with feeding difficulties need adaptive equipment; adaptive equipment should only be used when necessary and in the least intrusive manner possible. The decision to use adaptive equipment should be made by a feeding team that includes the educator, the therapists, the child, and the child's parents. Finally, adapted equipment does not have to be purchased commercially. Homemade adaptations can be the least expensive, easiest to use, and most appealing to the child and family.

Cary

Cary was an active and independent high school sophomore when he dove into a shallow pool and hit his head on the bottom, resulting in a C-3 quadriplegia spinal cord injury. Cary received comprehensive rehabilitation, including mouthstick training; he learned to turn pages of a book, type, and write (Garber et al., 1994). He also learned to direct another person verbally to feed him. Now a junior, Cary has returned to school. He chooses not to eat lunch in the school cafeteria. Cary has begun to think about life after high school—either going to college or living as independently as possible in his own apartment. For now, Cary is comfortable directing his mother to feed him at home. In the future, he wants to find a way to feed himself. He has asked for help in finding a way to feed himself.

- Why did Cary choose not to eat in the school cafeteria when he returned to school?
- What are your feelings about this choice? Was this decision appropriate for Cary's age?
- What factors need to be considered by the feeding team in preparation for Cary's transition to feeding himself?
- Will an electric self-feeder be an appropriate tool for Cary to use?

Cary apparently did not want his classmates to see someone feeding him, even though he was directing the interaction. Not wanting to appear "different" from classmates is age appropriate for a high school junior; in addition, not eating in school is a choice some high school students make. Unless there are specific issues relating to hydration and health, Cary's choice is fine.

An electric self-feeder would likely be an appropriate choice for Cary to use at home or in his own apartment; self-feeders are usually not portable enough to be used in a variety of environments. The team should consider the following issues in their discussions:

- Does Cary have the physical skills necessary (e.g., head control) to use a self-feeder?
- What type of self-feeder is best suited to Cary's specific physical abilities?
- Can Cary borrow an electric self-feeder to give him the opportunity to try one first before making a purchase?
- What resources are available to help pay for an electric self-feeder, which can cost several thousand dollars?
- What training will be required to teach Cary how to use a self-feeder?

REFERENCES

Campbell, P.H. (1993). Physical management and handling procedures. In M.E. Snell (Ed.), *Instruction of students with severe disabilities* (pp. 248–263). New York: Merrill.

Case-Smith, J. (1994). Self-care strategies for children with developmental deficits. In C. Christiansen (Ed.), *Ways of living: Self-care strategies for special needs* (pp. 101–156). Rockville, MD: American Occupational Therapy Association, Inc.

Case-Smith, J., & Humphry, R. (1996). Feeding and oral motor skills. In J. Case-Smith, A.S. Allen, & P.N. Pratt (Eds.), *Occupational therapy for children* (2nd ed., pp. 430–460). St. Louis: Mosby.

Erhardt, R.P., & Merrill, S.C. (1998). Neurological dysfunction in children. In M.E. Neistadt & E.B. Crepeau (Eds.), *Willard & Spackman's occupational therapy* (9th ed., pp. 582–607). Philadelphia: Lippincott-Raven Publishers.

Garber, S.L., Gregorio, T.L., Pumphrey, N., & Lathem, P. (1994). Self-care strategies for persons with spinal cord injuries. In C. Christiansen (Ed.), *Ways of living: Self-care strategies for special needs* (pp. 189–225). Rockville, MD: American Occupational Therapy Association, Inc.

Heller, K.W., Alberto, P.A., Forney, P.E., & Schwartzman, M.N. (1996). *Understanding physical, sensory, and health impairments: Characteristics and educational implications*. Pacific Grove, CA: Brooks/Cole Publishing Company.

Inge, K.J. (1992). Cerebral palsy. In P.J. McLaughlin & P. Wehman (Eds.), *Development disabilities: A handbook for best practices* (pp. 30–53). Boston: Andover Medical Publishers.

Klein, M.D., & Delaney, T.A. (1994). *Feeding and nutrition for the child with special needs: Handouts for parents.* San Antonio, TX: Therapy Skill Builders.

Morris, S.E. (1997). *Mealtimes: A resource for oral-motor, feeding and mealtime programs.* Faber, VA: New Visions.

Morris, S.E., & Klein, M.D. (1987). *Pre-feeding skills: A comprehensive resource for feeding.* San Antonio, TX: Therapy Skill Builders.

Orelove, F.P., & Sobsey, D. (1996). *Educating children with multiple disabilities: A transdisciplinary approach* (3rd ed.). Baltimore: Paul H. Brookes Publishing Co.

Reed, K.L. (1991). *Quick reference to occupational therapy.* Gaithersburg, MD: Aspen Publishers.

Sammons Preston. (1997). *Sammons Preston 1997: The premier source for rehabilitation professionals.* Bolingbrook, IL: Author.

York-Barr, J., Rainforth, B., & Locke, P. (1996). Developing instructional adaptations. In F.P. Orelove & D. Sobsey, *Educating children with multiple disabilities: A transdisciplinary approach* (3rd ed., pp. 119–159). Baltimore: Paul H. Brookes Publishing Co.

chapter nine

Behavior Strategies for Feeding

Dianne Koontz Lowman,
Mary Kientz, and Rebecca Anderson Weissman

Up to this point, the focus in this book has been on children with oral-motor feeding problems. This chapter focuses on feeding problems that are more behavioral in nature. Even though behavioral feeding problems are different in etiology, they can have a serious impact on children's health and growth, on interactions with caregivers, and on the enjoyment of mealtimes within families.

BACKGROUND INFORMATION

Before examining positive strategies for dealing with behavioral feeding problems, it is important to define the types of problems that are behavioral in nature and to understand why intervention is critical. In order to understand the need for positive strategies, a brief overview of intervention strategies utilized in the past is presented.

Types of Behavioral Feeding Problems

A review of the literature reveals a variety of feeding problems that are behavioral in nature, including food refusal, food selectivity by type or texture, mealtime tantrums, excessive meal duration, rumination, and pica (Babbitt, Hoch, & Coe, 1994). There are no exact prevalence statistics for children with developmental disabilities who have behavioral feeding problems; it has been estimated that as many as 50% of children with developmental disabilities also have behavioral feeding problems (Kedesdy & Budd, 1998). Behavioral feeding problems may be caused by a number of factors. Physical factors may include physiological abnormalities, neuromotor dysfunction, structural deficits, injury, mechanical obstruction, metabolic disorders, malabsorption problems, and food intolerance because of allergies (Babbitt et al., 1994; Luiselli & Luiselli, 1995). Another physical factor of behavioral feeding problems is apparent in the instances of children who are unable to orally receive sufficient nutrition for survival and who must depend on nonoral or tube feedings. Children who receive long-term tube feedings are at risk for developing a behavioral aversion to oral feedings (Foy, Czyzewski, Phillips, Ligon, Baldwin, & Klish, 1997). In addition, there are children with primarily medically based problems who are at risk for behavioral feeding problems. For example, rumination may first occur as a result of physical illness, but it may continue because of reinforcement (Babbitt et al., 1994; Christophersen & Hall, 1978). For this reason, behavioral factors should be considered during the assessment and treatment of most children with feeding problems, whether the problem originated as a medical or behavioral one (Babbitt et al., 1994). Last, behavioral feeding problems also can be caused by the feeding approaches of caregivers. Inappropriate feeding approaches include intrusive methods, forced feedings, excessive anxiety surrounding mealtimes, and behavioral mismanagement (Babbitt et al., 1994; Chatoor, 1997; Luiselli & Luiselli, 1995).

Rationale for Intervention

Behavioral feeding problems, whether common or rare, may have serious implications for nutrition and growth. The health and survival of the child may be compromised by inadequate nutritional intake. For example, long-term rumination of stomach acids can burn and damage the esophagus. Behavioral feeding problems can affect parent–child interactions by increasing parental anxiety about mealtimes (Babbitt et al., 1994). In addition, behavioral feeding problems such as food refusal, severe food selectivity, rumination, vomiting, and mealtime tantrums may interfere with the child's acceptance into an integrated environment such as child care, preschool, or school.

Intervention Strategies

A variety of behavior strategies have been employed in the past to deal with behavioral feeding problems; these strategies have been based in applied behavior analytic or learning theory approaches to intervention (Luiselli & Luiselli, 1995). Past behavior strategies have included positive reinforcement procedures, negative reinforcement procedures, prompting, modeling, extinction, and punishment (Babbitt et al., 1994). As described by Lovett (1996), behavior management techniques allow interveners (or adults) to act on how the behavior affects the adult rather than on what the child, who is exhibiting the behavior, might be trying to communicate. The following quotation from Dr. Lovett eloquently illustrates the problems with relying on behavior management techniques:

> If James becomes violently upset when people ask him why he is looking in the refrigerator, then I would be inclined to overlook mentioning it to him when he has the refrigerator door open. If he eats everyone else's food or eats until he makes himself sick, I might offer to make him a snack he enjoys before he goes into the kitchen or find something he likes doing that doesn't involve eating. If it seems he is eating out of boredom, anxiety, or for any of the many reasons that the rest of us eat when we aren't especially hungry, ignoring his behavior and the function it serves for him, or redirecting him to something that is irrelevant to him, seems pointless. The feeling and rationale that people need to be controlled distracts us from more compelling questions: Who loves this person? Is this person comfortable and happy living here? Are these people this person wants most to live with? These questions can create so much stress for service providers that it is often simpler—and not necessarily conscious—to ignore what people's behavior

is saying and control them simply to maintain business as usual. (Lovett, 1996, p. 57)

This chapter focuses on positive behavior strategies needed to address common as well as rare, yet serious, feeding problems not addressed in other chapters. First, the sensory-processing abilities of children who demonstrate the sensory basis of behavioral feeding problems are discussed. Behavioral issues discussed in this chapter include picky eating, refusing to eat, pica, and rumination. Children may demonstrate refusal to eat along a continuum from undereating to extreme food selectivity (i.e., picky eating) to total refusal to eat. *Pica* is the persistent eating of nonnutritive substances; children displaying this behavior typically eat paper, clothing, hair, and pebbles. *Rumination* is characterized by the regurgitation of food, which is then partially or completely rechewed, reswallowed, or expelled (Chatoor, 1997).

After a discussion of the child's sensory-processing abilities and their impact on behavior, positive behavior strategies to deal with behavioral feeding problems are explored. Literature describing the positive behavioral supports model, the communicative intent of behavior, and functional analysis of behavior (i.e., investigating the purpose or motivation behind the behavior) is presented. The last section of this chapter integrates the following information into the development of a behavioral support plan.

SENSORY-PROCESSING ABILITIES

As described in Chapter 6, children who demonstrate behaviors such as extreme food selectivity, picky eating, or refusal to eat may be doing so because of poor processing of sensory information. Other behaviors that may be indicative of poor sensory processing with feeding include spitting, choking, gagging, vomiting, pushing away (i.e., pushing the spoon or the adult's hand away, pushing him- or herself away from the situation), crying, and grimacing (Case-Smith & Humphry, 1996; Glass & Wolf, 1993). Other less obvious behaviors may include hitting, biting, and throwing food as a means to escape or change the feeding situation. As emphasized in the next section, this is why it is important for the feeder to determine the communicative function a behavior is serving the child. Behavior challenges, such as spitting or gagging, are frequently ways some children communicate a need for more or less oral stimulation from food or objects.

Children act in certain ways to seek or avoid sensory information to support their activities and performance (Dunn, 1997). As described in Chapter 6, the central nervous system regulates and modulates sensory stimuli to produce functional behaviors. If children do not modulate sensory information well (e.g., overrespond to sensory stimuli from a low-sensory threshold or underrespond to sensory stimuli from a high-sensory threshold), they may exhibit challenging behaviors. For example, a child needing more time or more stimuli to react may cram his mouth full of food because he needs the additional stimuli in his mouth to chew. A child who overresponds reacts more easily and readily to stimuli (Dunn, 1997). This child may be sensitive to touch, textures, tastes, and/or temperatures.

Based on how children react to sensory stimuli and their sensory thresholds, Dunn (1997) proposed four types of behavioral responses: 1) poor registration, 2) sensitivity to stimuli, 3) sensation seeking, and 4) sensation avoiding. The first behavior response type includes children who register sensory stimuli poorly. These children have difficulty registering stimuli because of high neurological thresholds; simply stated, they need more stimuli to react (Dunn, 1997). These children are often difficult to engage or appear withdrawn, and they may have poor endurance. They frequently need highly contrasting or novel stimuli to become involved in an activity (Dunn, 1997). When dealing with children who have difficulty registering stimuli while feeding, one should increase the contrast or novelty during mealtimes (e.g., use different colored bowls, change the environment to be more active, use new tastes and textures) as means to provide more stimuli.

The second behavior response type is comprised of those children who are sensitive to stimuli. They tend to be distractible, or they may have difficulty learning from their experience because they cannot block out stimuli to maintain attention (Dunn, 1997). These children respond to the use of calming techniques, such as the deep touch pressure described in Chapter 6.

The third behavior response type is comprised of those children who are sensory-seeking (i.e., children who have difficulty registering stimuli but counteract by seeking many sensory experiences) (Dunn, 1997). These children are the ones who may move constantly, chew on appropriate and inappropriate objects, or have a need to touch everything. It frequently benefits these children to be provided with the sensory stimuli they are seeking throughout their daily activities (Dunn, 1997). For example, children who mouth objects constantly because they are seeking proprioceptive input may benefit from chewing gum, eating snacks that are hard or crunchy (e.g., hard pretzels, carrots), or sucking on hard candies. These examples are ways these children can get oral input effectively throughout the day and ways educators can decrease in a positive way the challenging behavior of mouthing objects.

The fourth behavior response type is comprised of those children who act out in order to avoid sensation (Dunn, 1997). These children may be unwilling to try activities or participate in activities, especially those that are new and unpredictable, because they are trying to avoid overstimulation. They may avoid situations that they find uncomfortable. For example, a child who is sensitive to the tactile stimuli associated with feeding may scream or have a tantrum to try to avoid eating when he sees the spoon. These children often develop rituals while performing tasks that are thought to provide an acceptable pattern for them (Dunn, 1997). It is very helpful for the feeder to look at the rituals in which the child engages because the features of these rituals can offer information about the sensory stimuli the child seeks or avoids, which is helpful in planning intervention.

Teachers are encouraged to consult therapists to identify whether a child who is displaying behavioral feeding problems may have difficulty processing sensory input. If so, one way to assist the child is to examine closely the sensory features of the feeding or mealtime activity. Figure 1 allows the feeder to look at a routine task and determine the sensory qualities that the task entails (Dunn, 1996). For example, for a child who is hypersensitive with feeding, the feeder may find that objects and people in the environment influence the child's performance. The child may get more aroused in the cafeteria with its loud noises, large spaces, and bright lights than in the class-

ROUTINE/TASK SENSORY CHARACTERISTICS		WHAT DOES THE TASK ROUTINE HOLD?			WHAT DOES THE PARTICULAR ENVIRONMENT HOLD?	WHAT ADAPTATIONS ARE LIKELY TO IMPROVE FUNCTIONAL OUTCOME?
		A	B	C		
Somatosensory	light touch (tap, tickle)					
	pain					
	temperature (hot, cold)					
	touch-pressure (hug, pat, grasp)					
	variable					
	duration of stimulus (short, long)					
	body surface contact (small, large)					
	predictable					
	unpredictable					
Vestibular	head position change					
	speed change					
	direction change					
	rotary head movement					
	linear head movement					
	repetitive head movement-rhythmic					
	predictable					
	unpredictable					
Proprioceptive	quick stretch stimulus					
	sustained tension stimulus					
	shifting muscle tension					
Visual	high intensity					
	low intensity					
	high contrast					
	high similarity (low contrast)					
	competitive					
	variable					
	predictable					
	unpredictable					
Auditory	rhythmic					
	variable					
	constant					
	competitive					
	noncompetitive					
	loud					
	soft					
	predictable					
	unpredictable					
Olfactory/ Gustatory	mild					
	strong					
	predictable					
	unpredictable					

Task _____

Components: A = _____
B = _____
C = _____

Figure 1. Form for analyzing the sensory characteristics of task performance. (From Dunn, W. [1996]. The sensorimotor systems: A framework for assessment and intervention. In F.P. Orelove & D. Sobsey, *Educating children with multiple disabilities: A transdisciplinary approach* [3rd ed., p. 67]. Baltimore: Paul H. Brookes Publishing Co.; reprinted by permission.)

159

room, with its quiet noises, small spaces, and dimmer lights. He may tolerate more textures and feeding for a longer period of time, however, when he eats in a quieter and dimmer environment.

The form for analyzing the sensory characteristics of task performance (Figure 1) helps problem-solve to find the difficulty in performing a task and, therefore, helps decrease challenging behavior. If the basis of a behavior is thought to be sensory, this form can assist in analyzing the sensory qualities of the task, environment, and the child's interactions with others and objects (Dunn, 1996). A routine task is selected, and how a typical child under typical circumstances would complete the task is considered. The sensory qualities that are involved in the task are marked in the second column of the worksheet. The next three columns (A, B, and C) are provided to break down the task if it is complex. The next column takes into consideration the specific environment in which the child will perform the task. Using the previous example of the child eating in the cafeteria, it would be indicated in this column where the child is eating (e.g., in the cafeteria, in class), whether there are others (e.g., students, teachers) around, whether the child is finger feeding or using an eating utensil, what he is eating, and so forth. The last column in the form is provided to help the educator create intervention strategies and consider all possible modifications. Modifications, such as providing deep pressure input prior to the child's eating and having the child eat in a quieter environment, would be considered. The feeding team then changes one aspect at a time and notes any changes in the child's performance.

POSITIVE BEHAVIORAL STRATEGIES

Behavioral feeding problems within the context of the positive behavioral supports model are examined in this chapter. Two key components of this model, using person-centered planning and determining the communicative intent of the behavior, are discussed next.

Positive Behavioral Supports Model

The positive behavioral supports model emerged from the behavior management of the 1980s and was developed to help children with disabilities with methods that

- Are effective in changing undesirable patterns of behavior

- Are respectful of the child's dignity

- Are successful in promoting the child's capabilities, in expanding opportunities, and enhancing the quality of life (Koegel, Koegel, & Dunlap, 1996)

- Avoid the use of punishment (Anderson, 1990)

Before proceeding with more detail on the positive behavioral supports model, it is important to review the reasons punishment is not effective. All behavior occurs for a reason. *Punishment* is defined as any aversive action delivered with the "intent" of stopping a specific behavior (including timeout). Punishment does not work because it does not identify the communicative intent behind the child's behavior, and it does not teach a better way to resolve the problem for the learner. With punishment, the emphasis is on external versus internal controls of behavior for the learner. Punishment causes social disruption with relationships, and it does not generalize across people or environments. Punishment also increases the probability of aggression. Most important, the punished behavior (or similar behavior that expresses the child's identified "need") always recurs, so the punisher always needs to punish, which creates a negative interaction cycle. This negative interaction cycle occurs because the punisher is "lulled" into thinking that punishment works because the punisher is rewarded with a brief suppression of the problem behavior. This brief suppression is very temporary, at best, and does not teach a positive way for the learner to solve the problem. This is the reason it is so important for the educator to put extra effort into positive behavioral supports rather than punishment (Anderson, 1990). Essential features of the positive behavioral supports model are illustrated in Figure 2.

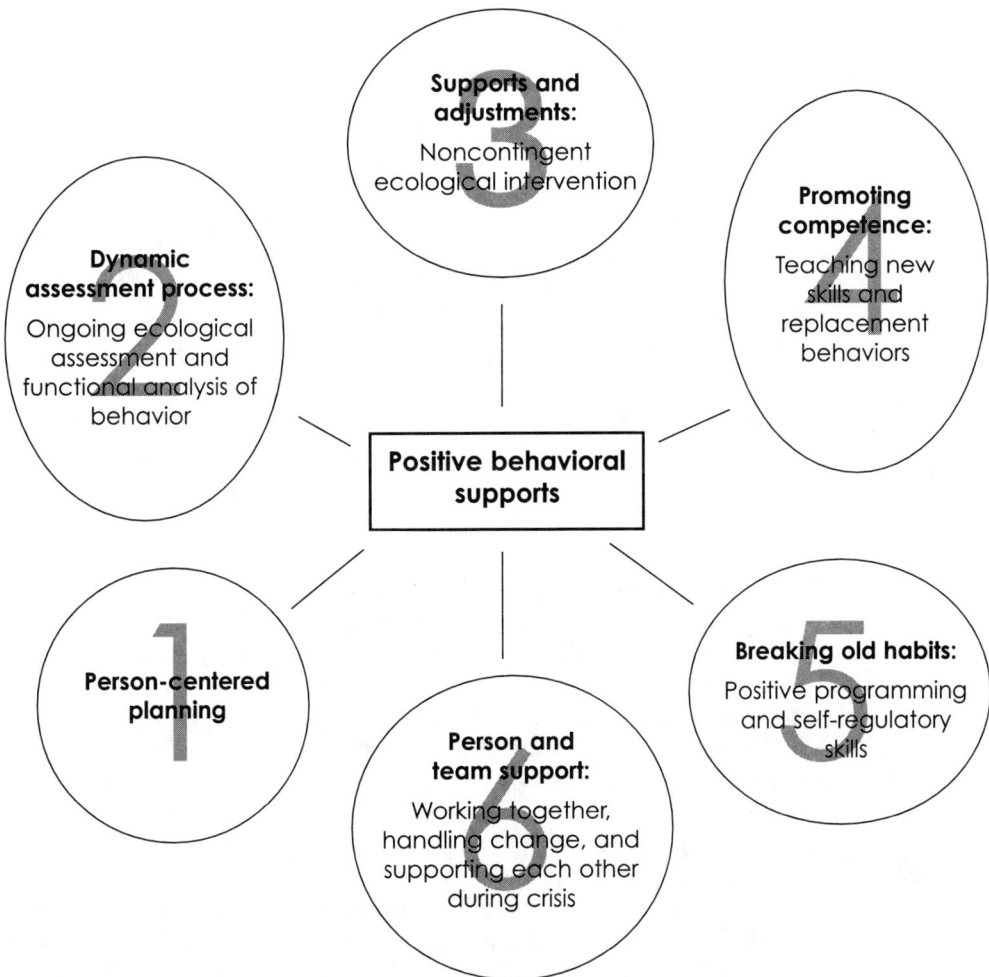

Figure 2. Positive behavioral supports model. (From Virginia Institute for Developmental Disabilities [1997]. *Positive behavioral support training module*. Richmond: Author; adapted by permission.)

The positive behavioral supports model is grounded in person-centered values. The assessment process is dynamic and ongoing, utilizing ecological assessment and a functional analysis of behavior. There is a commitment to multiple interventions and outcomes that are meaningful and that promote competence. The child and the feeding team are supported by multiple strategies (Koegel et al., 1996).

Person-Centered Planning

Person-centered planning is a process of learning how a person wants to live and then describing what needs to be done to help that person move toward that life (Smull, 1996). The life the person wants is the outcome rather than the plan. Good plans are rooted in what is important to the person while taking into consideration all of the other factors that have an impact on that person's life (e.g., the disability, the views of others around the person, the opportunities, the limitations presented by public funding) (Smull, 1996). Essential outcomes of person-centered planning include

- Participating in community life

- Maintaining satisfying relationships

- Expressing preferences and making choices in everyday life

- Having the opportunity to live with dignity

- Continuing to develop personal competencies (Kincaid, 1996)

What has been learned is that, with careful planning and implementation, most of the behaviors that have been labeled as "noncompliant, challenging," or "problem" behaviors go away when what is important to the person is present (Smull, 1996).

Communicative Intent of Behavior

Problem behaviors usually serve a purpose for the child (Carr et al., 1994; Meyer & Evans, 1989). Other phrases used to describe this concept include "the communicative intent of behavior" or "the need the behavior communicates."

All behaviors occur for a reason. The behaviors considered to be "problem" behaviors can be an effective strategy to accomplish something that the child needs or wants. Therefore, if the behavior serves a purpose for the child, the purpose must be identified in order for 1) the child's need to be addressed and 2) the problem behavior to be replaced with a more appropriate behavior (Meyer & Evans, 1989). Carr and Durand (1985) originally categorized problem behaviors according to three functions: 1) to gain something (e.g., attention, interaction, socialization), 2) to escape or avoid something (e.g., tangible object, interaction), or 3) to gain sensory or automatic effects that cannot be observed directly (e.g., self-regulatory effects) (Wacker, Berg, Harding, & Asmus, 1996). In addition, sometimes the purpose of the behavior is to play; the child may just like doing it. Functional analysis is the process used to identify the purpose of the child's behavior (Carr et al., 1994). Because problem behaviors may serve more than one purpose, multiple interventions may be needed. For example, crying during the meal may mean

Refusal—"I don't want this."

Request—"I want more."

Socialization—"Please talk to me."

Protest—"This just burned my tongue."

Sensory—"This feels awful in my mouth."

Once the purpose(s) of the child's behavior have been identified, the goal of intervention is to teach the child a replacement skill or a new way to meet his or her need (e.g., teaching the child to shake his head NO for a refusal).

FUNCTIONAL ANALYSIS

Functional analysis is a process of understanding the child's strengths, inclinations, and communication strategies. It is an assessment process that examines the stimuli and circumstances within the environment that influence a child's behavior. Based on the information gathered, hypotheses regarding the stimuli and circumstances influencing the child's behavior are then tested. The steps in conducting a functional analysis are described next (Carr et al., 1994; Meyer & Evans, 1989; O'Neill et al., 1997; Wacker et al., 1996).

Step 1: Identify the Target Behavior

The first step in a functional analysis is to identify the target behavior. Not all behaviors are "problem behaviors" that need to be changed. The following questions can assist the educator in deciding whether the child's behaviors should be changed (Weiss, 1980):

1.   Is the behavior potentially dangerous to the child or others?

2.   Does the behavior necessitate artificial means of control (e.g., medication, restraint)?

3.   Does the behavior interfere with the child's ability to learn new skills?

4.   Does the behavior impede the child's participation in integrated community activities?

5.   Is there agreement among feeding team members, family, advocates, and the child with the disability with regard to the need for change?

Step 2: Identify Circumstances of the Behavior's Occurrence

The second step in the functional analysis is to identify when, where, and under what circumstances the behavior is likely to occur and not occur. The Functional Analysis Observation Form in Figure 3 is one way to gather this information. This form allows the observer to collect the following data: 1) a frequency count of the behavior, 2) information on the times of day and the environments in which the behavior occurs, 3) information on the times of day and environments in which the behavior is not occurring, and 4) a record of the consequences being provided for the behaviors (O'Neill et al., 1997).

Step 3: Study the Child's History and Personal Attributes

In addition to directly observing the child's behavior, it is important to study the child's history, learning, and unique personal attributes in order to iden-

164

Person: _____ _____ to _____

Functional Analysis Observation Form

Time	Behaviors		Setting Events/Discriminative Stimuli								Perceived Functions									Actual Conseq.		
						Difficult task	Transition (task-task)	Transition (settings)	Interruption	Alone (no attention)				Get/Obtain				Escape/Avoid			Comments: (If nothing happened in period, write initials)	
	Demand/Request										Don't know/unclear	Attention	Desired item/Activity	Self-stimulation	Demand/Request	Activity ( )	Person ( )	Attention					

Figure 3. Functional analysis observation form. (From O'Neill et al., Functional assessment and program development for problem behavior: A practical handbook. © 1997 Brooks/Cole Publishing Company, Pacific Grove, CA. Used by permission of Wadsworth Publishing Co.)

tify other factors that may be contributing to the child's behavior. Caregivers can be interviewed about related factors that may affect the behavior by using the Functional Analysis Interview (O'Neill et al., 1997). Topics addressed during this interview include the child's medications, sleep cycles, eating routine and diet, predictability of activities, opportunity to make choices, variety of activities, density of people, staffing patterns, activities that are rewarding or pleasant, and activities that are unpleasant.

In addition, it is important to gather information about what the child's family wants and views as important. The Interview Protocol (Albin, Lucyshyn, Horner, & Flannery, 1996) is utilized to gather information aimed at understanding family characteristics, family values and goals, the way the family has constructed mealtimes, and the family's visions of successful meals.

Step 4: Identify Communicative Functions of the Behavior

Identify possible communicative functions of the child's problem behavior. The Functional Analysis Observation Form in Figure 3 is one tool for directing the observation of communication functions of behavior. The "Perceived Functions" and "Actual Consequences" sections of this form can assist in the identification of the purpose(s) of the child's behavior and what consequences are maintaining the behavior. In addition to direct observation, caregivers can be interviewed regarding the types of responses used by the child. An observation tool for analyzing the communicative functions of behaviors, which is shown in Figure 4, is another way to determine responses and possible functions (Donnellan, Mirenda, Mesaros, & Fassbender, 1984). When gathering information about communicative functions of behavior, it is important to observe the child regularly over time and across a variety of environments and situations. Ultimately, the observer wants to answer the questions "What is the motivation for the behavior?" and "What purpose is it serving?"

Step 5: Form a Hypothesis for the Behavior

Form a hypothesis regarding the function the child's behavior serves. Conduct a "function test" to test the hypothesis. For example, a function test for a child who ruminates after meals could take many forms, depending on the motivation underlying the behavior (i.e., the purpose the behavior is serving). A hypothesis must be based on extensive observation and caregiver interviews. Suppose the hypothesis is that the ruminating meets a *sensory* need. In this instance, the ruminating will decrease or stop only when the child's sensory need is met. Does the ruminating behavior decrease or stop when the child is given something more pleasurable or stimulating (from his or her perspective)? Does chewing on licorice or therapy tubing after meals decrease the behavior (the child must like this *more* than ruminating)? If not, after a few trials, move on to another hypothesis. Other example hypotheses include

Hunger (i.e., The child is ruminating to increase his or her sense of satiety while craving something tangible, like more food)

Escape (i.e., Does the child want to be left alone and successfully gains solitude by ruminating, or does the child find the feeding situation too overwhelming?)

FUNCTIONS \ BEHAVIORS	◆AGGRESSION	◆BIZARRE VERBALIZATIONS	◆INAPP. ORAL / ANAL BEHAVIOR	◆PERSEVERATIVE RITUALS	◆SELF-INJURIOUS BEHAVIOR	◆SELF-STIMULATION	◆TANTRUM	◆FACIAL EXPRESSION	◆GAZE AVERSION	◆GAZING / STARING	◆GESTURING / POINTING	◆HUGGING / KISSING	◆MASTURBATION	◆OBJECT MANIPULATION	◆PROXIMITY POSITIONING	◆PUSHING / PULLING	◆REACHING / GRABBING	◆RUNNING	◆TOUCHING	◆DELAYED ECHOLALIA	◆IMMEDIATE ECHOLALIA	◆LAUGHING / GIGGLING	◆SCREAM / YELL	◆SWEARING	◆VERBAL / PHYSICAL THREATS	◆WHINING / CRYING	◆COMPLEX SIGN / APPROXIMATION	◆COMPLEX SPEECH / APPROXIMATION	◆ONE WORD SIGN / APPROXIMATION	◆ONE WORD SPEECH / APPROXIMATION	◆PICTURE / WRITTEN WORD
I. INTERACTIVE																															
A. REQUESTS FOR Attention																															
Social Interaction																															
Play Interactions																															
Affection																															
Permission to Engage in an Activity																															
Action by Receiver																															
Assistance																															
Information / Clarification																															
Objects																															
Food																															
B. NEGATIONS Protest																															
Refusal																															
Cessation																															
C. DECLARATIONS / COMMENTS About Events / Actions																															
About Objects / Persons																															
About Errors / Mistakes																															
Affirmation																															
Greeting																															
Humor																															
D. DECLARATIONS ABOUT FEELINGS Anticipation																															
Boredom																															
Confusion																															
Fear																															
Frustration																															
Hurt Feelings																															
Pain																															
Pressure																															
II. NON-INTERACTIVE																															
A. SELF-REGULATION																															
B. REHEARSAL																															
C. HABITUAL																															
D. RELAXATION / TENSION RELEASE																															

Student: _____   Date: _____   Time: _____

Activity: _____

Figure 4.   Observation tool for analyzing the communicative functions of behaviors. (From Donnellan, A.M., Mirenda, P.L., Mesaros, R.A., & Fassbender, L.L. [1984]. Analyzing the communicative functions of aberrant behavior. *Journal of The Association for Persons with Severe Handicaps*, 9[3], 201–212; reprinted by permission.)

Attention (i.e., Does the child enjoy the "fuss" he or she receives from ruminating?)

Combination of all of the above

In a hypothesis, or function, test, the adult gives the child an abundance of the perceived need that the behavior is serving and looks for a decrease in the undesirable behavior. The function test is a very critical step in determining what new skill to teach the child.

Step 6: Develop the Behavioral Support Plan

Once the function test is successfully complete, the next step is to develop the behavioral support plan. At this point, all feeding team members involved should be aware that all behaviors occur for a reason, and the team members have completed all of the previous steps in the functional analysis.

BEHAVIORAL SUPPORT PLAN

The Behavioral Support Plan addresses multiple components, including ecological intervention, preventive strategies (usually manipulating antecedent variables), teaching new skills, effective consequences, and emergency procedures to prevent injury (Lucyshyn, Horner, & Ben, 1996). The Behavioral Support Plan may address one or all three components of a behavior: 1) antecedents, 2) behavior, and 3) consequences (Horner, O'Neill, & Flannery, 1993). If the antecedent is causing the behavior, the educator should alter something in the environment to preclude the occurrence of the behavior. In order to address the child's actual behavior, the educator can teach an alternative or replacement behavior or skill to serve the same purpose. Next, the educator needs to alter the consequences in order to strengthen or weaken the child's behavior. A collaborative team approach is imperative to address all issues and to develop a plan that not only looks at eliminating behaviors but also enhances a child's lifestyle. The collaborative team needs to listen and learn from each other about what has and has not worked for the child and specifics about each environment (Lucyshyn et al., 1996). A good support plan begins with the child's strengths and skills and then builds, including addressing issues not only related to the child but also related to the people implementing the plan and issues related to the environment (Albin et al., 1996; Horner et al., 1993).

When developing a behavioral support plan, context cannot be overlooked. Behavior and performance cannot be understood without looking at the context in which the behavior occurs (Albin et al., 1996; Carr, Reeve, & Magito-McLaughlin, 1996; Dunn, Brown, & McGuigan, 1994; Horner, Vaughn, Day, & Ard, 1996). A partial list of contextual factors to consider is included in Table 1. Manipulating something in the child's environment may prevent the occurrence of the child's behavior.

Because all behaviors serve a purpose, it is important that the educator never extinguish a behavior without first teaching a new skill or replacement behavior to serve the same purpose. If the function test determines a *sensory* need, the skill to teach the child might be how to chew on a given favorite object that meets his or her sensory needs. If this component (i.e., teaching a replacement skill) does not occur, ruminating will surely return. If *hunger*

Table 1. Factors to consider to ensure a contextual fit with the behavioral support plan

Child's expectations of the environment
Expectations of others concerning the child and mealtimes
Nature of materials
Nature of mealtime/feeding activity
Nature of instructions
Number of other children and students
Number of other adults
Behavior of other children
Environmental pollutants
Time of day
Student's physiological state
Effects of pain, fatigue, aversive events, and so forth
Length of mealtimes
Sudden changes in mealtime feeding activity, schedule, environment, or staff
Behavior of others toward child
Activity just completed
Activity to follow
Recent changes at home
Student's social ability
Communication system(s) used
Student's adaptive ability

is the actual motivation for the rumination, the feeding team might alter the child's diet with the help of a nutritionist and simultaneously teach the child to become aware of his or her hunger and communicate it to others. (School lunches are rarely suitable for children with severe disabilities or extreme behaviors.) If escaping the feeding situation is the motivation for the child's behavior, the feeding team might provide a more peaceful mealtime environment in terms of noise level and slower pace as well as teach the child to request a break or indicate that he or she is finished eating. If the motivation for the undesired behavior is attention, the feeding team can work out a plan to increase the child's receipt of attention while feeding as well as teach the child appropriate methods for asking for attention (e.g., the new skill taught must be more successful at meeting the child's attention needs than the ruminating). In most cases, a combination of strategies that are specific to the child's needs are employed in a behavior plan. It is important to change or add only one component at a time so it is easy to identify and maintain successful components.

A final step in completing the behavioral support plan is the maintenance and generalization plan, including generalization strategies across different environments, people, and materials as well as eventual elimination of the behavioral support plan. An example of a behavioral support plan is included in the vignette at the end of this chapter.

SUMMARY

Behavioral feeding problems have a serious impact on a child's health and growth, interactions with family members, and enjoyment of mealtimes. In order to gain a complete understanding of a child's behaviors, a functional analysis of the child's feeding difficulties is recommended. The functional analysis should include an examination of the child's ability to process sensory input and the communicative intent of the child's behavior. The result of the functional analysis is the development of a behavioral support plan.

Frank

Frank is 15 years old and recently began a new vocational program connected with his school program. Frank is good with his hands and usually likes doing simple assembly activities, such as folding towels sent to the vocational center by a nearby hotel. Frank has mental retardation requiring extensive support as well as serious limitations with both his vision and hearing. His mode of communication has always been a tactile sign language, such as stroking his throat in a downward fashion when he is thirsty.

Recently, Frank started ruminating daily after lunch. The vocational staff was puzzled by this new behavior. In order to do an in-depth assessment, or functional analysis, the vocational staff, the school staff, and Frank's family agreed to meet. Questions included

- What was the motivation behind Frank's ruminating, and what need was it meeting?

- In which environments does the ruminating occur? Was it occurring only after lunch in the vocational environment?

- What events occurred immediately prior to Frank's rechewing and then again swallowing his food?

- What happens immediately after Frank begins ruminating?

- What was the frequency and duration of the ruminating?

As a result of this preliminary meeting, data were collected over several days. The motivation for Frank's ruminating was not obvious, even after much observation across different environments. At this time, the ruminating occurred only in the vocational environment after lunch (the only meal provided there), although Frank's parents reported prior episodes occurring in Frank's early childhood. Frank's parents also reported that the behavior went away at that time without ever knowing why it occurred. The only event immediately prior to the target behavior was eating lunch itself. Frank ruminated for one episode each day for an average of 20 minutes over 3 days of data collection. Once Frank began ruminating, staff response was mixed. Some staff members avoided Frank, and some staff members gave Frank repeated verbal cues to stop, which were not effective. Frank also was not given any more towels to fold until his ruminating ceased.

At the next meeting with Frank's parents and the vocational and school staff, collected data were reviewed and discussed. The team brainstormed hypotheses for the motivation behind Frank's behavior. Did the ruminating bring Frank desired attention? The team felt that it probably did not because Frank is a bit of a loner. Although he does not turn attention away, he rarely seeks it except when hungry or thirsty. Could the ruminating be motivated by escape? Frank wasn't given any towels to fold until he was finished eating. If this was Frank's motivation, the team hypothesized, a fun activity immediately after lunch should cease his behavior. The team decided to try offering Frank tactile books immediately after lunch. Frank enjoyed touching and exploring different textures as the school staff told a story. This "hypothesis test" was given a try during the next 3 days with no results. Frank enjoyed his books but kept ruminating. If this hypothesis test had been successful, Frank would have stopped the ruminating in preference of the alternative activity.

The team also came up with another hypothesis to try. If the ruminating was sensory-motivated, in terms of taste, the team members could give Frank a wider choice of foods to select at lunch. Prior to each lunchtime, Frank was given a choice of at least three different foods. Because Frank's only method of selecting food was to smell it, those foods not selected were wasted. Although wasteful, it was Frank's only way to have more choice about what he ate. The team made an interesting discovery here. Although Frank did refuse some of the choices presented to him, he ate two servings of food most days. With enough food to satiate his hunger, he stopped ruminating. Although more work for everyone was involved, it clearly was in Frank's best interest to provide him with enough food along with a reasonable number of choices of food. The lunch provided by the vocational center was not typically Frank's favorite foods, and the quantity of lunch served was not enough for Frank.

Clearly, Frank was hungry and did not like some of his lunch choices; therefore, he was ruminating to ''feel'' more full. Now that the question of motivation behind Frank's ruminating was solved, how would the feeding team provide Frank's identified needs? At the next team meeting, the school staff reported what foods had been Frank's preferences in this prior environment. The vocational staff agreed to continue collecting data on which lunches Frank chose most frequently and to use some of their petty cash fund to keep extra food available for him as well as for other students. Frank's mother agreed to keep a close eye on the vocational program's lunch menu and to send a large bag lunch with Frank on days that the staff indicated that the planned lunch menu was not one of Frank's favorites, thereby providing Frank with an additional food choice.

Now that the functional analysis portion of his behavioral plan was complete and the environment was better tailored to meet Frank's needs, it was time to look toward selecting a new skill to teach Frank. Hopefully, during Frank's next transition, perhaps to employment, Frank can indicate his need for more food. All team members agree that teaching Frank the MORE sign (i.e., touching his two fists together for more food) would be beneficial because it is widely understood and would result in Frank's getting his needs met faster in a new environment. Team members contributed to the development of an educational plan, and all staff in all environments were trained to implement the MORE communication program for Frank.

The alternative desired behavior of learning to communicate MORE was successful because of Frank's internal desires and need for more food as well as the staff members' consistency in providing more food promptly when Frank requested it. In an effort to increase the strength of the behavioral support plan, tactile reinforcement was added for encouragement. This additional strategy included a pat on the back when Frank asked for more food as well as promptly providing his requested food. If the prompt response to Frank's request had not occurred, it is likely that Frank would have continued to ruminate for a sensation of satiety. To Frank, it was the best way to solve his problem until the team found a successful strategy to replace it with that was more effective rather than less effective from Frank's perspective.

The final step for success is generalization of Frank's new skill. The ultimate success of a behavioral support plan is not to need it. As the sign for MORE is utilized successfully at Frank's school, home, community at large, and the vocational program, this training can be systematically reduced.

PRACTICE EXERCISE

. . . .

- What philosophical orientation led to such a dignified method of addressing Frank's rumination behavior?
- Why is it so important to put the effort into functional analysis, or an in-depth assessment, of the motivation of the target behavior? How successful is a behavioral support plan without a functional analysis likely to be? Why?
- Why is it important to complete the hypotheses tests before beginning the behavioral support plan?
- Why teach an alternative desired behavior?
- Why add strategies, such as positive reinforcement?
- Why plan for systematic generalization as part of the behavioral support plan?

REFERENCES

Albin, R.W., Lucyshyn, J.M., Horner, R.H., & Flannery, K.B. (1996). Contextual fit for behavioral support plans: A model for "goodness of fit." In L.K. Koegel, R.L. Koegel, & G. Dunlap (Eds.), *Positive behavioral support: Including people with difficult behavior in the community* (pp. 81–98). Baltimore: Paul H. Brookes Publishing Co.

Anderson, J.L. (1990). *Research and training center on community referenced nonaversive behavior management trainer's manual.* Eugene: University of Oregon.

Babbitt, R.L., Hoch, T.A., & Coe, D.A. (1994). Behavioral feeding disorders. In D.N. Tuchman & R.S. Walter (Eds.), *Disorders of feeding and swallowing in infants and children: Pathophysiology, diagnosis, and treatment* (pp. 77–95). San Diego, CA: Singular Publishing Group.

Carr, E.G., & Durand, V.M. (1985). Reducing behavior problems through functional communication training. *Journal of Applied Behavior Analysis, 18,* 111–126.

Carr, E.G., Levin, L., McConnachie, G., Carlson, J.I., Kemp, D.C., & Smith, C.E. (1994). *Communication-based intervention for problem behavior: A user's guide for producing positive change.* Baltimore: Paul H. Brookes Publishing Co.

Carr, E.G., Reeve, C.E., & Magito-McLaughlin, D. (1996). Contextual influences on problem behavior in people with developmental disabilities. In L.K. Koegel, R.L. Koegel, & G. Dunlap (Eds.), *Positive behavioral support: Including people with difficult behavior in the community* (pp. 403–423). Baltimore: Paul H. Brookes Publishing Co.

Case-Smith, J., & Humphry, R. (1996). Feeding and oral-motor skills. In J. Case-Smith, A.S. Allen, & P.N. Pratt (Eds.), *Occupational therapy for children* (3rd ed., pp. 430–460). St. Louis: Mosby.

Chatoor, I. (1997). Feeding disorders of infants and toddlers. In S. Greenspan, S. Wieder, & J. Osofsky (Eds.), *Handbook of child and adolescent psychiatry: Volume I. Infants and preschoolers: Development and syndromes* (pp. 367–386). New York: John Wiley & Sons.

Christophersen, E.R., & Hall, C.L. (1978). Eating patterns and associated problems encountered in normal children. *Issues in Comprehensive Pediatric Nursing, 3,* 1–16.

Donnellan, A.M., Mirenda, P.L., Mesaros, R.A., & Fassbender, L.L. (1984). Analyzing the communicative functions of aberrant behavior. *JASH, 9*(3), 201–212.

Dunn, W. (1996). The sensorimotor systems: A framework for assessment and intervention. In F.P. Orelove & D. Sobsey, *Educating children with multiple disabilities: A transdisciplinary approach* (3rd ed., pp. 35–78). Baltimore: Paul H. Brookes Publishing Co.

Dunn, W. (1997). The impact of sensory processing abilities on the daily lives of young children and their families: A conceptual model. *Infants and Young Children, 9*(4), 23–35.

Dunn, W., Brown, C., & McGuigan, A. (1994). The ecology of human performance: A performance framework for considering the effect of context. *The American Journal of Occupational Therapy, 48*(7), 595–607.

Foy, T., Czyzewski, D., Phillips, S., Ligon, B., Baldwin, J., & Klish, W. (1997). Treatment of severe feeding refusal in infants and toddlers. *Infants and Young Children, 9*(3), 26–35.

Glass, R.P., & Wolf, L.S. (1993). Feeding and oral-motor skills. In J. Case-Smith (Ed.), *Pediatric occupational therapy and early intervention* (pp. 225–288). Boston: Andover Medical Publishers.

Horner, R.H., O'Neill, R.E., & Flannery, K.B. (1993). Effective behavior support plans. In M.E. Snell (Ed.), *Instruction of students with severe disabilities* (4th ed., pp. 184–214). New York: Merrill.

Horner, R.H., Vaughn, B.J., Day, H.M., & Ard, W.R. (1996). The relationship between setting events and problem behavior. In L.K. Koegel, R.L. Koegel, & G. Dunlap (Eds.), *Positive behavioral support: Including people with difficult behavior in the community* (pp. 381–402). Baltimore: Paul H. Brookes Publishing Co.

Kedesdy, J.H., & Budd, K.S. (1998). *Childhood feeding disorders: Biobehavioral assessment and intervention.* Baltimore: Paul H. Brookes Publishing Co.

Kincaid, D. (1996). Person-centered planning. In L.K. Koegel, R.L. Koegel, & G. Dunlap (Eds.), *Positive behavioral support: Including people with difficult behavior in the community* (pp. 439–465). Baltimore: Paul H. Brookes Publishing Co.

Koegel, L.K., Koegel, R.L., & Dunlap, G. (Eds.). (1996). *Positive behavioral support: Including people with difficult behavior in the community.* Baltimore: Paul H. Brookes Publishing Co.

Lovett, H. (1996). *Learning to listen: Positive approaches and people with difficult behavior.* Baltimore: Paul H. Brookes Publishing Co.

Lucyshyn, J.M., Horner, R.H., & Ben, K.R. (1996, July). Positive behavior support with families. *TASH Newsletter, 22*(7), 10–12.

Luiselli, J.K., & Luiselli, T.E. (1995). A behavioral analysis approach toward chronic food refusal in children with gastrostomy-tube dependency. *Topics in Early Childhood Special Education, 15*(1), 1–18.

Meyer, L.H., & Evans, I.M. (1989). *Nonaversive intervention for behavior problems: A manual for home and community.* Baltimore: Paul H. Brookes Publishing Co.

O'Neill, R.E., Horner, R.H., Albin, R.W., Sprague, J.R., Storey, K., & Newton, J.S. (1997). *Functional assessment and program development for problem behavior: A practical handbook.* Pacific Grove, CA: Brooks/Cole Publishing Company.

Smull, M.W. (1996, December). Person centered planning: Should we do it with everyone? *Community Service Reporter, 3*(12), 1.

Virginia Institute for Developmental Disabilities. (1997). *Positive behavioral support training module.* Richmond: Author.

Wacker, D.P., Berg, W.K., Harding, J., & Asmus, J. (1996). A functional approach to dealing with severe challenging behavior. In S. Stainback & W. Stainback (Eds.), *Inclusion: A guide for educators* (pp. 327–342). Baltimore: Paul H. Brookes Publishing Co.

Weiss, N. (1980). Positive behavioral programming. In J. Gardner & M. Chapman (Eds.), *Program issues in developmental disabilities: A guide to effective habilitation in active treatment* (pp. 59–77). Baltimore: Paul H. Brookes Publishing Co.

chapter ten

Feeding Children
with Complex Health Care Needs

Dianne Koontz Lowman

Children with complex health care needs compose a relatively new population of children receiving services in public schools (Knight & Wadsworth, 1994; Lowman, 1993, 1997; Mulligan-Ault, Guess, Struth, & Thompson, 1988; Virginia Departments of Education & Health, 1995). The purpose of this chapter is to describe children with complex health care needs, provide an overview of what educators need to know in order to safely feed these children in school, and answer educators' frequently asked questions.

DEFINITION OF COMPLEX HEALTH CARE NEEDS

Children with complex health care needs are those children with chronic conditions who require technology or ongoing support for survival (Bruder, 1990; Lowman, 1994; Virginia Departments of Education & Health, 1995). Children with complex health care needs may or may not require special education services (Lowman, 1994; Sirvis, 1988). Because children with complex health care needs may require a wide range of services and supports, some U.S. states have categorized the needs of children according to the level of supports needed. A method of categorization used in the state of Virginia is illustrated in Figure 1.

Children with complex health care needs who also have feeding difficulties usually require the administration of specialized feeding procedures intermittently throughout the school day. Specialized procedures may include nasogastric (NG) tube feedings, gastrostomy tube feedings, or oral feedings with monitoring for aspiration (Virginia Departments of Education & Health, 1995). These procedures may be the result of medical conditions that affect the child's ability to eat or drink by mouth, to digest food, or to ingest sufficient nutrition to survive and grow (Klein & Delaney, 1994). Medical advances have enabled children with complex health care needs to receive nutrition through supplemental tube feedings. As illustrated in Table 1, there are a number of types of feeding tubes, which are characterized by the point of insertion and destination.

Level A: Children with one or more conditions who require **continuous,** ongoing specialized health care procedures
These procedures include but are not limited to
- Mechanical ventilation
- Continuous administration of oxygen
- Continuous cardiopulmonary monitoring
- Combination of procedures, such as tracheostomy care, suctioning, and gastrostomy feeding

Level B: Children who require an **intermittent** specialized health care procedure or procedures
These procedures include but are not limited to
- Nasogastric feedings
- Gastrostomy feedings
- Oral feedings where a documented risk of aspiration exists
- Oral, nasal, and pharyngeal suctioning
- Tracheostomy care
- Urinary catheterization
- Ostomy care
- Medication via injection, inhalation, or complex regimens

Level C: Children with identified conditions of unusual severity who require specialized services **episodically** due to the potential for occurrence of a medical crisis
These conditions include but are not limited to
- Uncontrolled seizure disorders
- Unstable diabetes
- Poorly controlled asthma
- Allergies with a history of anaphylactic shock
- Severe immune deficiency

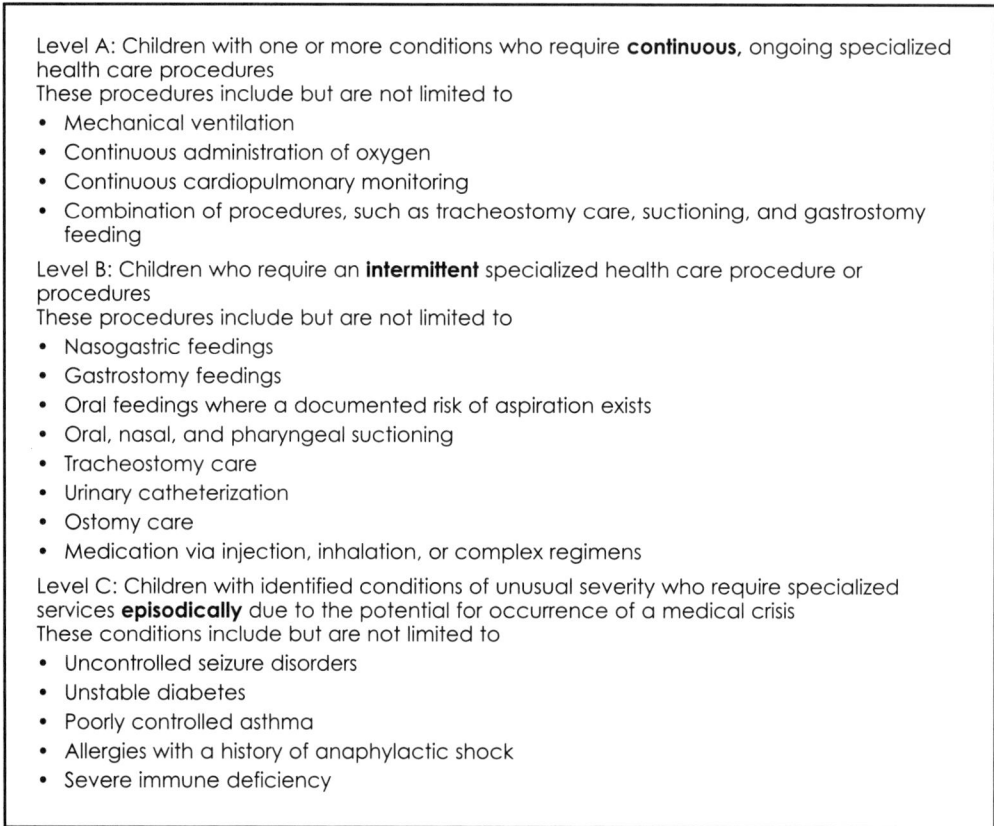

Figure 1.   Levels of services required by children with special health care needs. (From Virginia Departments of Education and Health. [1995]. *Report of the Departments of Education and Health. Report on the needs of medically fragile students to the governor and the general assembly of Virginia* (Senate Document No. 5). Richmond: Commonwealth of Virginia.)

Actual estimates of the number of children with complex health care needs are not available. In a 1993 study of early childhood special education (ECSE) teachers, Lowman reported that 14.5% of ECSE teachers in Virginia were performing gastrostomy tube feedings in the classroom. In 1995, the Virginia Departments of Education and Health reported that 7% of the schools in Virginia had students receiving tube feedings. In the Eighteenth Annual Report to Congress on the Implementation of the Individuals with Disabilities Education Act (1996), the U.S. Department of Education reported that the largest increases from 1990 to 1995 occurred in the number of students with other health impairments (an increase from 56,349 to 106,509 students) and students with orthopedic impairments (an increase from 49,340 to 60,604 students). Anecdotal reports from school personnel indicate that the prevalence of children receiving tube feedings in school is increasing.

EMOTIONAL ISSUES SURROUNDING
A CHILD'S INABILITY TO EAT ORALLY

Initially, when preparing for a student with complex health care needs to enter the classroom, teachers and teacher assistants sometimes voice very

Table 1. Comparison of supplemental feeding tubes

Type of feeding tube	Insertion/Destination	Strengths	Limitations
Nasogastric (NG) tube	Nose/stomach	No surgical placement required Oral feeding possible with tube in place	Insertion and presence in nose/throat is uncomfortable and may be aversive May trigger bradycardia May be cosmetically unacceptable for long-term use
Orogastric tube	Mouth/stomach	No surgical placement	Same as NG tube, plus difficult to feed orally with tube in place
Duodenal tube	Nose/duodenum	No surgical placement Bypasses stomach, so decreases risk of GE reflux	Same as NG tube, though softer, so may have fewer hypersensitive responses Must use continuous-drip feeding Difficult to place and maintain in correct position
Gastrostomy tube (e.g., standard, percutaneous, button, peg)	Surgically placed in stomach	No aversive oral-facial stimuli Despite surgical placement, can be removed easily when no longer needed	Requires surgical placement Site needs daily care and possibly trip to doctor if tube falls out Potential risk for increased GE reflux after tube placed
Jejunostomy tube	Surgically placed in jejunum, possibly in association with a gastrostomy tube	Same as gastrostomy tube Bypasses stomach, so reduces risk of GE reflux	Requires surgical placement Site needs daily care; requires trip to hospital if tube falls out Requires continuous-drip feedings

From Wolf, L.S., & Glass, R.P. (1992). Feeding and swallowing disorders in infancy: Assessment and management. Tucson, AZ: Therapy Skill Builders, a division of The Psychological Corporation; reprinted by permission. All rights reserved.

GE = gastroesophageal

emotional concerns. One reason for this initial reaction may be fear of the unknown because of the lack of training; many preservice university training programs have not prepared teachers to deal with specialized health care in the general classroom (Fauvre, 1988; Lehr, 1990; Sciarillo, Draper, Green, Burkett, & Demetrides, 1988).

Parents and families also experience emotional reactions to sending a child with complex health care needs to general schools. As first emphasized in Chapter 1 of this book, feeding and eating skills are essential to a child's survival. The inability to eat orally has a significant impact on families; it is critical for educators working with parents and families to acknowledge this impact and the possible consequences. (See Jan's story and Figure 1, Elements of family-centered care, presented in Chapter 1 of this book. The teacher, Jan, was frightened by Brittany's dangerous aspiration of food and misunderstood the parents' reasons for relying on oral feedings for Brittany rather than moving to tube feedings.)

Despite initial concerns, educators and parents report that children with complex health care needs enjoy coming to school and benefit from integration with peers (Lowman, 1994). Careful preparation and planning contribute to this successful integration.

PLANNING AND PREPARATION

Precise planning and preparation are essential for the safety and protection of the child with complex health care needs and for the adults who provide health-related services in the school environment. Two critical components that protect adults are careful documentation and training.

Protection Against Liability

Two of the most common reasons many educators initially voice fear about feeding children with complex health care needs in school are 1) Will I hurt the child by doing something wrong? and 2) Am I liable for injuries while feeding the child? There are few published court decisions addressing liability of educators for injuries that might occur while feeding students with complex health care needs (Lowman, 1997). Factors to consider related to liability of teachers and teacher assistants are described in Figure 2. Ways for school personnel to protect themselves from the charge of negligence include the following:

- Documentation
- Education and training
- Being alert to "product notices" (i.e., warning labels on equipment)
- Being alert to trends observed in the past in the student's health and taking specific steps to prevent future occurrences of health problems in school (Virginia Departments of Health & Education, 1992, p. 288)

Documentation and training through the development of a health services plan is emphasized in this chapter.

Documentation and Training

Check with your school system concerning the written policies and procedures regarding documentation and training for school personnel performing

Factors for school division to consider when developing local school policy for determining who will provide specialized health care procedures in the educational setting include
- Section 504 of the Rehabilitation Act of 1973 (PL 93-112)
- Individuals with Disabilities Education Act (IDEA) of 1990 (PL 101-476)
- Nurse Practice Act
- Third party payment
- Legal liability issues—In addressing the issue of personal liability, there are few published decisions that address school district liability for injuries to students who have special health care needs. In one case, Nance vs. Matthews (1993), a student brought a suit for damages against a school principal, school nurse, and special education aide. The complaint was based on the negligent supervision of training of the aide by the principal, nurse, and special education director as well as the aide's negligent failure to catheterize the student. The principal, nurse, and special education director were protected by discretionary function immunity from liability for negligent supervision.
- Sovereign immunity—One possible defense in a negligence suit is the doctrine of sovereign immunity. This doctrine protects governmental agencies and employees who commit acts of negligence while performing acts within the scope of their employment. Sovereign immunity applies only to negligent acts; it does not apply to intentional or malicious acts. The doctrine of sovereign immunity for governmental employees has been partially or completely eliminated by legislative or judicial decisions in some states. Consult the local school board attorney regarding the issue of liability, including the defense of sovereign immunity.
- In loco parentis—In determining who is qualified to dispense medication or conduct health care procedures, some school divisions have relied on the legal doctrine of in loco parentis (i.e., in place of the parents). Historically, the doctrine empowered school officials to exercise the same control over students at schools that parents could exercise at home. Many legal and societal events over the past years have led educators, attorneys, and judges to change their views of in loco parentis. Consult the local school board attorney before relying on the doctrine of in loco parentis.

Figure 2.   Liability issues. (From Virginia Department of Health [1996]. *Guidelines for students with specialized health care needs.* Richmond: Author.)

specialized health care procedures during the school day. The Health Services Plan presented in Appendix B at the end of this book is one example of a format for documenting planning, preparation, and training (Lowman, 1994, 1997; Lowman & Rosenkoetter, 1994). Other sample plans are available from a variety of sources (Haas, 1993; Porter, Haynie, Bierle, Caldwell, & Palfrey, 1997; Virginia Department of Health, 1996).

As stated throughout this book, the importance of team planning that involves the child's family is critical. It is important for classroom staff, who usually have primary responsibility for feeding, to remember that complex health care needs are medically based and may be life threatening. Feeding plans or programs should not be written or implemented without the involvement of an interdisciplinary team. The specific members of the team may vary, depending on the special needs of the child. For example, children who demonstrate a risk of aspiration of food should be evaluated by a physician and have a videofluoroscopic swallowing study, also known as the modified barium swallow (Wolf & Glass, 1992). Children who are not receiving adequate calories should have a nutritional evaluation and plan developed by a registered dietician.

A critical component of the Health Services Plan is the training of classroom personnel (Bennett, Haley, Smith, & Valluzzi, 1993; Lehr, 1990; Lowman & Rosenkoetter, 1994; Sherman & Rosen, 1990; Sobsey & Cox, 1996; Virginia Departments of Education & Health, 1995). In order to be successful, training should include the following components:

- Training should take place before the child enters school.

- Training should be provided by a health care provider with the child's parent(s) present.

- Training should be child specific.

- Training should include everyone who may be responsible for providing emergency care, including backups in case of staff absences.

- Training should include an opportunity for supervised practice and documentation of competency.

- Time lines should be established for regular review and retraining on the health-related procedures (Lowman, 1994, 1997; Lowman & Rosenkoetter, 1994; Virginia Department of Health, 1996; Virginia Departments of Education & Health, 1995).

The checklist included in Figure 3 is an example of one way to document that classroom personnel are trained and competent in the administration of health-related procedures.

An important component of preparing school personnel to conduct health-related procedures in school is understanding how to handle contact with body fluids. Universal precautions refer to ways to handle body fluids such as blood, feces, vomit, nasal secretions, urine, and saliva when blood is visible in these substances. In 1991, the Occupational Safety and Health Administration (OSHA) developed a standard for prevention of exposure to blood-borne pathogens. Educators should check with their local school division for policy related to applicable sections of the OSHA standard. One critical aspect of universal precautions is frequent hand washing, the most effective procedure to protect staff and other students from the transmission of infectious diseases (Giardina & Psota, 1997). The use of protective equipment, such as gloves, provides an additional measure of protection when in contact with blood. Gloves, however, may contain latex; allergic reactions to natural latex rubber have been reported in children with conditions such as spina bifida. School personnel should be aware of the possibility of allergic reactions; alternative, nonlatex gloves are available.

The Health Services Plan illustrated in Appendix B at the end of this book is one way to provide documentation. All health services plans do not need to be this inclusive; the plan will be based on the child's individual needs. The purpose of the plan is to provide for feedings in school that are safe for both the child and the feeder.

SPECIALIZED FEEDING PROCEDURES CONDUCTED IN SCHOOL

A number of specialized feeding procedures are conducted in school environments; the most frequently performed procedures include conducting NG and gastrostomy tube feedings, moving children from tube feedings to oral feedings, and feeding children with tracheostomies.

A. States name and purpose of procedure	Date	Date	Date	Date	Date	Date	Date
B. Preparation 1. Completes at _____ time(s)							
2. _____ cc (amount) _____ Formula/Feeding (type of feeding)							
3. Feeding to be completed in _____ minutes							
4. Position for feeding _____							
5. Identifies potential problems and appropriate actions							

C. Identifies Supplies:
  1. Catheter _____ (size)
      _____ (type)
      Balloon size _____ cc							

a. Small port plug							
b. Feeding port							
2. Clamp and plug							
3. 60 cc catheter-tipped syringe							
4. Formula at room temperature							
5. Small glass of tap water							
D. Procedure:							
1. Washes hands thoroughly							
2. Gathers equipment							
3. Positions child and explains procedure							
4. Removes plug from feeding tube							
Child-specific: Steps 5–11 need to be prescribed for each child							
5. Checks for proper placement of tube. Attaches syringe and aspirates stomach contents by pulling plunger back							
6. Measures contents							
7. Returns stomach contents to stomach							
8. If stomach contents are over _____ cc, subtracts from feeding							
9. If more than _____ cc, holds feeding							
10. Pinches or clamps off tube							
11. Removes syringe							
12. Attaches syringe without plunger to feeding port							
13. Pours formula (room temperature) into syringe (approx. 30–40 cc)							
14. Releases or unclamps tube and allows feeding to go in slowly							
15. When feeding gets to 5 cc marker, adds more formula							
16. Continues this procedure until the feeding has been completed							

(continued)

Figure 3.   Documentation checklist for gastrostomy bolus feeding. (From Caldwell, T.H., Todaro, A.W., & Gates, A.J. [Eds.]. [1989]. *Community providers guide: An information outline for working with children with special health care needs.* New Orleans, LA: National MCH Resource Center, Children's Hospital.)

Figure 3. (*continued*)

17. Takes about 30 minutes to complete feeding (the higher the syringe is held, the faster the feeding will flow)								
18. Lowers the syringe if feeding is going too fast								
19. Makes feeding like mealtime; young children may suck on a pacifier								
20. Flushes tube with _____ cc of water when feeding is complete								
21. Pinches off tubing, removes syringe, and closes off clamp								
22. Allows child to remain in feeding position for minimum of 1/2 hour after feeding								
23. Washes syringe with soap and warm water and puts in home container								
24. Reports any problems to parents								
25. Documents procedure and problems in log								

Checklist content approved by:

_____ Date _____
Parent/Guardian signature

_____ Date _____
Administrator

_____ Date _____

Conducting Tube Feedings in School

A number of resources are available for classroom staff who will be conducting tube feedings in school (Caldwell, Todaro, & Gates, 1989; Graff, Ault, Guess, Taylor, & Thompson, 1990; Porter et al., 1997; Urbano, 1992; Virginia Department of Health, 1996). As stated previously, training in the proper, step-by-step procedures for conducting tube feedings must be conducted by a health care professional and be specific to the individual child. Based on the needs of the individual child and whenever possible, tube feedings should be scheduled to coincide with routine mealtime activities (Urbano, 1992). If the child also receives food by mouth, the child should receive feedings by mouth simultaneously with tube feedings to help the child make the connection between oral feedings and feelings of being "full." If the child does not take any food by mouth, oral stimulation during tube feedings is critical for the child to continue to experience and tolerate sensation in his or her mouth.

Making the Transition from Tube Feedings to Oral Feedings

The prolonged use of tube feeding can delay the development of oral feeding skills, especially if the child has been fed exclusively with tube feedings without concurrent oral-motor stimulation (Luiselli & Luiselli, 1995). Moving from tube feedings to oral feedings must be done slowly and with respect for the child's needs and abilities; tube feedings should never be eliminated suddenly from the child's diet (Morris, 1987). A carefully designed transition plan should be developed by the feeding team. The studies highlighted in Table 2 list components that help move from tube to oral feedings.

When team members are developing this transition plan, the following points should be considered (Wolf & Glass, 1992):

- Determine the child's readiness for oral feedings (including understanding the original medical conditions that resulted in tube feedings).

- Determine the parental wishes regarding transition to oral feedings.

- Establish the level and quality of the child's oral-motor abilities.

- Establish the status of the child's swallowing abilities.

- Determine the child's nutritional needs.

- Explore ways to normalize hunger / satiation cycles.

- Determine any behavioral issues related to oral feedings.

A key feature of any intervention program designed to facilitate transition to oral feedings is oral-tactile normalization (Wolf & Glass, 1992). Many of the techniques described in Chapter 6 will be especially useful to educators. In addition to sensory opposition to oral feedings, many children who have had prolonged tube feedings have developed a behavioral opposition to oral feedings. The behavioral strategies described in Chapter 9 will also be helpful to educators.

Feeding Children with Tracheostomies

A *tracheostomy* is an opening in the trachea that allows air movement into and out of the lungs. A *tracheostomy tube* is a metal or plastic hollow tube that is placed into this opening. This tube allows the child to breathe through the trachea, rather than through the mouth or nose (Graff et al., 1990). Oral feedings are possible with a tracheostomy in place because oral-motor skills should not be directly affected. The presence of the tracheostomy tube can,

Table 2.   Overview of behavioral techniques used to intervene with feeding refusal

Reference	Behavioral technique
Discipio et al. (1978)	Shaping, deconditioning
Riordan et al. (1984)	Positive reinforcement, ignoring, guidance techniques
Luiselli et al. (1985)	Contingently reinforcing oral consumption
Blackman & Nelson (1985)	Exposure and response prevention
Geertsma et al. (1985)	Desensitization, positive reinforcement
Handen et al. (1986)	Desensitization, positive reinforcement
Blackman & Nelson (1987)	Exposure and response prevention
Hyman et al. (1987)	Positive reinforcement, guidance techniques
Lamm & Greer (1988)	Progressive physical prompts, reinforcement, repeated trials
Chamberlin et al. (1991)	Support group using extinction, positive reinforcement
Singer et al. (1991)	Positive reinforcement, time out, shaping, ignoring
Johnson & Babbitt (1993)	Manipulation of food texture
Babbitt et al. (1994)	Positive reinforcement
Hoch et al. (1994)	Maintaining food presentation until consumption occurred
Luiselli (1994)	Desensitizing the child to feeding demands
Foy (1997)	Exposure and response prevention

Adapted from Foy et al. (1997) and Luiselli & Luiselli (1995).

however, lead to impairments in swallowing (Wolf & Glass, 1992). Evaluation of swallowing function is critical when initiating oral feedings; educators who feed children with tracheostomies should be aware of the danger signs of aspiration. Ten indicators of aspiration include

1. Medical history (e.g., pneumonia, bronchitis, asthma)
2. Dramatic events have happened (e.g., food stuck in throat, required Heimlich maneuver)
3. Not enough intake of liquid (e.g., history of dehydration)
4. Coughing, gagging, or choking
5. Wheezing or asthma
6. Rapid breathing or fatigue with meals
7. Vomiting or regurgitation
8. Drooling or food falls out of mouth
9. Spurting or forceful ejection of food
10. Mealtime behaviors (e.g., fear, reluctance, eats slowly, eats in unusual way) (Hall, Yohn, & Reed, 1992, p. 7)

SUMMARY

Children with complex health care needs have specialized feeding procedures that are conducted during the school day. Teachers and teacher assistants initially voice fear and concern about performing "health-related" feeding procedures in school. After careful planning, preparation (including receiving specific training), and documentation, most educators are positive about the integration of children with complex health care needs into their classes. A carefully developed Health Services Plan ensures that educators are safely feeding children and that the experience is positive for both the feeder and the child.

Fred

Fred is a 20-month-old boy who has been receiving tube feeding since his birth. Fred was born more than 2 months premature, weighing less than 1,000 grams. He spent 2 months in the neonatal intensive care unit (NICU), where he was placed on a ventilator for respiratory distress. During his stay in the NICU, Fred also received NG feedings and was frequently suctioned in his mouth and nose. Fred left the hospital receiving gastrostomy tube feedings and supplemental oxygen via a nasal cannula (i.e., prongs that are inserted into the child's nostrils to deliver a low to moderate concentration of oxygen).

The infant educator and the therapists in the NICU worked closely with the family to ensure that Fred would continue to receive oral stimulation during tube feedings. While in the NICU, Fred's parents observed other infants who had become hypersensitive to oral stimulation and who would not allow anything to be placed in their mouths. Determined that would not happen to Fred, his parents have carefully continued the oral stimulation program at home. In addition to stroking Fred's face (techniques taught by the therapists), the parents encourage Fred to mouth toys dipped in food. Fred also sucks on a pacifier during tube feedings.

Fred can now tolerate larger amounts of food at one time; he has successfully moved from continuous-drip feedings to bolus feedings. Fred no longer receives supplemental oxygen. During the last home visit, the family asked about moving Fred from tube feedings to oral feedings.

P R A C T I C E · · · E X E R C I S E

Generate a list of questions you need to ask other team members to begin to develop a plan to move Fred from tube feedings to oral feedings.

- First, what questions would help determine whether Fred is ready for oral feedings?

  You need to understand the original medical conditions that resulted in tube feedings. Have those conditions been resolved?

  You need to establish the status of Fred's swallowing abilities. What kind of tests will be needed?

- Second, what questions will help determine parental wishes regarding Fred's transition to oral feedings?

  What concerns do Fred's parents have about nutritional needs during the transition?

  What concerns do Fred's parents have about the time, consistency, and perseverance that will be required during this transition?

- Next, what questions will help determine Fred's nutritional needs during the transition period? Whom will you seek out to ask these questions?

- What questions/observations are needed to help establish the level and quality of Fred's oral-motor abilities?

  An oral stimulation program has been conducted regularly by this family. How can this program be modified to facilitate the transition?

- What are some ways you can begin immediately to normalize hunger/satiation cycles in Fred?

  Because Fred is already receiving bolus feedings, the first step to establish this cycle has been taken. What else can be done?

- Are there any behavioral issues related to oral feedings?

  Are there any emotional issues surrounding mealtimes?

  Does Fred exhibit any oppositional behaviors related to feeding?

REFERENCES

Bennett, F.C., Haley, P., Smith, G., & Valluzzi, J. (1993). Inservice programs for related services teams serving medically fragile children. *OSERS News in Print*, 31–35.

Bruder, M.B. (1990, October). *Children with complex health care needs: Issues in policy and personnel preparation.* Paper presented by the International Early Childhood Conference on Children with Special Needs, Albuquerque, NM.

Caldwell, T.H., Todaro, A.W., & Gates, A.J. (Eds.). (1989). *Community provider's guide: An information outline for working with children with special health care needs.* New Orleans, LA: National MCH Resource Center, Children's Hospital.

Fauvre, M. (1988). Including young children with "new" chronic illnesses in an early childhood education setting. *Young Children, 43*(6), 71–77.

Foy, T., Czyzewski, D., Phillips, S., Ligon, B., Baldwin, J., & Klish, W. (1997). Treatment of severe feeding refusal in infants and toddlers. *Infants and Young Children, 9*(3), 26–35.

Giardina, R.G., & Psota, C.E. (1997). Universal precautions and infection control in a school setting. In S. Porter, M. Haynie, T. Barley, T.H. Caldwell, & J.S. Palfrey (Eds.), *Children and youth assisted by medical technology in educational settings: Guidelines for care* (2nd ed., pp. 74–93). Baltimore: Paul H. Brookes Publishing Co.

Graff, J.C., Ault, M.M., Guess, D., Taylor, M., & Thompson, B. (1990). *Health care for students with disabilities: An illustrated medical guide for the classroom.* Baltimore: Paul H. Brookes Publishing Co.

Haas, J.B. (Ed.). (1993). *The school nurse's source book of individualized health care plans: A compendium of I.H.P.s covering the most frequently encountered chronic and acute health issues.* North Branch, MN: Sunrise River Press.

Hall, S., Yohn, K., & Reed, P.R. (1992). *Feeding students in school: Providing guidelines and information on safe feeding practices for special students.* Salem: Oregon Department of Education.

Klein, M.D., & Delaney, T.A. (1994). *Feeding and nutrition for the child with special needs: Handouts for parents.* San Antonio, TX: Therapy Skill Builders.

Knight, D., & Wadsworth, D.E. (1994). Guidelines for educating students who are technology dependent. *Physical Disabilities: Education and Related Services, 13*(1), 1–8.

Lehr, D.H. (1990). Preparation of personnel to work with students with complex health care needs. In A.P. Kaiser & C.M. McWhorter (Eds.), *Preparing personnel to work with persons with severe disabilities* (pp. 135–151). Baltimore: Paul H. Brookes Publishing Co.

Lowman, D.K. (1993). Preschoolers with complex health care needs: A survey of early childhood special education teachers in Virginia. *Topics in Early Childhood Special Education, 13*(4), 445–460.

Lowman, D.K. (1994). *Integrating preschoolers with complex health care needs into early childhood special education programs: The teacher's perspective.* Unpublished doctoral dissertation, University of Virginia, Charlottesville.

Lowman, D.K. (1997). Students with special health care needs. In L.A. Power-DeFur & F.P. Orelove (Eds.), *Inclusive education: Practical implementation of the least restrictive environment* (pp. 245–258). Gaithersburg, MD: Aspen Publishers.

Lowman, D.K., & Rosenkoetter, S.E. (1994). Creating successful transitions for children with complex health care needs: New friends on the journey. In S.E. Rosenkoetter, A.H. Hains, & S.A. Flower, *Bridging early services for children with special health care needs and their families: A practical guide for transition planning* (pp. 181–196). Baltimore: Paul H. Brookes Publishing Co.

Luiselli, J.K., & Luiselli, T.E. (1995). A behavioral analysis approach toward chronic food refusal in children with gastrostomy-tube dependency. *Topics in Early Childhood Special Education, 15*(1), 1–18.

Morris, S.E. (1987). *Pre-feeding skills: A comprehensive resource for feeding development.* San Antonio, TX: Therapy Skill Builders.

Mulligan-Ault, M., Guess, D., Struth, L., & Thompson, B. (1988). The implementation of health related procedures in classrooms for students with severe multiple impairments. *Journal of The Association for Persons with Severe Handicaps, 13,* 100–116.

Occupational exposure to blood-borne pathogens, 56(235) Fed. Reg. 64004–64182 (1991) (to be codified at 29 C.F.R. § 1910.1030).

Porter, S., Haynie, M., Bierle, T., Caldwell, T.H., & Palfrey, J.S. (1997). *Children and youth assisted by medical technology in educational settings: Guidelines for care* (2nd ed.). Baltimore: Paul H. Brookes Publishing Co.

Sciarillo, W.G., Draper, S., Green, P., Burkett, K., & Demetrides, S. (1988). Children with specialized health needs in the special education setting: A statewide technical assistance approach. *Infants and Young Children, 1,* 74–84.

Sherman, L.P., & Rosen, C.D. (1990). Development of a preschool program for tracheostomy dependent children. *Pediatric Nursing, 16*(4), 357–361.

Sirvis, M. (1988). Students with special health care needs. *Teaching Exceptional Children, 20*(4), 40–44.

Sobsey, D., & Cox, A.W. (1996). Integrating health care and educational programs. In F.P. Orelove & D. Sobsey, *Educating children with multiple disabilities: A transdisciplinary approach* (3rd ed., pp. 217–251). Baltimore: Paul H. Brookes Publishing Co.

Urbano, M.T. (1992). *Preschool children with special health care needs.* San Diego, CA: Singular Publishing Group.

U.S. Department of Education. (1996). *Eighteenth annual report to Congress on the implementation of the Individuals with Disabilities Education Act* [On-line]. (Available: http://www.ed.gov/pubs/OSEP96AnlRpt/)

Virginia Department of Health. (1996). *Guidelines for students with specialized health care needs.* Richmond: Author.

Virginia Departments of Education and Health. (1995). *Report on the needs of medically fragile students to the Governor and the General Assembly of Virginia* (Senate Document No. 5). Richmond: Commonwealth of Virginia.

Virginia Departments of Health and Education. (1992). *School health guidelines.* Richmond: Author.

Wolf, L.S., & Glass, R.P. (1992). *Feeding and swallowing disorders in infancy: Assessment and management.* San Antonio, TX: Therapy Skill Builders.

Appendix
Resources to Aid in the Inclusion
of Students with Complex Health Care Needs

BOOKS

Batshaw, M.L. (Ed.). (1997). *Children with disabilities* (4th ed.). Baltimore: Paul H. Brookes Publishing Co.

Graff, J.C., Ault, M.M., Guess, D., Taylor, M., & Thompson, B. (1990). *Health care needs for students with disabilities: An illustrated medical guide for the classroom.* Baltimore: Paul H. Brookes Publishing Co.

Has, J.B. (Ed.). (1993). *The school nurse's source book of individualized health care plans: A compendium of I.H.P.s covering the most frequently encountered chronic and acute health issues.* North Branch, MN: Sunrise River Press.

Heller, K.W., Alberto, P.A., Forner, P.E., & Schwartzman, M.N. (1996). *Understanding physical, sensory, & health impairments: Characteristics and educational implications.* Pacific Grove: Brooks/Cole Publishing Company.

Porter, S., Burkley, J., Bierle, T., Lowcock, J., Haynie, M., & Palfrey, J.S. (1992). *Working towards a balance in our lives: A booklet for families of children with disabilities and special health care needs.* Boston: Project School Care, The Children's Hospital.

Porter, S., Haynie, M., Bierle, T., Caldwell, T.H., & Palfrey, J.S. (1997). *Children and youth assisted by medical technology in educational settings: Guidelines for care* (2nd ed.). Baltimore: Paul H. Brookes Publishing Co.

Rosenkoetter, S.E., Hains, A.H., & Fowler, S.A. (1994). *Bridging early services for children with special needs and their families: A practical guide for transition planning.* Baltimore: Paul H. Brookes Publishing Co.

Urbano, M.T. (1992). *Preschool children with special health care needs.* San Diego, CA: Singular Publishing Group.

MANUALS

Caldwell, T.H., Todaro, A.W., & Gates, A.J. (Eds.). (1989). *Community provider's guide: An information outline for working with children with special health needs.* New Orleans, LA: National MCH Resource Center, Children's Hospital.

California Department of Education. (1990). *Guidelines and procedures for meeting the specialized physical health care needs of pupils.* Sacramento: Author.

Epstein, S.G., Taylor, A.B., Halberg, A.S., Gardner, J.D., Walker, D.K., & Crocker, A.C. (1989). *Enhancing quality: Standards and indicators of quality care for children with special health care needs.* Boston: New England SERVE.

Haynie, M., Porter, S.M., & Palfrey, J.S. (1989). *Children assisted by medical technology in educational settings: Guidelines for care.* Boston: Project School Care, The Children's Hospital.

Heller, K.W., Alberto, P.A., Schwartzman, M.N., Shiplett, K., Pierce, J., Polokoff, J., Heller, E.J., Andrews, D.G., Briggs, A., & Kana, T.G. (1990). *Suggested physical health procedures of students with special needs.* Atlanta: Georgia State University.

Kluge Children's Rehabilitation Center. (1992). *The strawberry connection guide to supporting families of children with feeding tubes.* Charlottesville, VA: Author.

Mountain Plains Regional Resource Center and the Utah State Office of Education. (1992). *Guidelines for serving students with special health care needs.* Salt Lake City: Utah State Office of Education.

Parent Educational Advocacy Training Center (PEATC) and The ARC of Northern Virginia. (1993). *Taking charge: A parent's guide to health care for children with special needs.* Alexandria, VA: PEATC.

Tamari, P., Kempf, B., & Woodward, E. (Eds.). (1991). *Information and resource directory for children with special health care needs.* Selden, NY: Starting Early Childhood Division of Developmental Disabilities Institute.

Virginia Department of Health. (1996). *Guidelines for students with specialized health care needs.* Richmond: Author.

West Virginia Department of Education. (1990). *Basic and specialized health care procedure manual for West Virginia Public Schools.* Charleston: Author.

NEWSLETTERS

ACCH News. [Published bimonthly by the Association for the Care of Children's Health, 7910 Woodmont Avenue, #300, Bethesda, MD 20814, 301-654-6549]

Catch Quarterly. [Published by the American Academy of Pediatrics, 141 Northwest Point Boulevard, Post Office Box 927, Elk Grove Village, IL 60009-0927]

Families and Disability Newsletter. [Published three times a year by the Beach Center on Families and Disability at the University of Kansas, 3111 Haworth Hall, Lawrence, KS 66045, FAX 913-864-5323]

Springboard. [Published by the Center for Children with Chronic Illness and Disability, Box 721-UMHC, Harvard Street at East River Road, Minneapolis, MN 55455]

REPORTS: RESEARCH, TECHNICAL, PROCEEDINGS

Caldwell, J.H., Sirvis, B., Todaro, A.W., & Accouloumre, D.S. (1991). *Special health care in the school.* Reston, VA: Council for Exceptional Children.

Joint Task Force for the Management of Children with Special Health Care Needs. (1990). *Guidelines for the delineation of roles and responsibilities for the safe delivery of specialized health care in the educational setting.* Reston, VA: Council for Exceptional Children.

Koop, C.E. (1987). *Surgeon General's report: Children with special health care needs* (DHHS Publication No. HRS/D/MC 87-2). Rockville, MD: U.S. Department of Health and Human Services.

National Center for Education in Maternal and Child Health. (1990). *Children with special health needs: A resource guide.* Washington, DC: The National Maternal and Child Health Clearinghouse.

U.S. Congress, Office of Technology Assessment. (1987). *Technology-dependent children: Hospital v. home care—A technical memorandum* (OTA-TM-H-38). Washington, DC: U.S. Government Printing Office.

chapter eleven

Sensory Disabilities and Feeding Problems

Julie K. Jones

Children with feeding and/or eating problems who also have sensory disabilities (i.e., visual impairments, blindness, hearing loss, deafness, or deafblindness) present some unique challenges to caregivers, therapists, and educators. Although this chapter recommends some specific accommodations for these children, the information and techniques discussed in previous chapters in this book also apply to children with sensory impairments. The challenge for teachers is to make necessary accommodations during mealtimes for children in their classrooms who have sensory impairments.

Few teachers are trained to work with children with sensory impairments until these children are placed in their classrooms. It is important for teachers to keep in mind that each child with a sensory impairment is an individual, just as each child without a disability is an individual. No one accommodation or set of accommodations applies to all sensory impairments or to all children.

This chapter provides teachers and paraprofessionals with information about sensory impairments and their effects on feeding. This chapter includes information about techniques and accommodations that are specific to each sensory impairment and provides a framework for individualizing accommodations. Each disability area (i.e., visual impairments, hearing impairments, and deafblindness) is discussed separately.

VISUAL IMPAIRMENTS AND BLINDNESS

Sight is one of our distance senses (hearing and smell are the others) (McInnes & Treffry, 1982). Using sight, children can observe from nearby or far away and learn without directly participating. Infants and young children learn much through observation; Bower (1977) described how newborns inspect their environments visually and even imitate their mothers' facial expressions. It has been estimated that as much as 80% of a child's learning occurs through vision (Hart, 1974). When a child's vision is impaired, the child's primary channel for learning, especially incidental learning, is compromised. The extent of this compromise depends on the degree and type of vision loss and the age of the child when the vision loss occurs (Heward & Orlansky, 1992).

The term *blind* generally creates confusion. When people hear the word *blind*, most assume complete lack of sight. In reality, however, most individuals referred to as blind have sight, albeit impaired. The term *legally blind* refers to someone who, with the best possible correction in eyeglasses or contact lenses, needs to be 20 feet away to see an object that someone with unimpaired vision can see at a distance of 200 feet. *Visual acuity* refers to the measure of how well someone sees. *Unimpaired* visual acuity is 20/20, meaning that one can see clearly at 20 feet what one should see at that distance with unimpaired vision. Legal blindness begins with a visual acuity of 20/200. The only letter on the eye chart that someone with a visual acuity of 20/200 can see with sufficient clarity to read is the big "E" at the top of the chart. A child whose visual acuity falls between 20/70 and 20/200 is said to be *partially sighted.*

Some types of vision problems do not affect an individual's visual acuity. Instead, these problems affect how much of the environment the individual sees at any one time. When looking straight ahead, most individuals see objects out of the corners of their eyes within a range of approximately 200°. This sight out of the corners of the eyes is called *peripheral vision.* What one sees with peripheral vision as well as central vision is called the *visual field.*

When peripheral vision is impaired, an individual sees only part of the visual field. For example, everyone has had the experience of looking through binoculars. What he or she is looking at is clear, but the scope of what is seen is quite limited. The binoculars restrict the visual field—the peripheral vision. One must move his or her head in order to see the other parts of the scene. Anyone having a severely restricted visual field (20° or less) is also considered to be legally blind.

Effects of Vision Loss on Development

Sight plays an extremely important role in all aspects of a child's development. Cognitively, for example, children learn object permanence—objects and people continue to exist even though they are out of sight—by following the movements of people and objects in their environments as they appear, disappear, and reappear. Children learn cause-and-effect relationships because they are able to see that their actions affect others. They learn much socially and behaviorally by watching how others interact and by seeing the effects of their own actions. They learn facial expressions and body language through observing others and imitating what they see. For example, children learn to smile by imitating their mothers' smiles. Sight is even important in learning language. For example, children learn to make a shift in pronouns from "you" to "me" by watching as well as listening while others make the shift and by recognizing confusion when they do not. *Over, under,* and *between* are three concepts that are learned more easily, thanks to sight.

What role, then, does sight play in the development of feeding and eating skills? After all, isn't eating a basic instinct? Well, yes, eating is a basic instinct, but what we eat and how we eat are not. These are among the aspects of eating that are learned and that are affected by vision loss.

Very early in their lives, children learn to anticipate that food is coming or that they are finished eating by observing certain cues in their environments. They may see their mothers coming, bottles in hand. They may watch their mothers prepare cereal. They may observe their refrigerators being opened and see all of the food inside. They may recognize that they are being carried to the usual location for feeding. Even when being fed, children can anticipate each spoonful of food because they can see their mothers scoop food on the bowl of the spoon and watch as the spoon approaches. They can anticipate the meal coming to an end as they watch the amount of food dwindle. Often, mothers show their young children that food is "all gone" or "all finished" by showing their children the empty bowl, jar, or plate.

Children with sight realize that there is a wide variety of food and drinks available beyond what they receive by seeing people around them consuming and enjoying them. Children with sight also observe how these foods are consumed. For example, young children typically beg for a taste of food that is beyond their capabilities to handle when they see their parents or siblings enjoying it. Although they may react with uncertainty or even rejection when they are given a new food taste or texture, they see their mothers smiling and encouraging them to try the food again. Before children with sight receive foods that require chewing, they have had multiple opportunities to observe people chewing. Generally, their family members have made exaggerated chewing motions when interacting with them. Young children also observe people around them consuming food themselves, rather than being fed. Such an observation may lead children to want to self-feed, often before they or their parents are ready. Sitting up while eating and sitting at a table instead of running around are among the social skills of eating that young children with sight observe others doing.

Cues such as these may not be visible to children who have limited sight. For others, the cues are visible but require so much effort to see them that the children have not observed the necessary details. Thus, they have not had the usual incidental experiences that facilitate learning more advanced feeding and eating skills.

Accommodations for Children with Impaired Vision

There are a number of accommodations that can be made to help children with visual impairments learn the skills and concepts associated with eating. These accommodations include positioning (i.e., carrying and seating) children, providing environmental lighting, approaching children with food or drink, contrasting children's food and drink from the background, facilitating incidental learning, teaching the children to self-feed, and teaching the children to eat solid foods. Because each child is unique, these accommodations cannot be presented as specific recipes in cookbook fashion. Rather, their concepts will be discussed, the rationales and intended outcomes presented, and specific examples cited so that they can be used and adapted as needed.

Positioning

Proper positioning is especially important for children with visual impairments. Vision stimulates children with sight to hold up their heads and look around. Children with significant visual impairments or blindness do not have this stimulation. As a result, they develop head control later in their development and often display poor posture. Poor head control and posture affect a number of areas of development; it is more difficult to feed children with poor head control and posture and even more difficult for these children to learn to self-feed. Poor head control and posture also place children at greater risk for aspiration. If children also have cerebral palsy, problems with poor head control and posture are compounded.

Proper positioning of children with visual impairments is the same as that for other children. With regard to sitting, they should be seated so that their ankles, knees, and hips form right angles. They should be supported so that they do not fall to the side. If a child does not yet have good head control, high-chair trays or tabletops should be set at a height to support head control. If a child has good head control, then high-chair trays or tabletops should allow for easy hand and arm movement and object manipulation.

Lighting

Lighting needs to be considered when positioning a child with visual impairments. The lighting of the area in which the child eats, for example, can help or hinder the child's ability to see. Although the area should be well-lit to help the child use his or her vision, glare must be avoided. Often, children with visual impairments have increased sensitivity to light and glare, which is called *photophobia*. Trying to see in bright sunlight without sunglasses or turning on a light when waking in the middle of the night are experiences we all have had. These examples are similar to those that children with photophobia experience easily, although the intensity of the light need not be so great. Thus, a child with a visual impairment should be seated so that his or her back is to a window or bright light, rather than facing a light source.

The amount of light in the feeding area is also important. For example, a child with photophobia may require a feeding area with soft light because a brightly lit area may provide too much light. Classrooms tend to be lit with fluorescent lighting. Fluorescent lights are often too bright and produce too much glare. Natural lighting combined with incandescent lighting or halogen floor lamps generally provide better lighting with less glare.

Lighting requirements are unique for each child with a visual impairment. A vision specialist should be able to help caregivers and teachers determine the best lighting for each child. A good procedure to follow, however, is to observe the child's reactions when he or she is in different lighting situations. The caregiver should notice where the child seems to see better or more easily and where he or she has more difficulty seeing. If the child is old enough (generally at least 4–5 years old), the caregiver should ask the child where he or she sees more comfortably or "better" or which situation he or she likes the most. The older child may even be able to help experiment with different lighting arrangements.

Incidental Learning

Vision is a distance sense that allows children to learn incidentally. The importance of incidental learning cannot be overemphasized (Heward & Orlansky, 1992). For children with visual impairments, teachers and caregivers must be vigilant about situations in which concepts are not being learned because limited vision is inhibiting incidental learning. The feeding area is one area in which there are a number of such incidentally learned concepts.

Babies with sight quickly learn that mealtime is coming because they learn to associate certain visual cues with eating (e.g., seeing their bottles, watching as baby food jars are opened and the contents are placed in dishes). During meals, babies with sight learn that spoons being filled with food or full spoons coming toward them means that the next bites of food are on the way. These cues are not available to many children with visual impairments.

Often, children with visual impairments are startled when their mothers or caregivers appear from nowhere to feed them. Bottles seem to appear suddenly at their mouths because these children cannot see the bottles as they approach. Later, when these children are able to eat solid food, spoonfuls of food appear at their mouths in much the same way. These items also disappear just as "magically."

It is important to provide cues to children with visual impairments so that they can learn to anticipate the feeding process and not be startled. Providing cues with sound and touch and improving the visibility of the bottle, spoon, and plate are adaptations that can help these children. For example, a teacher or paraprofessional can call the child's name to let the child know that he or she is coming as he or she approaches the child. Shaking the child's crib or bed, gently touching the child, and letting the child feel the bottle before picking him or her up also can provide cues that it is mealtime to a child with visual impairments. When seated and ready to feed the child, the caregiver can let the child feel the bottle again and gently touch the bottle's nipple to the child's lips to let the child know that the bottle is there. Increasing the visibility of the bottle for the child may help him or her see and recognize it. Fortunately, many bottles come with simple, brightly colored pictures on them. If using standard white- and pastel-colored bottles, placing stripes of brightly colored tape around these bottles increases their visibility. Brightly colored bowls or plates placed on a solid-color background such as white, yellow, dark blue, or black can make bowls and plates easier for the child to see. Tapping against the side of the bowl or plate before each bite of food can signal to the child that another spoonful of food is on the way. Showing the child the spoonful of food by placing it in his or her range and field of vision can also alert the child that the next bite of food is coming.

Another simple, but important, accommodation for children with visual impairments is to be sure that they are present during food preparation. Young children who have unimpaired vision observe the whole food preparation process easily. For example, infants with unimpaired vision can be in another room while observing an adult getting a drink from the refrigerator because they have a clear line of sight to the refrigerator and adequate vision to see the event take place. Infants learn that food and drinks are stored in a refrigerator or a pantry. They learn that cooking involves putting food into vessels, perhaps adding other food, stirring it, cooking it on the stovetop or in an oven, and placing the food in serving dishes or directly on plates. Children with visual impairments, however, often do not learn these basic concepts unless an adult specifically ensures that they do. It may be necessary to carry these children to the refrigerator or pantry while getting out food or drinks, to hold these children while stirring food, or to carry these children along when putting a pot of food on the stove to cook. Young children with visual impairments who pretend to cook during play by making the noises they associate with cooking are demonstrating their concept of cooking. These sounds are what they hear their mothers make in the kitchen while preparing meals. They do not realize what actions accompanied the sounds.

Providing Contrast

Dishes provide the contrasting background for food items placed on them. Plates and bowls used during mealtimes with children who have visual impairments can either facilitate or hinder children in seeing the food. Thus, colors and patterns of plates and bowls are important considerations for children with visual impairments.

For the child who must be fed, dishes with a background that makes the food easier to see can help the child see when the parent is obtaining the next spoonful of food as well as what that spoonful of food will be. The child will learn that food does not magically appear from nowhere. He or she will also learn to anticipate the next spoonful of food. Later, when the child is old enough to self-feed, the contrasting background of a dish will facilitate locating the food.

There are other situations in which attention to contrast is important. First, when feeding a child with visual impairments, whoever is doing the feeding should wear clothing or a smock that facilitates seeing the bottle or spoon. Busy patterns, although fashionable, generally do not make good backgrounds. Solid colors of clothing, especially dark colors, generally work well. Experimenting with colors and the actual items to be seen by the child is the best way to determine the color or colors that will work best. Second, for the self-feeding child, the background against which dishes are placed helps the child see the dishes. Of course, if the child has a favorite place mat, honoring the child's preference is generally more important, even though it may not provide the best background. This rule applies to favorite dishes as well.

Contrast plays an important role in a child's ability to recognize and locate his or her own chair at the table. When a child with a visual impairment needs assistance, it is a good idea to provide some type of contrast so that the child's chair stands out from the others. A brightly colored high chair might be a better choice than a lightly colored one. The back of an existing chair can be covered with a brightly colored fabric by making a simple cover for it that is similar to a pillow case. The cover will slip easily over the chair back and slip off again for washing when dirty. A brightly colored bow or a brightly colored piece of paper or tag board attached to the chair could be used as well. The point is to make the chair stand out against the background of the area surrounding it.

Contrast for children who are blind is also important. In their case, however, the contrast needs to be textural. Marking the children's chairs and places at the table with distinct textures (e.g., one chair cover made from wide-wale corduroy, another chair cover made from swimsuit fabric) allows children to locate their seats independently. Matching pieces of cloth can mark other items such as cubbies, lockers, or backpacks. Giving place mats, cups, and glasses distinct textures permits these children to identify their own items.

Self-Feeding

Both children with sight and children with visual impairments begin to feed themselves first by finger feeding. Finger feeding is especially important for children with visual impairments, particularly children who have very little or no sight. Their hands take on the eyes' task of searching for the food. (The hands—instead of the eyes—locate the food item; then the child reaches for it, grasps it, and brings it to the mouth.) In general, these children should finger feed for a longer period than is usual. Because these children's visual limitations do not permit them to observe others eating with utensils, they need, in effect, to overlearn the process of bringing food to the mouth. Once learned, it will be easier to transfer these skills to bringing food to the mouth with a utensil. Finger feeding is also important because many children with visual impairments are reluctant to get their hands messy. They need to overcome this aversion. Using their hands to scan, locate, and identify replaces scanning and locating objects visually.

When a child with a visual impairment or blindness is reluctant to finger feed, it often helps to begin by finger feeding hand-over-hand with whomever is feeding the child. One of the child's hands is placed on top of one of the feeder's hands as the feeder locates, grasps, and brings pieces of food to the child's mouth. It helps if the food is one of the child's favorites because the child can share the food. After the feeder has fed a number of bites of food to the child, the feeder can place one of his or her hands over the child's hand and show the child how to finger feed.

Once a child has become successful and confident with finger feeding, he or she can move to using spoons and, later, forks and knives. Initially, the child will need to learn to use one hand to scoop bites of food with the spoon and the other hand to locate, push, and hold each bite of food so it does not get away from the utensil. Using the other hand in this manner is referred to as using the hand as a *pusher*. When older, the child should learn to use a piece of bread or a butter knife as a pusher. Eventually, the child should also learn to locate food on his or her plate by positions on a clock face (e.g., the carrot sticks are at 1:00, the hamburger is at 4:00, and the french fries are at 9:00). Teaching utensil use can be accomplished in much the same way as teaching finger feeding.

Plates with highly raised sides are helpful because the individual with significantly limited vision can use these sides to push food onto the fork or spoon. Bowls can facilitate getting food onto a utensil because their sides are curved. Of course, the degree of assistance that any plate or bowl provides depends on the food itself as well as the structure of the dish.

It is important that the plate or bowl does not slide around when the child is trying to eat. It is frustrating for anyone to try to get food on a utensil while the dish slides around. This situation is even more frustrating for one who cannot see. Using a surface that keeps dishes stationary is particularly important to the beginning self-feeder with a visual impairment. If slippage is an issue and place mats do not help, a piece of nonslip material like that made to line shelves or to keep throw rugs from sliding can serve as a place mat. Therapists often use a special product called Dycem, a material that is specifically designed to keep items and even people from slipping around on a surface. Dycem's usual blue color provides a nice contrast for light-colored dishes.

There are other accommodations that can help children with visual impairments become independent eaters. It is important to keep in mind that these accommodations can work with children with and without disabilities. For example, using Dycem to keep a dish in place is an accommodation that is useful and appropriate not only for children with visual impairments but also for children with many different disabilities and even children without disabilities who are learning to feed themselves. Musical utensils and cups are accommodations that are commercially available. These are especially useful for children with visual impairments to entice them to self-feed and help in locating the utensils. Musical utensils and cups are designed for all young children, regardless of disabilities, as motivators for feeding themselves.

When children need utensils that are easier to grasp, physical therapists can adapt their handles so that they are bigger. Children with visual impairments, mental retardation, deafblindness, or cerebral palsy who need larger utensil handles benefit from this accommodation. It is important to draw on other disciplines when making accommodations for children who have visual impairments. It is also important to weigh carefully any accommodations that make the children look different or stand out, and the age appropriateness of accommodations needs to be considered. Musical utensils, for example, often have larger handles. Young children using such utensils do not look out of place. Older children using such utensils, however, would look out of place. It is important to revisit accommodations periodically to ensure that they are still needed, that they remain age appropriate, and that they are not isolating the children or labeling them as "different."

Feeding Problems

Feeding problems encountered in children with visual impairments mirror those encountered in other children with disabilities. Jones (1982) identified five broad areas of feeding problems in children with disabilities: 1) drinking, 2) eating, 3) self-feeding, 4) social, and 5) self-injurious. Social problems involved such actions as stealing food, throwing tantrums during mealtimes, messy eating, eating too fast, using utensils for eye poking or light gazing, throwing food, and showing aggression toward others. Self-injurious problems involved pica, rumination, and regurgitation. Jones classified the causes of these feeding problems as behavioral, neurological, or physical. He considered the social and self-injurious areas as being primarily behavioral in etiology, whereas the other three problem areas (i.e., drinking, eating, and self-feeding) could be behavioral, neurological, or physical.

Children with visual impairments, especially visual impairments combined with other disabilities, can display any of these feeding problems. There are a few problems, however, that are particularly common. If not addressed when they arise, these problems can become significant issues. The next section focuses on these common feeding problems.

Sometimes young children with visual impairments have problems with learning to drink from a cup or glass. The reasons may be behavioral, neurological, physical, or a combination, depending on the presence of other disabilities in addition to the vision loss. Although suggestions for addressing drinking problems have been described elsewhere in this text, it is important to review the following suggestions in the context of children with visual impairments.

Generally, children with visual impairments resist drinking from cups or glasses for one of two reasons: 1) the cup rims have bumped their noses, and being bumped on the nose without seeing the bump coming may have startled them; or 2) the cup rim may come too close to their eyes. Many children with visual impairments have had painful or frightening experiences associated with their eyes. As a result, they often dislike being touched around their eyes. A simple solution to this drinking problem is using a plastic cup or glass with a portion of the front cut away to create a large nose hole. (See Figure 2A on page 146.) The cup will not touch the nose or eye area as it tips to deliver its contents.

Many children who are drinking from cups and glasses for the first time are surprised when the liquid sloshes on their faces. They may even choke and gag because they are startled. Children with visual impairments are particularly prone to surprise because they do not see the liquid coming. Reacting from fear, frustration, or change of routine, they may refuse liquids unless permitted to drink them from their bottles. Thickening liquids with applesauce, yogurt, or a thickening agent allows these children to control the flow more easily when drinking from a cup or glass.

Some mothers have made learning to drink from a cup more fun by using a favorite drink in the cup. Thickening one of the child's favorite beverages and presenting it in a cut-out cup often overcomes the child's resistance and facilitates learning to use a cup. As the child becomes more experienced, liquids can be thinned gradually until the child will accept a liquid consistency. As the child becomes a more experienced cup drinker, he or she will accept regular cups and glasses. School personnel may find using such encouragement helpful with some of their students with visual impairments.

Two additional feeding problems encountered frequently in children with visual impairments involve eating—refusal to eat solid foods or eating only a limited repertoire of solid foods. These problems seem to be behavioral in origin because the children who exhibit these behaviors are capable of chewing and swallowing normally. Either situation creates problems for these children, both at home and at school. Fortunately, with intervention, these children can learn to chew and swallow and eat a more broad array of foods.

There are a number of intervention techniques that have been used over the years to address behavioral feeding problems. One technique involves hiding or camouflaging the undesirable food under or behind a desirable food and gradually decreasing the presence of the desirable food (Jones, 1982). Another technique involves gradually increasing food texture until the child refusing to eat solid foods is able to do so (Campbell, 1976; Hart, 1974; Morris, 1977; Schmidt, 1976). Various behavior modification techniques, sometimes in combination with other techniques, have proven successful (Hoch, Babbitt, Coe, Krell, & Hackbert, 1994; Iwata, Riordan, Wohl, & Finney, 1982; Jones, 1983; Luiselli, Evans, & Boyce, 1985; Singer, Nofer, Benson-Szekely, & Brooks, 1991). For example, Luiselli and Gleason (1987) taught a young child with multiple disabilities, including visual impairments, to eat solid food by combining reinforcement techniques with gradually increasing food texture. For each bite of food accepted, the child was permitted to gaze at light while rocking in a swing. As the study progressed, the texture of the food increased from strained baby food to regular foods such as squash, scrambled egg, hamburger, and macaroni. Reinforcement was modified until the child sat in a chair at a table with other children and fed herself. Jones (1978, 1983) used behavior modification techniques and compared a "solid food only" approach to an approach of gradually increasing food texture. He studied 20 school-age children with mental retardation, many of whom had other disabilities including visual impairments. After 15 consecutive meals, 2 of the 10 children who received gradually increasing food textures were eating regular foods, whereas 8 of the 10 children who received solid foods from the beginning were eating regular foods. Follow-up studies conducted 1 month later found the same results.

There are some important factors for caregivers to keep in mind when deciding how to address a child's eating problem. First, a caregiver should be sure that there are no physical or neurological reasons for the eating problem. If the child had been a solid food eater and then stopped, a physical condition might be the cause. Perhaps the child has a sore throat, sore teeth, or an upset stomach. Second, a caregiver should examine what purposes refusing to eat regular food may serve for the child. What is the child trying to communicate with his or her refusal? Perhaps the reason is more about exercising control over the only situation in which he or she can be in control, rather than being uncomfortable with or scared of solid foods. If so, providing the child with many opportunities for choice making throughout the day—a more typical situation—may reduce or even eliminate the eating problem. Third, the caregiver should try simpler techniques first. It is important to always use a meaningful reinforcer as part of the chosen approach. Fourth, the caregiver should remember that each of these techniques has worked with some children. An important key to success is consistency. A camouflage technique worked with some children because the camouflage food was something the children liked eating. Positive reinforcement was built into each spoonful of food and was being paired consistently with the new food. Over time, less and less camouflage food was used—the reinforcement was faded—until the children ate all of their food before receiving their reinforcement (i.e., dessert). A behavior modification program coupled with increasing textures worked (Luiselli & Gleason, 1987) because the highly motivating sensory reinforcers (i.e., swinging and light gazing) were paired with *each* bite of food at *each* meal *every* day. Then the reinforcement schedule became varied while the texture was increased, but the procedures continued to be implemented at *every* meal *every* day.

Consistency in implementation is a key to the success of any intervention procedure. At no time is this statement more true than when implementing an intervention for a feeding problem. Remaining positive, not becoming angry, and providing frequent reinforcement are also key elements to success.

Characteristics of visual impairments and blindness, how these disabilities can limit children's learning, and accommodations caregivers can make to reduce or eliminate their impact on the learning experiences associated with feeding and mealtimes have been discussed. It is important to reiterate that many of the techniques discussed in this section may be beneficial not only for children with visual impairments and blindness but also for children without visual impairments. The following section discusses hearing loss and deafness and accommodations necessary to compensate for these disabilities. A number of the accommodations discussed will sound familiar to the reader.

HEARING LOSS AND DEAFNESS

Hearing, like vision, is a distance sense. It permits children to observe—in this case, eavesdrop—without being directly involved in an interaction. Adequate hearing is vital to learning an oral language. Thus, language acquisition is a primary focus of educational programs for children with hearing loss.

There are four factors that are used to classify hearing loss: 1) degree of loss, 2) age at onset, 3) cause of loss, and 4) structures affected (Sobsey & Wolf-Schein, 1991). When a child cannot understand speech through his or her ear, even with a hearing aid, then that child is considered *deaf*. When a child can understand speech through the ear—albeit with difficulty—with or without a hearing aid, then that child is considered *hard of hearing* (Moores, 1987). A child has *prelingual deafness* when the deafness occurs before spoken language develops. When deafness occurs after speech and language acquisition, the child has *postlingual deafness*.

Sounds are measured by their *frequency,* which is cycles per second, or *hertz* (Hz), and their *intensity,* or loudness, which is *decibels* (dB). Of course, how well a child hears speech is especially important, so losses between 500 Hz and 2,000 Hz negatively affect spoken language learning the most. A child's hearing loss is classified by the amount or degree of hearing loss experienced. A loss of 35–54 dB is considered to be *mild,* 55–69 dB is *moderate,* 70–89 dB is *severe,* and 90 dB or greater is *profound* (Moores, 1987).

There are many pre- and postnatal causes of hearing loss and deafness, including illness, injury, and genetics. These can result in *conductive, sensorineural,* or *mixed losses* or in *central auditory disorders.* Conductive hearing losses result when something (e.g., wax buildup, fluid from an infection, hole in the eardrum, bony growth of the small bones in the ear, birth defect) interferes with sound waves reaching the nerves of the inner ear. Sensorineural losses refer to hearing losses due to nerve damage. This damage may occur in the inner ear or along the eighth cranial (i.e., vestibulocochlear) nerve that transmits sound information to the brain. Mixed losses involve both conductive and sensorineural losses. Central auditory disorders refer to an inability to respond meaningfully to sound in the absence of damage to the auditory system (i.e., outer, middle, and inner ear and vestibulocochlear nerve).

Effects of Hearing Loss on Development

Hearing permits children to interact with the sound features of their environments. Over time, they attach meaning to these sounds. This learning begins early in their lives. For example, as infants, children learn to recognize the sound of someone approaching their rooms because of the frequent pairing of the sound with receiving attention from a caregiver. When the children are crying, their parents may call to them as they approach to let them know they are coming, which is also a sound cue.

As children grow, they interact more with their environments, and people around them talk about these interactions; therefore, children learn the names of objects, people, features, and events associated with the interactions. They acquire important information and concepts. Language mediates their experiences, but hearing loss may reduce or distort these experiences and information if the children do not have access to visual or auditory language (Prickett & Welch, 1995).

Young children learn many concepts from the feeding experience. Consider the number of items related to this experience that young children learn to label. They learn the names of a large array of foods as well as all of the items associated with cooking and eating food. Food and associated items have many attributes (e.g., color, temperature, texture, taste), so children learn to describe them as well as to associate and categorize them. Social aspects of the feeding experience are also important to consider. For example, children learn how to make requests during mealtimes. Very early during the requesting process, children learn that their cries will result in others' responding. Later, children discover that their cries can be refined to a sound or a look and still achieve the same result. Later still, children discover that they can point and pantomime to make a request, and they can respond to others' requests as well. For example, children might share cookies with friends or siblings when asked to do so. One important social aspect of the feeding experience is mealtime itself. Mealtime is often the time when families discuss what will be happening and what has happened to each family member. These discussions not only help children learn to conceptualize the meanings of *past* and *future* but also serve as part of the bonding experience among family members.

Hearing loss and deafness place children at a disadvantage for fully experiencing and learning from mealtimes if the only language available is spoken. Thus, although feeding and eating problems are not associated with hearing loss per se, children with hearing loss and deafness are at significant risk for altered conceptual and socioemotional development in addition to the significant oral language problems associated with hearing loss and deafness.

Accommodations for Hearing Loss and Deafness

Providing complete information on accommodating for hearing loss in children is beyond the scope of this chapter. Teachers are advised to read some of the excellent textbooks that focus on facilitating language acquisition in children with hearing loss and deafness and to consult with specialists in hearing loss and deafness from their school systems. This chapter does, however, discuss some important accommodations that will facilitate learning while children with hearing loss and deafness are eating. These accommodations have been discussed previously for children with visual impairments; much of the same information applies to children with hearing loss and deafness as well.

Lighting

Providing adequate lighting and controlling glare are important considerations for children with hearing loss and deafness. Because their hearing is limited, these children place more reliance on their sight to provide them with environmental information. For example, they learn to pay particular attention to speakers' lips, faces, and body language to help them understand what they may be hearing. Lighting and glare are also inhibiting or supporting factors when using sign language. Hand shape and movement, facial expression, body movements, and use of environmental space are used together to express communications in sign language, especially American Sign Language, which is also called ASL (Adams, 1997; Radetsky, 1994).

Everyone has had the experience of trying to watch someone while he or she stands in front of a sunny window or a bright light. It is difficult, visually fatiguing, and even headache producing. When young children find it hard to see well, they generally turn their attention elsewhere. Older children may struggle and persevere to see, but they also tire. In either case, information and incidental learning will be limited or lost because these children do not see well. They must rely on their other senses, especially their hearing. When these children have hearing loss and deafness, however, neither of the distance senses that permit environmental contact beyond their fingertips is providing input. Therefore, teachers must be sure that the areas where their students eat are well-lit but without glare or shadows that make seeing difficult and uncomfortable.

Providing Contrast

Providing background contrast is also important for children with hearing loss and deafness. Contrast should be provided between teachers' and aides' clothing and their hands and faces. Busy patterns of clothing make reading signs more difficult and visually fatiguing. Generally, solid colors of clothing work better, with darker colors providing better contrast for teachers and aides with light skin tones and lighter colors providing more contrast for those teachers and aides with dark skin tones.

Positioning

Because children with hearing loss and deafness rely so heavily on vision to augment their residual hearing and compensate for what they do not hear, they need to be positioned properly. For example, it is difficult to observe the environment visually or read someone's facial expressions, body language, or signs while struggling to maintain head control or being forced into an abnormal reflex because of the need to turn far to one side. Proper positioning not only facilitates head control and vision functions (e.g., looking, following, tracking) but also allows children to point, gesture, and sign. When poorly positioned, children's balance may be unstable—their hands and arms are available only for maintaining body position against gravity. Their shoulders may be held back so that they cannot bring their hands together at the middle of their bodies (i.e., mid-line) to grasp utensils or make signs. Many signs are formed with both hands chest high at mid-line. For example, the sign for CUP involves placing one hand in the shape of the letter C in the palm of the other hand as it is held flat and palm up. COOKIE is signed by using these same hand shapes and having the open side of the letter *C* appear to cut a cookie from the palm of the open hand. The signs for SPOON, FORK, KNIFE, PLATE, GLASS, MEAT, EGGS, CAKE, BREAD, and BUTTER are some other signs that require having one's hands together at mid-line.

In addition to positioning children properly to help them see well and use their hands freely, teachers need to attend to how children position themselves at mealtimes in relation to children with hearing loss and deafness. Teachers need to be able to see their children's faces and vice versa. Often, teachers need to sit behind children because they need to use jaw control procedures or teach hand-over-hand feeding. Doing so in front of a mirror allows for face-to-face communication, even though the teacher and child sit one behind the other. When using a mirror is impractical, such as in a school cafeteria or a restaurant, sitting behind but slightly to the side of the child permits the teacher to lean around and establish face-to-face contact with the child.

Incidental Learning

Mealtimes provide all sorts of opportunities for incidental learning. Family conversation at the dinner table is significant for family bonding and for making children feel that they are accepted, important family members (Adams, 1997). Unfortunately, in homes where only spoken language is used, children with hearing loss and deafness miss out on these learning and bonding opportunities. Deaf adults often describe being unable to follow the rapid-fire spoken conversations of their families at mealtimes and feeling left out of the family circle (Adams, 1997).

Teachers must be concerned with compensating for hearing loss so that children with hearing loss and deafness can understand concepts typically learned from eavesdropping on others. Teachers should also help families to compensate for children's hearing loss. Helping with meal preparation is an excellent language- and communication-building activity for both home and school. It provides multiple opportunities for learning vocabulary, learning the language associated with various concepts (e.g., *under, behind, thick, thin, hot, cold, spicy, mild, more, less, how many, how much*) and practicing communication (e.g., "I need more milk," "Please give me the spoon"). It also provides a topic for conversation at mealtimes and later, at school or home, when teachers or parents ask what the children did during the day.

First, teachers must understand the impact that hearing loss and deafness have on children in order to accommodate for them. Next, teachers must be alert to spoken language and sounds in the environment. Finally, teachers must ensure that children with hearing loss and deafness have visual access to language and sounds. Such access helps the children give meaning to sounds they hear and, more important, permits language mediation of their experiences.

DEAFBLINDNESS

Children with deafblindness present unique challenges to educators. Whereas hearing is available to assist children with visual impairments and blindness and vision is available to assist children with hearing loss, both of these senses are impaired in children with deafblindness.

There are approximately 10,000 children and youth, from birth to 21 years of age, who have deafblindness (Baldwin, 1994). The degree of their visual impairments ranges from partial sight to total blindness, and their hearing losses range from mild to profound. As many as 70% of these children also have concomitant disabilities, such as cerebral palsy and mental retardation. Of those with mental retardation, many have cortical blindness or cortical deafness. Children with *cortical blindness* are unable to see but have no apparent damage to the eye or visual mechanism. Likewise, children with *cortical deafness* are unable to hear but have no damage to the auditory mechanism.

Effects of Deafblindness on Development

Deafblindness is not simply a vision loss plus a hearing loss (McInnes & Treffry, 1982). The resulting disability is one in which both distance senses are compromised; neither sense has remained intact to pick up the slack for the other (i.e., to permit the child to fill in lacking information due to the missing sense) (Prickett & Welch, 1995). For example, when a visual disability is present, children learn much about eating because they can use their hearing to notice what is going on around them. Their parents also tell them what is going on, so voice expression and language help these children learn. In addition, these children can ask questions and discuss the process because they have acquired a spoken language that they have learned to use to get information about something they cannot see. When a hearing disability is present, children still have their sight to allow them to observe others eating, observe and make decisions about the food that is offered, imitate the social skills of eating that they see, and react to the facial expressions and gestures of others. When deafblindness is present, however, children are more cut off from their environments. The sights of eating are not seen and the sounds of eating are not heard, or the sights and sounds are so distorted that these children ignore them. Language cannot be used to mediate the experience until these children have acquired sufficient language skills. For most children with deafblindness, acquiring sufficient language skills to mediate learning will take longer than learning to eat. In general, children with deafblindness rarely learn communication skills and language without much intervention.

There is a rule of thumb to follow when working with children who are deafblind: Assume that whatever the children will know and whatever skills they will have will happen because someone will make the effort to show or teach them. One cannot assume that a child with deafblindness will learn incidentally because intact sight and hearing are not available to the child. Although this rule may seem extreme, it serves children with deafblindness well. Their worlds extend only as far as their fingers reach, as far as their residual vision sees, and as far as their residual hearing hears.

Fortunately, total deafblindness—no sight and no hearing—is rare. Most children with deafblindness have some remaining sight and hearing (Downing & Eichinger, 1990; Fredericks & Baldwin, 1987; Hart, 1974; McInnes & Treffry, 1982; Prickett & Welch, 1995). This residual vision and hearing, as the remaining senses are called, are available to help these children learn about eating. How much assistance these senses provide depends on the amount of residual vision and hearing remaining and how well the children have learned to use them. For example, children with deafblindness who can see things held extremely close to one of their eyes will examine their food visually, but they will also use their sense of smell (olfactory sense). If being fed, these children may refuse the food and grab their teacher's arm to bring the food closer to their faces so they can look at it. They may lean forward and tilt their heads to examine the offered food carefully. They will probably also smell the food, and they may touch it gently. These children are supplementing their limited vision with their other senses. Likewise, if children with deafblindness have no vision available but only moderate hearing loss, they may examine their food by smelling and touching it and be encouraged by hearing the tone of their teachers' voices.

Accommodations for Children with Deafblindness

Touch (tactile input), smell (olfactory input), and movement (kinesthetic input) are especially important to children with deafblindness. They rely on these senses to help them learn about and organize their worlds even more than children with single sensory disabilities. Accommodating for deafblindness requires combining the various accommodations for vision and hearing disabilities with tactile, olfactory, and kinesthetic input. In order to demonstrate how combining various accommodations might be achieved, some students with deafblindness are discussed in the following vignettes.

Ivan

Ivan is a 7-year-old boy who attends a class for first graders in a general education school. Ivan's deafblindness is due to maternal Rubella syndrome. Rubella is an unusual cause of deafblindness in young children in the United States but is still a leading cause of deafblindness in other countries, especially in developing countries. Ivan was born in Russia and adopted by an American family at 3 years of age.

Both Ivan's vision and hearing are quite impaired. He has a profound, bilateral hearing loss for which he uses two hearing aids. He has not yet demonstrated any awareness of sound. He had cataract surgery and now wears eyeglasses with thick lenses. Although his doctors have been unable to test his vision, they think Ivan has better vision in his left eye and no usable vision beyond light perception in his right eye. He wears his eyeglasses willingly, both at school and at home, but he wears his hearing aids at school only. Ivan engages in such stereotypical behaviors as light gazing and finger flapping. He has even climbed adults like trees to get closer to light sources. Ivan does not exhibit sound making, however. When Ivan began his school program last year, he communicated by physically manipulating others and by screaming, crying, throwing things, and stomping his feet. He was ambulatory and ran and jumped with ease. Jumping while holding an adult's hands was a favorite activity. Ivan still drank from a bottle and ate mainly soft food, although he did like cheese puffs and cheese crackers.

Rebecca

Rebecca is a 6-year-old child who attends an elementary school that houses a tri-county regional program for children with hearing loss and deafness. She has four classmates, all 5–7 years old. Rebecca's records indicate a severe sensorineural hearing loss, cortical blindness, quadriplegic cerebral palsy, and mental retardation requiring pervasive support. She is nonambulatory. Rebecca lives with her grandmother and grandfather, who are her legal guardians. Rebecca's parents are dead, and she has no siblings. She has three cousins near her age whom she sees frequently. Rebecca's grandparents describe skills that Rebecca exhibits at home with her cousins, but the school staff have seen little evidence that Rebecca has many skills. The staff know that Rebecca recognizes her grandmother's voice, but she does not seem to attend to or recognize other sounds at school. Sometimes she has appeared to look at the windows in the classroom. Also, Rebecca has appeared to follow one of her classmates as he walked by, but the school staff are not sure. She usually sits in her wheelchair with her head resting on her chest. Rebecca smiles and laughs when the other children tickle and play with her. Her grandmother says that she finger feeds at home, but she has not done so at school. Rebecca eats most foods, including chewing and swallowing, and drinks from a cup when it is held to her lips.

Juan Carlos

Juan Carlos is a 10-year-old boy whose deafblindness is due to prematurity. He has light perception, a severe sensorineural deafness, mild cerebral palsy, and mental retardation. He is ambulatory, although he generally does not move around unless it is required. He has attended a segregated school for children with mental retardation requiring extensive or pervasive support since he was 3 years old. School staff sign to Juan Carlos by placing their hands over his hands and making the signs together. Juan Carlos understands about 30 signs and signed phrases—perhaps more. He drinks from cups, glasses, soda bottles, and cans and through straws. Although messy, he feeds himself but eats only soft foods, especially Cream of Wheat.

All three of these children have deafblindness. Each child presents differences in the degree of sensory impairments and extent of additional disabilities. Most important, each child is an individual whose unique characteristics and personality must be considered when making accommodations (Stremel & Schutz, 1995). Fortunately, the staff of each of the programs that these children attend are well-trained professionals who are able to orchestrate appropriate accommodations for each child. Comparing accommodations illustrates how the variables for each child were considered.

Positioning

Proper positioning is important for Ivan, Rebecca, and Juan Carlos. Both Ivan and Juan Carlos are ambulatory; therefore, they have sufficient trunk and head control to sit in regular chairs. Rebecca, however, is nonambulatory; she generally sits in her wheelchair, often without maintaining head control. All three children need to sit so that there are 90° angles at their hips, knees, and ankles. All three children should have their feet resting on the floor or on a platform so that they feel secure. Table height for Ivan and Juan Carlos should be appropriate so that they do not have to lean over too far or reach up too high to eat.

Proper seating at a table of appropriate height will help Ivan remain in his seat while he eats. Ivan likes to eat a few bites of food, go to the windows to look at the sunlight, return for a few more bites of food, go back to the windows, and so on. At home, Ivan's parents seat him in a high chair to keep him at the table while he eats. Remaining in his seat while eating is not an issue with Juan Carlos. Because he does not see and is not yet comfortable with his position in space, however, he feels insecure when not sitting in a stable position.

Lighting

These three children share some lighting needs, but some lighting needs are different among the three. Glare should be controlled for each child. In Ivan's case, glare makes it more difficult for him to see. In addition, as typical of children with Rubella syndrome, Ivan loves to light gaze (i.e., stare at light) and to light gaze while finger flapping (i.e., waving his hand back and forth in front of his eyes). Glare encourages such stereotypical behaviors. In Juan Carlos' case, glare may be uncomfortable and annoying. In Rebecca's case, glare may discourage her from learning to use her vision. Rebecca has cortical blindness, which means that her lack of sight is not due to any observable problem with her vision system. Its cause is unknown. (Frequently, children with cortical blindness learn to use their sight through intervention and encouragement.)

Keeping the eating area well-lit with a nonglare light source is important for both Ivan and Rebecca. It helps Ivan see better, and it encourages Rebecca to use her vision. For Juan Carlos, lighting in the eating area provides a location clue when he enters the eating area. Different lighting arrangements, including different locations of lighting sources, help a child with light perception to recognize different rooms or areas of a room. For example, the assigned table in the dining room might be located on the side of the cafeteria nearest the windows. Unlike children who are blind but have intact hearing, Juan Carlos cannot rely on sound to provide location clues. He can use gross differences in lighting, however, because he has light perception. Although Ivan has residual vision that he relies on to move through his environment, he also has a significant hearing loss. Lighting can provide additional location information to supplement the information Ivan receives through his eyes.

Providing Contrast

Providing background–foreground contrast is important for all three children. Juan Carlos needs texture contrasts. In Juan Carlos' classroom, his chair has been marked with a unique texture, a piece of fine sandpaper. Although Juan Carlos and his classmates eat lunch in the cafeteria, they have drinks and snacks available in their classroom. Juan Carlos' place mat and plastic drinking glass have textures that help him locate them easily. Both color and texture contrasts help Ivan and Rebecca. Ivan's sight is limited, and what he sees is blurry. His royal purple place mat stands out against the light color of the tabletop, and it permits the light color of the plastic containers that his mother sends in his lunches to show up well. The plastic drinking glass that Ivan uses is yellow to help him see it on the purple place mat and has a bumpy surface that he can feel. Ivan's teacher has covered his chair in purple corduroy and taped a 3″ × 5″ rectangle of the same corduroy above the latch for his locker. The texture provides another avenue of input for Ivan. Ivan often does not use his vision, which is typical of many children with maternal Rubella syndrome. Texture encourages him to look and reinforces that he is seeing contrasts. Rebecca's place mat is a piece of bright blue Dycem. Dycem has a distinctive feel to it, so Rebecca is learning to identify her place tactually. Like Ivan's purple place mat, the bright blue Dycem contrasts well with the table, with the containers that Rebecca brings from home, and with the school cafeteria's food trays. Rebecca uses a red plastic cup with a rough surface and a nose hole to facilitate drinking. Rebecca's teacher and classroom aide have her feel the textures to identify her lunch items. The bright colors and color contrasts encourage Rebecca to use her vision. Ivan's and Rebecca's teachers use calendar boxes to help them organize their days and communicate what is upcoming and what is finished. Ivan has a small piece of a purple place mat that matches his larger place mat to indicate mealtime. Rebecca uses a matching cup identical to her own cup at mealtime for the same purpose. Often, children use items from the calendar boxes in their beginning, expressive, symbolic communications. Ivan quickly learned the meaning of his small piece of purple place mat. When it was the next item in his box, he would smile and immediately get his larger place mat, put it at his place at the table, get his lunch, sit down, and eat. Within a short period of time, Ivan began selecting his small piece of purple place mat out of order or going to the calendar box spontaneously to get the small piece of place mat and give it to his teacher to indicate he wanted to eat. Although he does not eat solid foods, Ivan enjoys eating and drinking, especially yogurt and fruit juices. Staff reinforced these early symbolic communications with a small drink or some yogurt, even though it was not mealtime. Had they not done so, Ivan might never have tried any other symbolic forms of communication and may have continued to rely on tantrums. It did not take long for Ivan to begin selecting either his cup or place mat to indicate whether he wanted a drink or something to eat. Soon staff were able to tell Ivan that he could have his request when he had finished an activity.

Juan Carlos had used a calendar box when he was younger. Because he learned to respond to so many signs, it had been discontinued when he was about 7 years old. Juan Carlos does not use any signs expressively, however. In fact, he rarely asks for anything from the classroom staff. He behaves differently with Mike, one of the after-school child care workers. He and Mike have a special bond. Juan Carlos generally communicates with Mike by pushing or pulling him and putting Mike's hand on something with which he thinks Mike can help him. Juan Carlos even finds his cup and hands it to Mike to indicate that he wants a drink. Mike does not anticipate Juan Carlos' needs. He waits for Juan Carlos to ask. Juan Carlos knows that when he asks, no matter the form, Mike will respond.

Using Touch and Movement

Touch and movement are extremely important avenues of input for children with deafblindness. Both require close contact between the child and another person. Whether signing hand-over-hand (tactile signing) or teaching the child to scoop a bite of food onto a spoon, the child and the adult must share space and be in physical proximity. Yet the U.S. culture is one in which touching is reserved for close relationships (Stremel & Schutz, 1995). Those interacting and working with children with deafblindness will need to become comfortable with sharing their space and learning how vital touch is to these children. The next section explains some ways in which touch and movement have been used with Ivan, Juan Carlos, and Rebecca during feeding.

Touch

A gentle touch, perhaps on the shoulder, should be used to indicate that someone has approached and is about to do something with the child. Because of their dual sensory impairments, children with deafblindness can be startled easily. For example, Juan Carlos may not realize when someone has approached him until that person begins to sign with his hands. Although Ivan has some residual vision, he does not hear someone who approaches him from behind. Rebecca has a significant amount of residual hearing, so she may hear someone approaching if the person makes sufficient noise. Often, there is so much going on that Rebecca does not realize when some of the sounds she hears come from someone approaching her. At lunchtime, for example, the classmate assigned to push Rebecca's wheelchair generally walked up to the back of her chair and simply began taking her to the cafeteria. Rebecca always jumped, and sometimes she cried. Once the child learned to touch Rebecca's shoulder and greet her before pushing the wheelchair, Rebecca no longer became startled. When someone is about to interact with a child with deafblindness, making the intention known to the child with a touch cue is the tactile equivalent of catching one's eye or saying one's name before beginning to converse.

Touch cues can be used to communicate a variety of messages. Tapping fingers might mean GIVE ME, lightly tapping fingertips on the lips could indicate MEALTIME, and tapping the hand holding the spoon could mean KEEP EATING. Touch cues are especially important if the child with deafblindness does not understand signs or tangible symbols (Rowland & Schweigert, 1989).

When Juan Carlos was younger and still being fed, he received a touch cue before each bite of food so he would know that it was available. Whoever was feeding him would gently touch the tip of the spoon to the middle of his lower lip and then move it away just slightly. Therefore, Juan Carlos learned that another bite of food was available. He also had time to smell the food. If he wanted the food, he had to open his mouth, lean forward to get the spoon in his mouth, close his lips around it, and remove the food himself. Juan Carlos was an active participant in feeding.

All too often, children like Juan Carlos become passive participants because they have to do little beyond keeping their mouths open to receive food. Spoonfuls of food arrive, and their contents are dropped into the children's mouths or scraped off by the children's teeth. Juan Carlos could well have been a passive feeder had it not been for the input from his first teacher, who showed Juan Carlos' mother how to feed him so that he had to participate in the process. The first tactile sign Juan Carlos learned to understand was EAT, which is signed by touching the fingertips of one hand to the lips. An important touch cue for Juan Carlos is a gentle tap on the back of a hand. This touch cue indicates that someone wants to tell him something. Telling

Juan Carlos something is done through tactile signing, which involves signing with and within Juan Carlos' hands.

Touch is also used to help children learn things they would usually learn through visual observation if their visual channels were intact. Children with sight observe self-feeding, eating and enjoying a variety of solid foods, and chewing and swallowing long before they are introduced to these skills. Children with deafblindness need to place their hands over the hands of trusted adults in order to observe the adults self-feeding and place their hands over the adults' cheeks and throats in order to observe chewing and swallowing and the pleasure the adults take in eating. A teacher might permit these experiences while eating a food that the child might enjoy. After every few bites, the teacher could offer a bite to the child. The reinforcement of the pleasurable taste might overcome the initial dislike for the food's texture.

Movement

Because their visual information is limited, children with deafblindness rely on motor or kinesthetic memory (i.e., how skills feel when doing them) to execute certain skills. Obtaining a cup or glass from the table is a good example. A child with residual vision can combine looking with his motor memory to reach for and secure his drink during mealtime. For a child without sufficient residual vision, motor memory makes locating the beverage easier. He will not have to search all over his space because he will remember reaching with his right or left hand a certain distance for the glass. The wrist rotation necessary to self-feed is another good example of using motor memory. Finger feeding, using utensils, and drinking from a cup or glass require rotating the wrist in order to get the food to the mouth and rotating the wrist again when returning to obtain more food or to place the glass on the table. Children without disabilities learn this rotation themselves. Many children whose sight is impaired need intervention.

Providing intervention requires that the child and the teacher sit in the same plane so that the child feels the movement exactly as he or she will feel it during independent execution. So when teaching self-feeding or drinking, the teacher needs to sit behind the child and work in a hand-over-hand fashion. The teacher must be careful to guide the child's movements exactly as the child would make the movements him- or herself.

Both Juan Carlos' and Ivan's teachers and paraprofessionals used this hand-over-hand technique to teach self-feeding. How they did so demonstrates individualized accommodations of the basic technique used to address each child's needs and personalities. In addition, the different choices they made with regard to addressing each child's refusal to accept solid foods illustrate the choices that parents and teachers sometimes must make. The apparent disparity between Rebecca's feeding skills at home and at school illustrates yet another feeding problem that parents and teachers encounter.

FEEDING PROBLEMS

Juan Carlos
. . . .

Juan Carlos has no vision; therefore, he has had no opportunities to see others feed themselves. Because he refused to eat solid foods, finger feeding was problematic. He could be encouraged to put his hands in his food and then eat food from his hands. His mother and staff discussed the pros and cons of such a step and decided against it. The con of teaching him it was all right to play in his food outweighed the pro of experiencing hand-to-mouth movement. They knew that Juan Carlos made this connection because he routinely brought toys and other items to his mouth. They decided to begin with using a spoon. They agreed to revisit finger feeding if using the spoon proved unsuccessful.

Because Juan Carlos ate breakfast, lunch, and snacks at school, his parents and teacher began at breakfast with the help of one of Juan Carlos' favorite classroom paraprofessionals, Helga. Helga greeted Juan Carlos at the table and showed him she had her own bowl of farina and was sitting next to him to eat. Next, she showed Juan Carlos that she had a spoon just like Juan Carlos' by helping him to compare both spoons and signing SAME with his hands. Then the teacher helped Juan Carlos feel that Helga had grasped her spoon and was scooping a bite of farina, taking it to her mouth, moving it around in her mouth, swallowing it, and returning to the bowl for more. They repeated this procedure for several bites until Juan Carlos indicated that he wanted his farina. The teacher then helped him find his bowl and spoon. Sitting behind Juan Carlos and slightly to his right, she pantomimed Juan Carlos scooping a bite of his cereal and bringing it to his mouth. She then signed SAME with his hands, guided him to touch Helga's hand holding her spoon, and signed SAME again. Next, the teacher guided Juan Carlos to scoop his own bite of farina and bring it to his mouth. She touched his lips gently, as usual, to indicate to Juan Carlos that a bite of food awaited him. Juan Carlos thought about this new experience briefly, then opened his mouth and took his food. His teacher then guided him to return his spoon to the bowl for another bite. She also patted him on the shoulder to indicate that he had done well. This pat was a well-established touch cue to indicate GOOD. Juan Carlos and his teacher proceeded through his breakfast, following these same steps. Periodically, after touching the back of one of Juan Carlos' hands to indicate that she wanted to communicate with him, Helga would take his hands, touch her bowl and face, touch his bowl and face, and sign SAME to indicate that he was eating just like her. Juan Carlos' teacher and classroom aide followed the same procedures with snacks and lunch. Juan Carlos' parents and teacher had arrangements with the after-school program to have Juan Carlos eat his dinner before his parents picked him up. Mike, Juan Carlos' favorite after-school child care provider, followed the same procedures at dinner. By Friday of that week, Juan Carlos was feeding himself independently.

In his classroom and in the room for the after-school program, Juan Carlos ate at a table that had been placed against a large mirror mounted on the wall. This mirror allowed staff to communicate with the children while helping them learn to eat. Although Juan Carlos had no sight and could not use the mirror himself, his teacher used the mirror to see how Juan Carlos was handling the experience of self-feeding; to time when to begin the next bite; to have eye contact with Helga, other staff, and children; and to observe other children. It was because of the mirror that Juan Carlos' teacher had observed Juan Carlos' thinking posture and waited for him to decide to take his first self-fed bite of farina. There were no wall-mounted mirrors in the school cafeteria, and Juan Carlos' class sat at a table near the middle of the room. There, his teacher used a portable mirror.

Ivan

Ivan's sight appeared quite limited, although his selective use of sight made the actual degree of limitation difficult to determine. Certainly, Ivan had no visual input prior to removal of his cataracts and learning to wear his eyeglasses. He had accepted eating cheese puffs and goldfish-shaped cheese crackers, apparently from his sister's encouragement. Other foods had to be soft. In addition to puddings, yogurt, and applesauce, Ivan ate foods such as mashed potatoes, mashed butternut squash with butter and brown sugar, mashed plantains, various mashed fruits, and baby food meats. Except for the cheese puffs and crackers, Ivan did not feed himself, and he still used a bottle.

Learning to eat and drink like others his age was a goal that Ivan's family, members of the school staff, the special education director, and a consultant in deafblindness (i.e., Ivan's special education team) set for Ivan soon after he entered school. One objective of this goal was teaching Ivan to drink from a cup or glass; a second objective was teaching Ivan to feed himself; and a third objective was helping Ivan to eat regular food. The team decided to begin teaching Ivan how to drink from a cup or glass, then work on teaching him to self-feed, and finally work on teaching him to eat regular food.

School staff explained that they did not allow children who were Ivan's age to use a bottle at school. Because he liked to drink, they thought that he would accept a cup at school fairly easily. They also explained that they could begin with a cut-out cup and thickened liquid or a regular cup with a top that limited the amount of liquid that came out. Because they preferred to make only those accommodations that were necessary (Stratton, 1990), they leaned toward beginning with the regular cup and nonthickened liquid. Ivan's parents agreed; they pointed out that Ivan's bottles had large holes in the nipples and that he sometimes took sips of soda from his sister. Once Ivan discovered that there were not bottles for him at school, he accepted drinking from the school's cups. After 1 month of drinking with the lids on the cups, he began using the cups without their lids. He took one of the school cups home with him and began using it at home also.

Next, Ivan's special education team focused on self-feeding. Because they knew that Ivan could finger feed cheese puffs and crackers, the team decided to begin with spoon feeding. Ivan's sister and a friend volunteered to encourage him to feed himself at home by showing Ivan (visually) how they fed themselves. Because they had convinced Ivan to eat cheese puffs and take sips of soda from a can, they thought they might be successful at encouraging him to self-feed. The team agreed that systematic instruction would begin at school and then be transferred to home. Ivan's sister and her friend would encourage Ivan at home during the weekends.

On the following Monday morning, Ivan's mother sent a note saying that the girls had encouraged and cajoled Ivan all weekend, but Ivan refused to feed himself. The entire family was convinced, however, that Ivan knew exactly what they wanted. He had cooperated with his sister and her friend until they wanted him to use his spoon. Then he had stomped his foot in anger and stubbornness and cried. At school, the teacher and classroom aides tried to show Ivan the other children using their spoons. Ivan refused to look.

Ivan's response is not surprising. Children with maternal Rubella syndrome often display autistic-like behaviors and are uncooperative about changes in routine. Intervention requires motivating them sufficiently while showing them that the new routine will continue. Because Ivan's parents found it difficult to overcome his resistance at home, school staff suggested teaching him at school and moving the new skill to home later.

Ivan's teacher had Ivan follow his usual mealtime routine. When he was ready to eat, however, Ivan's teacher placed three spoonfuls of Ivan's yogurt into a bowl, placed the bowl in front of him, and handed him a spoon. Ivan's teacher moved Ivan's other food back to the lunchbox, which she placed open at the upper left corner of Ivan's purple place mat. She wanted Ivan to see that the lunch remained for him to eat. Ivan's teacher then indicated to Ivan that he should eat his yogurt. Each time Ivan tried to get food from his lunchbox, his teacher gently but firmly returned Ivan's attention to the spoon and yogurt. She ignored Ivan's foot stomping and sounds of obvious displeasure. She encouraged Ivan by scooping some yogurt onto the spoon, showing it to him, replacing it in the bowl, and taking Ivan's hand to grasp the spoon handle together. Ivan and his teacher had other, similar encounters when changing demand levels, so his teacher knew that Ivan would soon cooperate after he finished protesting. Ivan ultimately cooperated and, within a few days, accepted feeding himself a few bites of yogurt, pudding, or applesauce before eating the remainder of his lunch.

Ivan's teacher had been careful to place a small amount of one of Ivan's favorite foods in the bowl in beginning his intervention. She wanted Ivan to receive immediate reinforcement with each bite of food he fed himself and to achieve initial success easily. After Ivan grew accustomed to the routine of beginning his lunch with feeding himself a few bites of his favorite foods, his teacher gradually increased the amount he had to eat. By the time Ivan was accustomed to feeding himself all of his favorite foods first, he accepted eating the remainder of his lunch independently. Of course, he also received much praise from his teacher, the classroom aides, and his classmates.

Transferring the skill to home required a classroom visit by Ivan's parents at lunchtime, followed by a home visit at dinnertime from Ivan's teacher and a classroom aide on the same day. Ivan was not thrilled that his family would no longer feed him, but he accepted his parents' decision and smiled at the praise they and his sister gave him. Whenever his grandmother took care of him, however, Ivan ate only if his grandmother fed him.

Teaching Ivan to eat regular food did not prove as successful as teaching him to use a cup and self-feed. Children with Rubella syndrome often find it difficult to tolerate textures in food. Although they can learn to become good eaters of regular foods, much consistency is needed to teach them. Ivan's parents and school staff thought that they could follow the same protocol of teaching Ivan at school first and then transferring the skill to home use. This time, the technique did not work. After investigation of the research literature (i.e., Jones, 1978, 1982, 1983), they discovered the level of consistency necessary to be successful. Ivan's family would have to be involved at the same time, using the same techniques. Unfortunately, Ivan's family had several things happen that prevented them from being able to participate with the required level of consistency. Ivan's parents and school team decided to address the feeding issue at a later date when they would be able to provide the necessary consistency to be successful.

Rebecca

Rebecca's feeding problems were minor or major, depending on whether her mother or the school staff discussed them. At home, Rebecca was a good eater who finger fed herself all of the foods 6-year-olds typically eat. At school, however, Rebecca had to be fed. The teacher, educational interpreter, and itinerant vision specialist had discussed among themselves the possibility that her grandparents reported what they wanted Rebecca to be doing rather than what Rebecca actually did. Her grandparents also reported that Rebecca responded to her name and recognized the names of her cousins, but the school staff had seen no evidence of name recognition at school.

Early in the school year, the state's consultant in deafblindness began working with the staff of Rebecca's school. Rebecca began going to the kindergarten classroom for center time each morning and afternoon in order to have contact with hearing children. Rebecca responded enthusiastically to the kindergartners, and they responded well to her. Before long, the educational interpreter who accompanied Rebecca began to notice that Rebecca seemed to look at one of the windows in the classroom. As the kindergartners began to interact more with Rebecca, the educational interpreter spent more time observing until she was sure that Rebecca was not only looking at the window but also visually tracking children as they walked in front of it. The educational interpreter also noticed that Rebecca was spending increasing amounts of time holding her head up in the kindergarten classroom. One day, before she could stop the child, a little girl offered Rebecca a piece of cookie. Rebecca reached directly for the cookie, took it, and ate it.

When the state consultant visited Rebecca's classroom 3 weeks later, Rebecca had changed considerably. She exhibited much better head control, and it was obvious to everyone that she was seeing. When the teacher said her name, Rebecca turned toward the teacher's voice. She bunny-hopped on the floor and was balancing on her knees for increasingly longer periods of time for the physical therapists. In the kindergarten classroom, she looked at the brightly colored pictures in the book that one of the kindergartners ''read'' to her. It was clear that Rebecca was seeing the pictures. At lunchtime, she removed the items from the lunchbox and gave them to her teacher. After her teacher placed her food on her tray, Rebecca fed herself the food that she could eat with her fingers. When the consultant asked what had happened to change Rebecca, the teacher and educational interpreter explained that once they realized that Rebecca could do at least some of the things her grandparents said, they changed their expectations of her. They began having Rebecca participate, even partially, in all activities in the classroom. Their genuine pleasure at everything Rebecca did pleased (i.e., reinforced) Rebecca. Her classmates began to encourage and praise her also. Rebecca began to protest if left out of an activity. Within 2 months, Rebecca was indicating where she wanted to be pushed in her wheelchair by pointing, walking with support from the bathroom, pulling the aide toward the children seated on the floor, and learning to feed herself with a spoon. Rebecca's 11-week transformation occurred because the school staff realized that they had been fooled by her appearance into thinking she could have few skills. Rebecca had lived up to their low expectations. When they increased those expectations, they provided a more interesting and enriching atmosphere for Rebecca. Rebecca responded to this atmosphere, to their encouragement, and to their genuine enthusiasm for what she did.

SUMMARY

Children like Ivan, Juan Carlos, and Rebecca, whose distance senses are impaired, cannot gather information from their environments as readily as their peers, whose distance senses remain intact. Restricted sensory input and experiences limit their learning (McInnes & Treffry, 1982), even for such natural, life-sustaining skills as feeding. Moreover, the natural motivation to do what others do—a motivation on which teachers often rely—can remain undeveloped. Understanding how sensory impairments restrict children's experiences, recognizing what considerations need to be made for the sensory impairments, knowing what accommodations to make, and realizing that each child with sensory impairments is an individual unlike any other will effectively facilitate meeting the challenges these children pose.

PRACTICE EXERCISE

....

1. Children who are said to be blind generally have vision. What accommodations can be made at mealtimes to stimulate and help them use their residual vision and to maximize learning during this everyday activity?

2. Describe a mealtime routine that would provide many learning opportunities for a child who has light perception only and a severe sensorineural hearing loss in both ears.

3. Why is proper positioning so important for a child who has a significant vision loss, a hearing loss, and cerebral palsy?

REFERENCES

Adams, J.W. (1997). *You and your deaf child: A self-help guide for parents of deaf and hard of hearing children* (2nd ed.). Washington, DC: Clerc Books, Gallaudet University Press.

Baldwin, V. (1994). *Annual deaf-blind census.* Monmouth: Teaching Research Division, Western Oregon State College.

Bower, T.G.R. (1977). *A primer of infant development.* San Francisco: W.H. Freeman.

Campbell, P.H. (1976). *Problem-oriented approaches to feeding the handicapped child.* Akron, OH: The Children's Hospital of Akron.

Downing, J., & Eichinger, J. (1990). Instructional strategies for learners with dual sensory impairments in integrated settings. *Journal of The Association for Persons with Severe Handicaps, 15*(2), 98–105.

Fredericks, H.D.B., & Baldwin, V.L. (1987). Individuals with sensory impairments: Who are they? How are they educated? In L. Goetz, D. Guess, & K. Stremel-Campbell (Eds.), *Innovative program design for individuals with dual sensory impairments* (pp. 3–12). Baltimore: Paul H. Brookes Publishing Co.

Hart, V. (1974). *Beginning with the handicapped.* Springfield, IL: Charles C Thomas.

Heward, W.L., & Orlansky, M.D. (1992). *Exceptional children: An introductory survey of special education* (4th ed.). New York: Macmillan.

Hoch, T.A., Babbitt, R.L., Coe, D.A., Krell, D.M., & Hackbert, L. (1994, January). Contingency contacting. *Behavior Modification, 18*(1), 106–128.

Iwata, B.A., Riordan, M.M., Wohl, M.K., & Finney, J.W. (1982). Pediatric feeding disorders: Behavioral analysis and treatment. In P.J. Accardo (Ed.), *Failure to thrive in infancy and early childhood: A multidisciplinary team approach.* Baltimore: University Park Press.

Jones, T.W. (1978). An experimental comparison of two methods for remediating behavioral eating problems of handicapped children. (Doctoral dissertation, University of Pittsburgh, 1978). *Dissertation Abstracts International, 39* (University Microfilms No. 7902707).

Jones, T.W. (1982). Treatment of behavior-related eating problems in retarded students: A review of the literature. In J.H. Hollis & C.E. Meyers (Eds.), *Life-threatening behavior: Analysis and intervention* (pp. 3–26). Washington, DC: American Association on Mental Deficiency.

Jones, T.W. (1983). Remediation of behavior-related eating problems. *Journal of The Association for Persons with Severe Handicaps, 8,* 62–71.

Luiselli, J.K., Evans, T.P., & Boyce, D.A. (1985). Contingency management of food selectivity and oppositional eating in a multiply handicapped child. *Journal of Clinical Child Psychology, 14*(2), 153–156.

Luiselli, J.K., & Gleason, D.J. (1987). Combining sensory reinforcement and texture fading procedures to overcome chronic food refusal. *Journal of Behavior Therapy & Experimental Psychiatry, 18*(2), 149–155.

McInnes, J.M., & Treffry, J.H. (1982). *Deaf-blind infants and children: A developmental guide.* Toronto, Ontario, Canada: University of Toronto Press.

Moores, D. (1987). *Educating the deaf: Psychology, principles, and practices* (3rd ed.). Boston: Houghton Mifflin.

Morris, S. (1977). *Program guidelines for children with feeding problems.* Edison, NJ: Childcraft.

Prickett, J.G., & Welch, T.R. (1995). Adapting environments to support the inclusion of students who are deaf-blind. In N.G. Haring & L.T. Romer (Eds.), *Welcoming students who are deaf-blind into typical classrooms: Facilitating school participation, learning, and friendships* (pp. 171–193). Baltimore: Paul H. Brookes Publishing Co.

Radetsky, P. (1994, Summer). Silence, signs, and wonder. *Discover,* 60–68.

Rowland, C., & Schweigert, P. (1989). Tangible symbols: Symbolic communication for individuals with multisensory impairments. *Augmentative and Alternative Communication, 5,* 226–234.

Schmidt, P. (1976). Feeding assessment and therapy for the neurologically impaired. *AAESPH Review, 1*(8), 19–27.

Singer, L.T., Nofer, J.A., Benson-Szekely, L.J., & Brooks, L.J. (1991). Behavioral assessment and management of food refusal in children with cystic fibrosis. *Developmental and Behavioral Pediatrics, 12*(2), 115–120.

Sobsey, D., & Wolf-Schein, E.G. (1996). Children with sensory impairments. In F.P. Orelove & D. Sobsey, *Educating children with multiple disabilities: A transdisciplinary approach* (3rd ed., pp. 411–450). Baltimore: Paul H. Brookes Publishing Co.

Stratton, J. (1990). The principle of least-restrictive materials. *Journal of Visual Impairment and Blindness, 84*(1), 3–5.

Stremel, K., & Schutz, R. (1995). Functional communication in inclusive settings for students who are deaf-blind. In N.G. Haring & L.T. Romer (Eds.), *Welcoming students who are deaf-blind into typical classrooms: Facilitating school participation, learning, and friendships* (pp. 197–229). Baltimore: Paul H. Brookes Publishing Co.

chapter twelve

The Overall Feeding Plan
Pulling It All Together

Dianne Koontz Lowman and Rebecca Anderson Weissman

This final chapter describes how to incorporate all of the necessary components for the development of a comprehensive, holistic feeding plan for children. This overall feeding plan results from 1) collaborating with the family, the child, and other professionals; 2) embedding communication and social skills in the learning process; and 3) providing needed motor, sensory, and behavioral accommodations as well as identifying necessary adaptive feeding equipment. The goal of this final chapter is to help the practitioner synthesize all of the information that is presented in previous chapters of this book. A vignette is presented for each component of the feeding/mealtime process to encourage review of the chapters' contents; a sample Holistic Feeding Observation Form (see the appendix at the end of this chapter) is also provided.

DEVELOPMENT OF A FEEDING PLAN

Throughout this book, we recommend the use of the Holistic Feeding Observation Form (see Appendix A at the end of this book) as a guide to gather as much information as possible about all aspects of the feeding/mealtime process when conducting the observation/interview. This form helps the team consider all components that might interfere with or have an impact on a child's feeding or eating skills. The bulleted checklist in the Completed Holistic Feeding Observation Form (see the appendix at the end of this chapter) presents key questions to ask when gathering information about each component of the feeding/mealtime process. (See the corresponding chapter for a detailed description of each component.)

Collaboration with the Family

Shirin
....

Shirin is 3 years old. She has recently been identified as having global developmental delays. She attends a center-based preschool and recently joined your classroom. Her father speaks some English, but Farsi is the primary language spoken in Shirin's home. Because of cultural and religious beliefs, pork is not allowed in Shirin's diet, and self-feeding is not yet expected of Shirin. Shirin's motor and oral-motor skills, which are necessary for self-feeding, are adequate, however. The family is most concerned about the lack of variety in Shirin's diet. How would you work with this family concerning lunch in school and assist with feeding skills in Shirin's home?

The first step in the development of a holistic feeding plan is to start communicating with the family. Determine whether a feeding routine has been established, and understand what this routine involves. Feeding routines are different at home, in school, and in other environments in which a child is fed. The Ecological Worksheet presented in Figure 3 of Chapter 2 is one way to gather information about feeding routines in different environments. While looking closely at the specifics of the feeding routine, determine the satisfaction of the family with this overall process. Be sure to determine what aspects the family would like to keep, what they would like to change, and what they would like to discard. Although it is critical to note the pleasurable aspects of the feeding process, be careful not to interfere with these aspects; instead, build on their positive contributions to the feeding process (Lowman & Lane, 1998).

It is important to understand the specific feeding issues identified by the caregivers who feed the child. From a family-centered perspective, intervention should begin by addressing these issues. The team should look at the priorities set by the family and, when possible, establish these as priorities for the child's feeding plan. There may be times when, for health and safety reasons, this is not possible. In these instances, the feeding team must address these issues with the family and establish priorities that are safe and promote the child's health (Lowman & Lane, 1998).

Collaboration with the family involves acknowledging and accepting the cultural values of the family. Because cultural implications affect all interactions with children and families, interventionists should be mindful of the family's cultural practices during all aspects of observing, planning, and working with children with feeding problems. Before developing any specific feeding plan, be sure to determine the family's cultural norms for food type, food preparation, utensils, time of meals, talking during mealtimes, and eating with the family. Be sure to share your suggestions for improving the feeding plan with the family before implementing them to ensure that they are consistent with the family's beliefs and values (Lowman & Lane, 1998).

Respiratory Issues

Bruce

Bruce was born at a very low birth weight and, because of medical complications, received a tracheostomy and gastrostomy tube. Medical clearance has been granted to begin oral feedings again for the first time since his tracheostomy. Bruce can clearly indicate his preferences with facial expressions and gestures, and he is just beginning to learn how to produce sounds by covering his tracheostomy tube.

What is the next step for a team to take in developing a feeding plan for Bruce? After the first step of communicating with the family, the second step in planning for a child with feeding and eating problems is to rule out any medical problems. Respiratory issues, in particular, can have very serious health and safety implications for a child and should always be evaluated medically. Some observations that should be noted include the presence of an over- or underresponsive gag reflex; an inhibited or delayed swallow reflex; and swallowing with gagging, coughing, or aspiration. Determine who sets the feeding pace (i.e., the child or the feeder). Does this pace allow extra time for coordination of breathing and swallowing? It is especially important to note the child's ability to coordinate breathing, swallowing, and talking; children who have difficulty with smoothly coordinating swallowing and breathing are in danger of aspirating food and inadequate intake of nutrients needed for growth (Wolf & Glass, 1992). Educators feeding children who may have possible respiratory problems should be familiar with the 10 indicators of aspiration (Hall, Yohn, & Reed, 1992) (see p. 182). Children with any of these problems should be referred for a medical evaluation. As described in Chapter 3, problems affecting respiration should be ruled out through the use of a modified barium swallow study.

Sometimes children have respiratory problems that are severe enough to warrant specialized health care (e.g., children with tracheostomies, children fed through tubes, children who must be monitored closely for aspiration). We recommend the development of a Health Services Plan (see Appendix B at the end of this book). A completed Health Services Plan is especially helpful in specifying warning signs and emergency procedures for children who have respiratory problems.

Oral-Motor Development

Shelia

Shelia has severe cerebral palsy. Her trunk has predominately low muscle tone, but high muscle tone is frequently present in her extremities. Shelia has a strong tongue thrust, despite achieving a good position in her wheelchair (a position that reduces her muscle tone fluctuations and helps promote muscle tone that is closer to neutral). What oral-motor assistance for Shelia can be provided?

Consult with the speech-language pathologist (SLP) and/or occupational therapist (OT) to establish whether the child's overall muscle tone has been determined (e.g., low, normal, high, fluctuating). Note which activities help normalize the child's overall muscle tone. Also, determine whether there are muscle tone issues specific to the child's face and mouth. Ask the SLP or OT if needs for oral-motor treatment for the child have been identified. As described in Chapter 4, some common examples of oral-motor considerations include the jaw (e.g., thrust, clenching, retraction, instability), the tongue (e.g., retraction, thrust, limited movement), the lips and cheeks (e.g., low muscle tone, lip retraction), and the palate (e.g., nasal reflux, cleft). Note whether any internal and external methods for providing oral support are currently being used with the child.

Physical Development / Positioning

Jennifer
···

Jennifer is a little girl with bright eyes who loves to socialize and explore her world visually. She has cerebral palsy and, because of her low muscle tone, has trouble maintaining a neutral head position for an effective swallow. Jennifer works so hard just to keep her head and trunk stable that eating is a frustrating experience due to both motor fatigue and lack of social interaction. What will help Jennifer reduce fatigue and increase her social opportunities?

The position of the child for feeding and eating is critical; the 90°–90°–90° upright position is usually the most efficient for school-age children (Lowman & Lane, 1998). Key points for seating are highlighted in Appendix C at the end of this book, the Postural Alignment Checklist for Sitting Positions.

Key points to note during observation include keeping the child's head upright and at mid-line; keeping the child's shoulders and arms in a neutral or slightly forward position; keeping the child's hips, knees, and ankles flexed to approximately 90°; and keeping the child's feet flat on the floor or on a foot rest (Lowman & Lane, 1998). In addition, note the seating position(s) and equipment that are currently being used for the child and the apparent effectiveness of this equipment. For example, note whether the child is fed while sitting on a chair, in a high chair, in a car seat, in a travel chair, on the parent's lap, and so forth. Which position / equipment appears to be most effective? Which position / equipment does the child's family prefer? As has been stated previously, always consult the physical therapist and / or the OT before observing and reporting the child's positioning. (See Chapter 5 for a detailed discussion of the specifics of positioning and seating.)

Sensory Development

Jonathon
···

Jonathon is having trouble accepting new, lumpy textures, such as scrambled eggs. He also hates cold temperatures and prefers familiar tastes. How do you expand Jonathon's experiences with new foods?

First, rule out any limitations of the sensory modalities present (i.e., visual, auditory, tactile, gustatory, olfactory, proprioceptive). Next, consider the child's reaction to sensory input in the mouth and around the face. As emphasized in Chapter 6, many children with feeding difficulties show sensory sensitivity to textures, tastes, temperature, and touch. Note the presence of any of the following: refusal of specific foods, picky eating, gagging, vomiting, stuffing food into the mouth, and sucking (rather than chewing) food. Determine which textures are most easily tolerated by the child (e.g., thick liquids, thin liquids, smooth solids, lumpy solids, chewy solids, crunchy textures, mixed textures). Which tastes are most easily tolerated by the child (i.e., likes versus dislikes)? Which temperatures are most easily tolerated by the child (e.g., hot, cold)? Which type(s) of touch are most easily tolerated by the child (arousing versus calming)?

Communication, Behavioral, and Socialization Skills

Patrick and Keisha

It is snacktime in your classroom. Most of the children are verbal and quickly tell you which type of drink and food item they want. Patrick has Down syndrome. He is shy and uses sign language to communicate his basic desires. Patrick also has trouble eating as quickly as the other students. Another child in your class, Keisha, uses an electronic communication device. What accommodations need to be incorporated in order to ensure maximum socialization opportunities for both children?

At the heart of successful mealtimes is a respectful interaction between the feeder and the child. This can be accomplished only through communication. Communication takes place through the use of sounds, words, gestures, facial expressions, body language, physical contact, and many other behaviors (Orelove & Sobsey, 1996). Through observation, note how the child communicates. How does the child indicate the following: 1) hunger (with and without food present), 2) the need for a change of pace or a pause in eating, 3) a choice of food or liquid, 4) readiness for more food, and 5) that he or she is finished eating? Does the child have the maximum control possible? Is the feeding interaction pleasurable? (See Chapter 7 for further discussion of the communication strategies for feeding.)

Use the Observation Tool for Analyzing the Communicative Functions of Behaviors (Figure 4 in Chapter 9) to note which of the child's behaviors communicate the following: refusal, request, socialization, protest, and reaction to sensory issues. Are any of the following behaviors present: food refusal, severe food selectivity, rumination, vomiting, or mealtime tantrums? (See Chapter 9 for a discussion of the communicative intent of children's behaviors.)

Feeding Process and Implementation Plan

A number of resources that are available to assist feeding teams are listed in Appendix D at the end of this book. The holistic process described in this book involves a team of people conducting observations and interviews in a variety of environments across time. After these observations and interviews have produced a vast amount of information, the feeding team is ready to begin developing a feeding plan. This process pulls all components together into one comprehensive feeding plan. A sample Holistic Feeding Observation Form is provided in the appendix at the end of this chapter. During the development of the feeding plan, be sure to answer the following questions:

- Did the family, the child, all feeders, and needed specialists participate in the development of this plan?

- Was needed medical information (including physician orders and nutrition requirements) received and factored into this feeding plan?

- Is any additional medical information needed?

- What is the most effective sequence for the feeding process?

- What feeding equipment will be needed?

SAMPLE HOLISTIC FEEDING OBSERVATION REPORT

A sample written report of a holistic feeding observation is provided in the appendix at the end of this chapter. Written reports will vary, based on the nature and complexity of the child's feeding problems.

SUMMARY

Educators are being asked to feed an increasing number of students with disabilities who also have feeding problems. In this book, we discuss an ongoing process of gathering information from a variety of sources about

- The family's feeding routine, issues, and cultural implications
- The presence of any respiratory issues
- Physical development and positioning during feeding and eating
- The child's oral-motor and sensory development
- Communication, behavioral, and socialization skills during the feeding process

This process involves a team of individuals, including the family and the child. The goal of this process is to make feeding children with disabilities as safe and pleasant as possible for both the child and the adult feeder.

REFERENCES

Hall, S., Yohn, K., & Reed, P.R. (1992). *Feeding students in school: Providing guidelines and information on safe feeding practices for special students.* Salem: Oregon Department of Education.

Lowman, D.K., & Lane, S.J. (1998). Children with feeding and nutritional problems. In S. Porr & E.B. Rainville, *Pediatric therapy: A systems approach.* Philadelphia: F.A. Davis Company.

Orelove, F.P., & Sobsey, D. (1996). *Educating children with multiple disabilities: A transdisciplinary approach* (3rd ed.). Baltimore: Paul H. Brookes Publishing Co.

Wolf, L.S., & Glass, R.P. (1992). *Feeding and swallowing disorders in infancy: Assessment and management.* San Antonio, TX: Therapy Skill Builders.

Appendix
Completed Holistic Feeding Observation Form

Child's Name: *Sheama*   Age: *2 years, 6 months*

Date(s) Observed: *January 12, 19, and 26*   Time: *11:30 A.M.–1:00 P.M.*

Environment(s) Observed: *Home*   Observer(s): *D.K. Lowman*

Reason for Referral:

Sheama is 2¹/₂ years old and has cerebral palsy. Sheama was observed during a series of home visits; her mother and the preschool teacher were present during each visit. Sheama's family is from Afghanistan. The home-based preschool teacher initiated this referral. The reasons for referral involved determining 1) the most appropriate position for feeding and 2) Sheama's readiness for making the transition from bottle to cup drinking.

I. Collaboration with the Family

Sample Questions

- What is the feeding routine at home? What is the feeding routine in school?
- How is the child fed? What equipment is used?
- What are the feeding issues identified by the family?
- What is pleasurable specific to the feeding interaction?
- What is difficult specific to the feeding interaction?
- What cultural implications are important to consider?
- Are there medical or nutritional issues that must be addressed?

Observations:

Sheama's mother participated in each observation. She indicated that she usually holds Sheama on her lap while bottle feeding. She agreed that Sheama was getting too large to hold, but it is considered that Sheama must drink enough to stay healthy and to grow. It is suggested that team members working with this family learn more about families from Middle Eastern cultures. It would be helpful to understand the feeding and health care, proximity and physical contact, and attachment and individualization beliefs of this family.

II. Respiratory Issues

Sample Questions

- Is the gag reflex present and effective (i.e., not over- or underresponsive)?

- Is the swallow reflex present and effective (i.e., not inhibited or delayed; no paralysis)?
- Is the feeding pace determined by the child (i.e., not the feeder)?
- Is swallowing relaxed and without gagging, coughing, or aspiration?
- If a respiratory infection is present, is enough extra time allowed for coordination of breathing and swallowing?
- Is the coordination of breathing, swallowing, and talking difficult?

Observations:

The snug seat caused a noticeable difference in Sheama's respiration for the better. When she was sitting upright in the snug seat, her respiration sounded clear and easy. When positioned backward on someone's lap, Sheama sounded congested and appeared to have difficulty with coordinating swallowing with breathing. It is important that Sheama always be fed slowly. Because of limited oral-motor control, she needs extra time to coordinate swallowing with breathing.

It appears appropriate to request a videofluoroscopy to help determine the timing and components of Sheama's swallow response. This will provide very helpful information important to her feeding program. It may, in fact, be difficult for Sheama to coordinate swallowing because of restrictive movement patterns.

III. Oral-Motor Development

Sample Questions

- Has overall muscle tone been determined (e.g., low, normal, high)?
- Have muscle tone issues specific to the face and mouth been determined?
- Have needs for oral-motor treatment been identified?

Observations:

Sheama has limited motor ability and, hence, limitations with oral-motor skills. Sheama's family should work with the speech-language pathologist and/or occupational therapist to identify appropriate oral-motor techniques. They should begin by working to improve lip closure and a consistent suck and swallow with the bottle. The therapists can help develop a specific and detailed plan to move, with oral supports, from the bottle to a cup.

IV. Physical Development/Positioning

Sample Questions

- Is 90°–90°–90° position achievable?
- Are feet and arms supported by a flat surface (i.e., not dangling)?
- Are knees at a comfortable 90° angle?
- Are hips resting symmetrically against a supportive surface?
- Is trunk upright and symmetrical?
- Is a neutral head position assured for most effective swallow and eye contact?

Observations:

The safest feeding position for Sheama appears to be her snug seat. This seat provides a flexed position that is very helpful in breaking up her high muscle tone. It is difficult to hold Sheama in one's lap and maintain a good therapeutic position for feeding. (She is getting bigger, and her high muscle tone presents difficulty with maintaining an appropriately flexed position.) Encourage Sheama's mother to rock her prior to feeding and to hold her and tell her a story afterward so that they may still enjoy physical contact at feeding time. Therapists should use the positioning checklist when explaining positioning and its importance to Sheama's mother and other caregivers. Also, they should be sure to present food calmly and at mid-line to reduce eliciting Sheama's strong asymmetric tonic neck reflex.

V. Sensory Development

Sample Questions

- Are any limitations of the sensory modalities present (e.g., visual, auditory, tactile, gustatory, olfactory, proprioceptive)?
- Which **textures** are most easily tolerated?
- Which **tastes** are most easily tolerated (likes versus dislikes)?
- Which **temperatures** are most easily tolerated? (Note preferences.)
- Which type(s) of **touch** are most easily tolerated (arousing versus calming)?

Observations:

It is important that Sheama's mother and caregivers continue to provide Sheama with puréed textures of food that vary in taste. The homemade puréed food will more closely approximate "typical tastes." This will be important later, when Sheama moves to thicker textures of food. Until more medical information is available, it would be wise for Sheama's mother and caregivers to continue to feed her the puréed textures that are easy for Sheama to swallow, feed her slowly at a pace that follows Sheama's lead, and be extra cautious when she has a cold or might be congested.

VI. Communication, Behavioral, and Socialization Skills

Sample Questions

- Does the child have the maximum control possible?
- How does the child indicate hunger with food present?
- How does the child indicate hunger when food is not present?
- How does the child indicate his or her need for a change of pace/pause in feeding?
- How does the child indicate a choice of food or liquid?
- How does the child indicate readiness for more food?
- How does the child indicate that he or she is finished eating?
- How does the child indicate a desire for social closeness/distance?

Observations:

Sheama demonstrates a nice readiness for her next spoonful of food (e.g., makes eye contact, opens mouth). Sheama's mother and caregivers should consider teaching the following communication skills that pertain to feeding: indicating the desire to eat (when food is present and not present), indicating the need for a pause in feeding, indicating choices of food and liquid, and indicating when finished eating. It might be helpful to develop a communication dictionary so all feeders respond appropriately.

VII. Feeding Process and Implementation Plan

Sample Questions

- Have the family, all feeders, and needed specialists participated in the development of this plan?

- Has needed medical information (including physician orders and nutrition requirements) been received and factored into this feeding plan?
- Has needed feeding equipment been identified and obtained?
- Has the most effective sequence (i.e., the best order of feeding) been determined?

Observations:

1. Be sure to rule out or clarify any medical issues related to swallowing.
2. Develop a feeding team for Sheama that includes her mother and all other direct services providers. As a team, develop a plan of action specific for improving oral-motor skills, moving from drinking from the bottle to drinking from the cup, and increasing textures that Sheama can handle.
3. The following is a suggested feeding sequence:
   Begin with relaxation (rocking with mom), if desired. Position Sheama in her snug seat for best stability and motor control. Ensure clear respiration and a neutral head position. Wait for her readiness response (i.e., eye contact and open mouth). Work to improve Sheama's communication initiations and lip closure. Encourage Sheama's mother to hold Sheama after she has finished eating instead of during the feeding process.

The Educator's Guide to Feeding Children with Disabilities by Dianne Koontz Lowman and Suzanne McKeever Murphy © 1999 by Paul H. Brookes Publishing Co., Baltimore

G L O S S A R Y

....

Anterior   In front of or the forward part of an organ.

Apnea   A temporary or permanent cessation of breathing.

Aspiration   Breathing food or liquid into the lungs.

Asymmetric tonic neck reflex   A postural reflex typically characterized by the head turning to one side, with resulting extension (i.e., straightening) of the limbs on one side (face side) and bending of the limbs on the other side (skull side). This reflex is typically seen at the age of 2 months but may persist and influence a child's posture and motor control.

Ataxic cerebral palsy   A type of cerebral palsy that is characterized by impaired motor coordination, poor balance, and unsteady movements. These characteristics may limit postural control and stability and prevent the execution of accurate and precise movements.

Athetoid cerebral palsy   A type of cerebral palsy characterized by excessive, involuntary movements that are often irregular and flailing. Such movement characteristics may prevent a child from sustaining postural control or demonstrating accurate control during functional tasks.

Bolus   A soft mass of food that is ready to be swallowed.

Bradycardia   A heart rate that is below normal.

Cerebral palsy   A nonprogressive disability resulting from an insult to the brain prior to, during, or shortly after birth. Children with this condition frequently exhibit delays or disorders in their motor functioning. Children with cerebral palsy are typically classified according to their most apparent motor dysfunction (e.g., spastic, athetoid, ataxic) or areas of the body involved (e.g., quadriplegia, diplegia, hemiplegia).

Dissociation   When two body parts move independently of each other.

Distal   Used when describing a part of the body as one moves farther away from the trunk.

Down syndrome   A chromosomal anomaly that results in generalized low muscle tone and other postural, motor, communication, and feeding difficulties.

Dynamic techniques   Therapy techniques that encourage active movement from the child.

Dysphagia   Difficulty with swallowing.

Extension   Movement that straightens out the body or specific body parts.

Failure to thrive   When a child fails to gain weight according to his or her age and body size. This lack of growth can cause delays in emotional, intellectual, and physical development. This condition can be caused by physical as well as emotional problems.

Feeding tube   A tube placed in the child's mouth or nose or directly into the stomach that allows nutrition to be given by a means other than the mouth.

Flexion   Movement that bends the body or a specific body part.

Gastroesophageal reflux   When contents of the stomach flow back into the esophagus because of the improper closure of the muscle where it enters the stomach.

Gastrostomy   A surgical opening in the stomach where a feeding tube is placed.

Handling   Specific techniques used when helping a child to move in therapy.

Head and neck extension   Active or passive motion of the head and neck joints that allow for movement of the chin upward so that the back of the head moves toward the upper back.

Head and neck flexion   Active or passive motion of the head and neck joints that allows for movement of the chin toward the chest.

Hyperreaction   An exaggerated reaction to a stimulus.

Hypertonicity   Increased tension (i.e., stiffness, rigidity) in a muscle.

Hyporeaction   A less-than-normal reaction to stimuli.

Hypotonicity   Significant lack of tension (i.e., stiffness, rigidity) in a muscle.

IEP (individualized education program)   A specific set of short- and long-term goals set up for a child in an education environment that dictates what the educator or therapist should address for a particular school year.

IFSP (individualized family service plan)   A specific set of short- and long-term goals set up for the child and family in a program designed to address the needs of infants, birth to 3 years of age, that dictates what the infant specialist should address with the family for the calendar year.

Key points of control   Areas of the body that can be stimulated to encourage proper alignment in a position. These areas are thought to influence more distal regions of the body. They are typically centrally located and include the trunk, shoulders, and pelvis.

Lactation consultant   A specially trained professional who helps mothers with breast-feeding issues.

Lateral   The side farthest from the middle of the body.

Limbic system   A set of nerve cells located in the center of the brain that are involved in automatic regulation of body functions, emotions, and the sense of smell.

Mobility   The process of allowing the body or specific body parts to move.

Motor control   Processes involved in the emergence of movement skills involving the interaction between a child and his or her environment to meet the goals of a task.

Neonate   A newborn child.

Neurodevelopmental Treatment Approach   A therapeutic approach developed in 1959 by Berta and Karl Bobath that focuses on the child as a whole. This approach includes facilitation of functional sequences of movement and a more normal sensory foundation from which improved quality of posture and motor control are targeted.

Oral-motor movements   Movements pertaining to the muscles of the mouth.

Oral-pharyngeal area   The area within the mouth pertaining to the back of the mouth (i.e., pharynx).

Peristalsis   Wave-like contractions by which food contents are moved from one area of the body to another.

Phasic bite–release reflex   Rhythmical up-and-down movement of the jaw typically seen in the first weeks of life.

Pica   A craving to eat nonnutritive materials.

Posterior   In reference to the back part of the body.

Postural adjustments   Automatic use of postural muscles before, during, and after movement.

Postural alignment   The relationship and orientation of body parts to one another.

Postural control   The ability to assume and maintain stable positions against gravity and the ability to maintain and control the relationship of body parts to each other.

Postural insecurity   The fear or inability to assume and maintain stable positions against gravity.

Prone   Lying on one's stomach.

Proprioceptive   The body's ability to receive information about where it is in relation to the environment around it. The information is used to make necessary adjustments in the contraction of muscles in order to maintain stable positions.

Protraction   Moving forward from a neutral position.

Proximal   Used when describing a part of the body closer to the middle (i.e., trunk).

Retraction   Drawing back a body part.

Rumination   The purposeful act of bringing food back from the stomach into the mouth.

Spastic cerebral palsy   A type of cerebral palsy characterized by excessive "stiffness" that may be felt when attempting to move or reposition a child. When spasticity is combined with other motor impairments, slow and labored movements may be observed.

Spina bifida   A congenital disorder that may affect the spinal cord, vertebrae, and skin. Motor and sensory impairments are commonly associated with this condition.

Stability   The use of muscles and structures that form a base for other muscles to work. A stable base of support is fixed and unmoving.

Static positioning   Descriptive term that indicates that a child's body is not in motion.

Supine   Lying on one's back.

Symmetry   A descriptor used to indicate equal or balanced alignment and control of the whole body or body parts in relation to each other.

Tactile   Pertains to touch.

Tongue lateralization   The movement of the tongue to the side.

Tonic bite   A bite with increased tension that the child typically has difficulty releasing.

Tracheostomy   Surgical opening into the trachea through the neck where a tube is placed to aid in breathing. Suctioning of secretions is also done at this site.

Ventilator   A machine that takes over respiration for a child who is unable to breathe independently.

Appendix A
Holistic Feeding Observation Form

Child's Name: _____   Age: _____

Date(s) Observed: _____   Time: _____

Environment(s) Observed: _____   Observer(s): _____

Reason for Referral:

I. Collaboration with the Family

Sample Questions
- What is the feeding routine at home? What is the feeding routine in school?
- How is the child fed? What equipment is used?
- What are the feeding issues identified by the family?
- What is pleasurable specific to the feeding interaction?
- What is difficult specific to the feeding interaction?
- What cultural implications are important to consider?
- Are there medical or nutritional issues that must be addressed?

Observations:

II. Respiratory Issues

Sample Questions
- Is the gag reflex present and effective (i.e., not over- or underresponsive)?
- Is the swallow reflex present and effective (i.e., not inhibited or delayed; no paralysis)?
- Is the feeding pace determined by the child (i.e., not the feeder)?
- Is swallowing relaxed and without gagging, coughing, or aspiration?

- If a respiratory infection is present, is enough extra time allowed for coordination of breathing and swallowing?
- Is the coordination of breathing, swallowing, and talking difficult?

Observations:

III. Oral-Motor Development

Sample Questions

- Has overall muscle tone been determined (e.g., low, normal, high)?
- Have muscle tone issues specific to the face and mouth been determined?
- Have needs for oral-motor treatment been identified?

Observations:

IV. Physical Development/Positioning

Sample Questions

- Is 90°–90°–90° position achievable?
- Are feet and arms supported by a flat surface (i.e., not dangling)?
- Are knees at a comfortable 90° angle?
- Are hips resting symmetrically against a supportive surface?
- Is trunk upright and symmetrical?
- Is a neutral head position assured for most effective swallow and eye contact?

Observations:

V. Sensory Development

Sample Questions

- Are any limitations of the sensory modalities present (e.g., visual, auditory, tactile, gustatory, olfactory, proprioceptive)?
- Which **textures** are most easily tolerated?
- Which **tastes** are most easily tolerated (likes versus dislikes)?
- Which **temperatures** are most easily tolerated? (Note preferences.)

- Which type(s) of **touch** are most easily tolerated (arousing versus calming)?

Observations:

VI. Communication, Behavioral, and Socialization Skills

Sample Questions
- Does the child have the maximum control possible?
- How does the child indicate hunger with food present?
- How does the child indicate hunger when food is not present?
- How does the child indicate his or her need for a change of pace/pause in feeding?
- How does the child indicate a choice of food or liquid?
- How does the child indicate readiness for more food?
- How does the child indicate that he or she is finished eating?
- How does the child indicate a desire for social closeness/distance?

Observations:

VII. Feeding Process and Implementation Plan

Sample Questions
- Have the family, all feeders, and needed specialists participated in the development of this plan?
- Has needed medical information (including physician orders and nutrition requirements) been received and factored into this feeding plan?
- Has needed feeding equipment been identified and obtained?
- Has the most effective sequence (i.e., the best order of feeding) been determined?

Observations:

Appendix B
Health Services Plan

Student: _____

Parents/Guardians: _____

This Health Services Plan will be in effect from _____ to _____.

This plan should be completed *before* the child comes to school or the child care center. Because health needs can change frequently, this plan should be developed at a meeting *separate* from the individualized family service plan (IFSP)/individualized education program (IEP) meeting.

Members of planning team:

Members of the planning team should include the parents or guardian, the child (if appropriate), the service coordinator, the primary teacher, the class paraprofessional, the school administrator, the special education administrator, other related-services staff as appropriate (e.g., speech-language pathologist, occupational therapist, physical therapist), the school nurse or school health contact person, the transportation director, the transition nurse from the discharging hospital or the local health department, the Medicaid waiver case manager, and the representative from the equipment company.

Description of child's medical condition:

This section should contain a complete description of the child's current medical condition, including relevant medical history, the child's needs for growth and development, and the effect of the medical condition on the child's performance in school.

Strategies to support the child in the school- or center-based environment:

In this section, specify activities in which the child may participate and any adaptations or modifications that may be needed (e.g., no contact sports; avoid contact with particles such as sand, powder).

Feeding and nutritional needs:

Describe the child's current diet, food allergies, food likes and dislikes, fluid in-take requirements, feeding plan, and oral-motor interventions.

Transportation arrangements:

This section should address whether the child will ride the bus or whether special transportation arrangements will be made. Is there a need for an assistant to accompany the student? Does the bus driver need to receive special training?

Medication to be dispensed, amount, time, and person administering:

This section should include the type of medication; the dosage to be dispensed; time, how, where, and who will administer medication; and the effect of the medication on the child's performance in school. Define a procedure for record keeping.

Procedure(s) to be performed by school/center personnel:

This section should outline the child's needs. The planning team should decide which procedure(s) can and cannot be done in school. Each procedure should be described in detail.

Where and when the procedure(s) should be performed:

Include the location, frequency, and time of day involved with the procedure(s).

Who will perform the procedure(s):

What are the qualifications of the individual who should perform the procedure(s)?

Training that is to take place prior to the child's entering class:

List in detail who will be providing the training and how often the training will be monitored and reviewed. Note that the training must be provided by a health care provider. The parents and a health care provider can work as a team to provide the training.

Schedule for review and monitoring of training:

Include time lines for regular review and retraining of the procedures. This should include a schedule for regular review as well as provisions for retraining if the child's needs change.

Emergency procedures:

Describe the expected emergency in terms of how the child typically reacts, if known. List specifically what to do, whom to call, and the order in which people should be notified. Who has a copy of the emergency plan? Where is it filed/posted? Be sure to notify the local rescue squad about procedures and location of the child in the school.

Plan for absences:

Outline the plan for dealing with instances when the teacher and/or the paraprofessional are absent, such as specific training of a substitute.

Outline the plan for home-based instruction if the child becomes too ill to attend school. Be sure to build this plan into the child's IFSP/IEP.

Outline the plan for receiving current medical information before the child returns to school from an extended illness/hospitalization.

Plan for change:

Plan for change and review frequently.

Revise plan after a major illness or hospitalization.

Signature

We have participated in the development of this Health Services Plan and agree with the contents:

_____   _____
Parents/Guardians   Date

_____   _____
School Administrator   Date

_____   _____
Health Care Professional   Date

_____   _____
Teacher   Date

REFERENCE

Lowman, D.K. (1994). *Integrating preschoolers with complex health care needs into early childhood special education programs: The teacher's perspective.* Unpublished doctoral dissertation, University of Virginia, Charlottesville.

Appendix C
Postural Alignment
Checklist for Sitting Positions

Child's Name: _____ Age: _____

Date: _____

	Lower half of the body			
Body part	Alignment considerations	Yes	No	Comments
Pelvis and hips	a. Is the pelvis upright in a neutral or slightly anterior tipped position?	☐	☐	
	b. Are the pelvis and hips symmetrical with equal distribution of weight on the "sit bones" (i.e., ischial tuberosities) and the knees facing forward?	☐	☐	
	c. Are the hips flexed to approximately 90°?	☐	☐	
	If no to a, b, or c:			
	Does the pelvis tip too far backward with excessive hip extension with or without asymmetry?	☐	☐	
	Does the pelvis tip too far forward with excessive hip flexion with or without asymmetry?	☐	☐	

Thighs and legs	a. Are the thighs well-supported in slight abduction with the seat surface 1–2 inches behind the knees?	☐	☐	
	b. Are the knees flexed to at least 90°?	☐	☐	
	If no to a or b:			
	Do the legs press tightly together?	☐	☐	
	Do the legs spread apart excessively?	☐	☐	
	Are the knees extended excessively?	☐	☐	
	Are the knees flexed excessively?	☐	☐	
Feet and ankles	a. Are feet and ankles well-supported and ankles positioned under or slightly behind the knees?	☐	☐	
	b. Are ankles flexed to 90°?	☐	☐	
	c. Are feet and toes facing forward?	☐	☐	
	If no to a, b, or c:			
	Are feet not flat and not resting on a supporting surface?	☐	☐	

Upper half of the body

Body part	Alignment considerations	Yes	No	Comments
Trunk	a. Is the trunk upright?	☐	☐	
	b. Is the trunk symmetrical?	☐	☐	
	If no to a or b:			
	Is the trunk rounded excessively?	☐	☐	
	Does the trunk fall forward?	☐	☐	

	Does the trunk arch backward?	☐	☐
	Does the trunk fall to one side?	☐	☐
Shoulders and arms	a. Are shoulders level and relaxed?	☐	☐
	b. Are the arms forward and in mid-line?	☐	☐
	If no to a or b:		
	Do the shoulders elevate?	☐	☐
	Are the shoulders asymmetrical?	☐	☐
	Are the shoulders excessively protracted with arms turned inward?	☐	☐
	Are the shoulders excessively retracted with arms pulling back?	☐	☐
Head and neck	Is head in mid-line with a slight chin tuck?	☐	☐
	If no:		
	Do the head and neck extend excessively with or without asymmetry?	☐	☐
	Do the head and neck flex excessively with or without asymmetry?	☐	☐

Always consult the physical and/or occupational therapist before observing and reporting the child's physical development and positioning.

From Snyder, Breath, & DeMauro. Positioning Strategies for Feeding and Eating. In *The Educator's Guide to Feeding Children with Disabilities* by Dianne Koontz Lowman and Suzanne McKeever Murphy © 1999 by Paul H. Brookes Publishing Co., Baltimore

Appendix D
Resource List

BOOKS AND CHAPTERS

Reference Books About Medical Conditions
Accardo, P.J., & Whitman, B.Y. (1996). *Dictionary of developmental disabilities terminology.* Baltimore: Paul H. Brookes Publishing Co.

Agins, A.P. (1998). *Teachers' drug reference: A guide to medical conditions and drugs commonly used in school-aged children.* Lancaster, PA: Technomic Publishing Co., Inc.

Bagnato, S.J., Neisworth, J.T., & Munson, S.M. (1997). *LINKing Assessment and early intervention: An authentic curriculum-based approach.* Baltimore: Paul H. Brookes Publishing Co.

Batshaw, M.L. (Ed.). (1997). *Children with disabilities* (4th ed.). Baltimore: Paul H. Brookes Publishing Co.

Berkow, R., & Fletcher, A.J. (Eds.). (1992). *Sixteenth edition—The Merck manual of diagnosis and therapy.* Rahway, NJ: Merck Research Laboratories.

Capute, A.J., & Accardo, P.J. (Eds.). (1996). *Developmental disabilities in infancy and childhood* (2nd ed.). Baltimore: Paul H. Brookes Publishing Co.

Clayman, C.B. (1989). *The American Medical Association encyclopedia of medicine.* New York: Random House.

Stedman's medical dictionary (26th ed.). (1995). Baltimore: Williams & Wilkins.

Books About Typical Development
Alexander, R., Boehme, R., & Cupps, B. (1993). *Normal development of functional motor skills.* San Antonio, TX: Therapy Skill Builders.

Bly, L. (1994). *Motor skills acquisition in the first year: An illustrated guide to normal development.* San Antonio, TX: Therapy Skill Builders.

Books About Feeding and Eating
Arvedson, J.C., & Brodsky, L. (1993). *Pediatric swallowing and feeding: Assessment and management.* San Diego, CA: Singular Publishing Group.

Bray, M., Beckman, D., & Barks, L. (1987). Mealtime interventions for persons with compromised oral-motor function. In *Problems with eating: Interventions for children and adults with developmental disabilities* (pp. 85–107). Rockville, MD: American Occupational Therapy Association, Inc.

Caldwell, T.H., Todaro, A.W., & Gates, A.J. (Eds.). (1989). *Community providers guide: An information outline for working with children with special health care needs.* New Orleans, LA: National MCH Resource Center, Children's Hospital.

Case-Smith, J., & Humphry, R. (1996). Feeding and oral motor skills. In J. Case-Smith, A.S. Allen, & P.N. Pratt (Eds.), *Occupational therapy for children* (pp. 430–460). St. Louis: Mosby.

Christiansen, C. (Ed.). (1994). *Ways of living: Self-care strategies for special needs.* Rockville, MD: American Occupational Therapy Association, Inc.

Clark, G.F. (1993). Oral-motor and feeding issues. In C.B. Royeen (Ed.), *AOTA self-study series: Classroom applications for school-based practice* (Vol. 9) [Booklet]. Rockville, MD: American Occupational Therapy Association, Inc.

Glass, R.P., & Wolf, L.S. (1993). Feeding and oral-motor skills. In J. Case-Smith (Ed.), *Pediatric occupational therapy and early intervention* (pp. 225–288). Boston: Andover Medical Publishers.

Hall, S., Yohn, K., & Reed, P.R. (1992). *Feeding students in school: Providing guidelines and information on safe feeding practices for special students.* Salem: Oregon Department of Education.

Heller, K.W., Alberto, P.A., Forney, P.E., & Schwartzman, M.N. (1996). *Understanding physical, sensory, and health impairments: Characteristics and educational implications.* Pacific Grove, CA: Brooks/Cole Publishing Company.

Kedesdy, J.H., & Budd, K.S. (1998). *Childhood feeding disorders: Biobehavioral assessment and intervention.* Baltimore: Paul H. Brookes Publishing Co.

Kessler, D.B., & Dawson, P. (Eds.). *Failure to thrive and pediatric undernutrition: A transdisciplinary approach.* Baltimore: Paul H. Brookes Publishing Co.

Klein, M.D., & Delaney, T.A. (1994). *Feeding and nutrition for the child with special needs: Handouts for parents.* San Antonio, TX: Therapy Skill Builders.

McClanahan, C. (1987). *Feeding and care for infants and children with special needs.* American Occupational Therapy Association, Inc.

Morris, S.E., & Klein, M.D. (1987). *Pre-feeding skills: A comprehensive resource for feeding development.* San Antonio, TX: Therapy Skill Builders.

Nelson, C.A., Meek, M.M., & Moore, J.C. (1994). *Head-neck treatment issues as a base for oral-motor function.* Albuquerque, NM: Clinician's View.

Orelove, F.P., & Sobsey, D. (1996). *Educating children with multiple disabilities: A transdisciplinary approach* (3rd ed.). Baltimore: Paul H. Brookes Publishing Co.

Porter, S., Haynie, M., Barley, T., Caldwell, T.H., & Palfrey, J.S. (1997). *Children and youth assisted by medical technology in educational settings: Guidelines for care.* Baltimore: Paul H. Brookes Publishing Co.

Shelton, T.L., & Stepanek, J.S. (1994). *Family-centered care for children needing specialized health and developmental services.* Bethesda, MD: Association for the Care of Children's Health.

Tuchman, D.N., & Walter, R.S. (1994). *Disorders of feeding and swallowing in infants and children: Pathophysiology, diagnosis, and treatment.* San Diego, CA: Singular Publishing Group.

Urbano, M.T. (1992). *Preschool children with special health care needs.* San Diego, CA: Singular Publishing Group.

Wolf, L.S., & Glass, R.P. (1992). *Feeding and swallowing disorders in infancy: Assessment and management.* San Antonio, TX: Therapy Skill Builders.

CATALOGS

Abilitations, One Sportime Way, Atlanta, Georgia 30340 (1-800-850-8603)
[whistle sippers, no-spill bubble tumbler, whistler kit]

Achievement Products, Inc., Post Office Box 9033, Canton, Ohio 44711 (1-800-373-4699)
[scoop bowl, plate, spoons, utensil cuffs, Dycem]

adaptAbility Products for Independent Living, Post Office Box 515, Colchester, Connecticut 06415-0515
[Dycem nonslip products]

Collis Curve Toothbrush Catalog, 302 North Central Avenue, Brownsville, Texas 78521 (1-800-298-4818)
[Collis Curve toothbrush]

DeRoyal/LMB, 200 DeBusk Lane, Powell, Tennessee 37849 (1-800-541-3992)
[plate guards, cups, weighted and soft-grip utensils, universal cuff]

Equipment Shop, Post Office Box 33, Bedford, Massachusetts (1-800-525-7681)
[maroon spoons]

Exceptional Parent, Post Office Box 3000 Department EP, Denville, New Jersey 07834 (1-800-562-1973)
[This magazine for parents reviews and advertises a variety of adapted equipment.]

Flaghouse, Inc., 601 Flaghouse Drive, Hasbrouck Heights, New Jersey 07604 (1-800-793-7900)
[utensils, cups, plates]

Mealtimes: A resource for oral-motor, feeding and mealtime programs. New Visions, 1124 Roberts Mountain Road, Faber, Virginia 22938 (http://www.new-vis.com)
[variety of massagers, chew toys, and utensils]

Medela, Inc., Post Office Box 660, McHenry, Illinois 60051-0660 (1-800-435-8316)
[Haberman Feeder]

Rifton, Box 901, Rifton, New York 12471 (1-800-777-4244)
[variety of adapted equipment]
Sammons Preston, Post Office Box 5071, Bolingbrook, Illinois 60440-5071 (1-800-323-5547)
[scooper bowls, cups, sure-grip utensils, universal cuff, Dycem, electric self-feeder]
Sassy, Inc., 1534 College SE, Grand Rapids, Michigan 49507
[Sassy training cup]
Smith & Nephew Rolyan, Inc., One Quality Drive, Post Office Box 1005, Germantown, Wisconsin 53022 (1-800-558-8633)
[variety of utensils, cups, plates and plate guards, toothbrushes, and oral swabs]
Southpaw Enterprises, Post Office Box 1047, Dayton, Ohio 45401 (1-800-228-1698)
[oral stimulation kit]
The Kennedy Cup, Providence Spillproof Container, Post Office Box 40672, Providence, Rhode Island 02940 (1-888-THE-KCUP)(http://www.kcup.com)
[spillproof cup with straw]
Therapy Skill Builders, 555 Academic Court, San Antonio, Texas 78204 (1-800-211-8378)
[maroon spoons, dysphagia cup, flex cups]

VIDEOTAPES

Feeding and Swallowing Videotape Series (1991).
University of Nebraska Medical Center, Meyer Rehabilitation Institute, Medica Resource Center, 600 South 42nd Street, Omaha, Nebraska 68198-5450 (402-559-7467)
Feeding with Love and Good Sense: The Infant, the Older Baby, the Toddler, and the Preschooler (1989). Produced by Ellyn Satter.
Ellyn Satter Associates, 4226 Mandan Crescent, Madison, Wisconsin 53711 (1-800-808-7976)
Feeding Your Baby with Love (1993). Produced by Whiteford-Hadary.
University of Maryland at Baltimore Video Press, 100 Penn Street, Baltimore, Maryland 21201 (1-800-328-7450)
Home Gastrostomy Care for Infants and Young Children (1991). Produced by University of Colorado Health Sciences Center School of Nursing.
Feeding Infants and Young Children with Special Needs (1990). Produced by University of Colorado Health Sciences Center School of Nursing.
Nutrition for Infants and Toddlers with Special Needs (1992). Produced by University of Colorado Health Sciences Center School of Nursing.
Universal Precautions in Schools: Protection from Blood-Borne Diseases (1996). Produced by University of Colorado Health Sciences Center School of Nursing.
Lerner Managed Designs, Inc., Post Office Box 747, Lawrence, Kansas 66044 (1-800-467-1644)
Let's Eat: Feeding a Child with a Visual Impairment (1994). Produced by Chris Richta and Chris Starr, S.C.O.R.E. Media.
Blind Childrens Center, 4120 Marathon St., Los Angeles, California 90029 (1-800-222-3566)
Therapeutic Management of Children with G-Tubes (1994). Produced by Clinician's View.
Clinician's View, 6007 Osuna Road, NE, Albuquerque, New Mexico 87109 (505-880-0058)

Index

n and Youth Assisted by Medical
~~Technology~~ in Educational Settings
Guidelines for Care, *Second Edition*

Edited by Stephanie Porter, M.S.N., R.N., Marilynn Haynie, M.D.,
Timaree Bierle, B.S.N., R.N., Terry Heintz Caldwell, Ed.D.,
& Judith S. Palfrey, M.D.

Containing detailed daily care guidelines and emergency-response techniques, this hands-on reference covers step-by-step procedures for providing crucial care and support to students with special health needs. You'll find valuable information on training personnel, meeting legal requirements, planning transitions, and anticipating transportation issues. Forms and checklists will help you organize your record keeping and guide your program planning.

This new edition examines working with a range of students including those who:

- have HIV infection
- utilize tube feeding
- rely on ventilators
- require catheterization

Reviewed by experts across the country to ensure accuracy and usability, this book is an important guide for school nurses, teachers, parents, school administrators, and health aides.

Stock #2363 • Price: $52.00 • 1997 • 432 pages • 8 1/2 x 11 • spiral bound • ISBN 1-55766-236-3

PLACE YOUR ORDER NOW! FREE shipping and handling on prepaid check orders (US only).

Please send me ____ copy(ies) of **Children and Youth Assisted by Medical Technology in Educational Settings**/Stock #2363/$52.00

___Bill my institution (PO must be attached) ___ Payment enclosed (checks payable: **Brookes Publishing Co.**)

___ VISA ___ MasterCard ___ AMEX Credit Card #: _____ Exp. date:_____

Signature: _____ Daytime telephone: _____

Name: _____

Address: _____

City/State/ZIP:_____

Maryland orders add 5% sales tax. Yours to review 30 days risk free. Prices subject to change without notice. Prices may be higher outside the United States.

Photocopy this form and mail to: Brookes Publishing Co., P.O. Box 10624, Baltimore, MD 21285-0624; FAX to (410) 337-8539; call toll-free (8 AM–5 PM ET) 1-800-638-3775; or e-mail custserv@pbrookes.com.

Source code: BA11

For more information, or to browse our entire catalog, visit us at **www.pbrookes.com**